TOUCHSTONES

52 GAMES AND 52 GIGS, FEATURING ...

Accept AC/DC Airbourne Anthrax Australia Avignon
Carl Barron Black Sabbath Black Stone Cherry
Brighouse Rangers Brisbane British Army Buckcherry
Buzzcocks Canada Canberra Canterbury Carcassonne
Castleford Clutch Couple of Dead Bodgies Crobot
Cronulla Dan Reed Network Dead Daisies Devine Electric
Dio Driver Dokken Dragon England Ferrals Fiji France
Frankie's World Famous House Band Gold Coast Goo
Goo Dolls Guns N' Roses Huddersfield Glenn Hughes
Hull FC Hull Kingston Rovers Illawarra Iron Maiden Italy
John Coghlan's Quo Ryan Koriya Last in Line Leeds Lock Lane
London Broncos London Skolars Sarah McLeod Manly
Melbourne Mr Big Newcastle Newtown New Zealand
North Queensland Oldham Oxford Palace of the King
Papua New Guinea Parramatta Penrith Queens Reef
Rival Sons Romeo's Daughter Russia St George Illawarra
Salford Samoa Scotland Screaming Jets Serbia
Sharlston Rovers Shihad Songhoy Blues South Sydney
Steel Panther Stryper Sydney Roosters Geoff Tate The Angels
The Answer The Last Vegas The Lazys The Poor The Quireboys
The Vapors Tonga Toronto Wolfpack Tyketto UFO
United States Villefranche Vintage Trouble Wakefield Trinity
Wales Warrington Warriors Wests Tigers Widnes Wigan

TOUCHSTONES

Welcome to the
Land of Oz!

Steve Muscad, 2017 World
Cup

TOUCHSTONES

RUGBY LEAGUE, ROCK'N'ROLL, THE ROAD AND ME

STEVE MASCORD

STOKE HILL PRESS

First published in 2017

by Stoke Hill Press
c/ 122 Wellbank Street
Concord NSW Australia 2137

National Library of Australia Cataloguing-in-Publication entry:

Mascord, Steve, author

Touchstones: rugby league, rock'n'roll,
the road and me/Steve Mascord.

ISBN: 978 0 9945 0083 0 (paperback)

Includes index.

Mascord, Steve.
Journalists—Australia—Biography.
Sportswriters—Australia—Biography.
Music journalists—Australia—Biography.
Rugby League football—Australia.
Heavy metal(Music)—Australia.

Edited & Produced by Geoff Armstrong
Cover and Internal Design by Luke Causby, Blue Cork
Typesetting by Kirby Jones
Printed in Australia by the OPUS Group

touchstone, n. 1. a test or standard by which something is judged ... 2. a physical or intellectual entity, often from childhood, by which the legitimacy or value of an obsession is measured or justified ...

CONTENTS

PRELUDE

I was conceived in an insane asylum and don't know for sure who my natural father is.

Bet you didn't expect this book to start like that, right? If you are part of the comparatively small group that has heard of me, you were no doubt anticipating something about Axl Rose or Brad Fittler. Or maybe a nightclub in Wakefield …

And I sympathise with you. I really do. Because that's exactly what I planned to write.

This project started as a treatise on how you can enjoy life more by being more independent, less encumbered by convention, less beholden to others. It wasn't shaping as *I Hope They Serve Beer in Hell*, but it was in the same postcode. However, as I slaved over a dilapidated laptop, things started to change. It took a long time for me to arrive at this conclusion but I guess the reason I am the way I am and got to the point where I was ready to write a book must, in some part, be linked to that first sentence.

Don't worry, you haven't opened up a tear jerker. But there's some stuff I need to get out of the way early, for purposes of context, OK?

As a child in Wollongong, Australia, I was told that I was adopted. My mother and father, Betty and Norm Mascord, told me my natural parents had died in a car accident. I always wondered if I'd been in the car at the time but never asked. Why? Well, I use the term 'always wondered' loosely. Like many adopted children who don't care about their circumstances before they arrive in their current home, I was just anxious to get on with life.

Being adopted empowered me. It meant I couldn't blame genetic predispositions for anything: 'Oh, I am bad at sports because my dad was' ... 'I have my mum's fair skin, I must stay out of the sun'. In many ways, it almost gave me a Jesus complex — I had been placed on earth with no family history, no flaws that would kick in later in life, no inherent weaknesses *or* strengths. The word 'inherent' did not apply to me. Immaculate.

When Stephany contacted me in 2006, I cut her off by saying. 'I was told I had no living parents or siblings but you are probably my sister, right?' (No, my biological mother did not name her children Stephen and Stephany. I was born Andrew John Langley, if you please.)

Deep down, I had long known I'd probably been lied to and that this conversation with someone from my biological family would happen eventually. *Why* was I lied to? For five years, my birth mother, Elizabeth, who was a patient at Gladesville Mental Hospital in Sydney where controversial shock treatment was used in the 1960s, refused to sign the papers to release me to Norm and Betty.

Norm and Betty lied because they didn't want me frightened every time 'Mr Tierney' from the adoption agency came to the door, worried that he would take me away. When Elizabeth eventually signed the papers, I guess Norm and Betty kept lying because they didn't want to admit they had done so in the first place. Elizabeth was on her deathbed, riddled with cancer, when she asked Stephany to find me.

Betty, too, was fighting a terminal illness around the time I found all this out. I did not want to burden her by saying I knew about her 40-year-old fib. But I mentioned it to my father on the way home from Betty's funeral. 'Your grandfather was a doctor, you know,' he said to me, as if being told a gigantic lie my entire life was akin to getting corned beef on your salad sandwich.

Yes, Elizabeth's father actually has a wing of a hospital on Sydney's north shore named after him. I won't go into further detail; that's another book.

Does all this make me sad, angry, wistful or resentful? No. It just is. As I said, the way I see it right now, my independence from traditional familial bonds has been a blessing. It's provided me with an endlessly interesting, stimulating life without boundaries. But by the end of this tome, I may feel differently. Its writing just happens to coincide with many belated discoveries about exactly where I came from.

If there are more unexpected turns in the pages ahead, don't blame me. They'll happen by themselves. Rest assured they will be as big a shock to me as they are to you.

On with the frivolity.

INTRODUCTION

SPORT, MUSIC AND THE REMINISCENCE BUMP

What the Hell have I done with my life? And, more to the point, should 'Hell' take a capital H if the person typing it does not believe in its existence?

Yesterday was an archetypal day, representing the last 25 years for me pretty well. The taste of last night's kebab and six pints of bitter lingered as I wrote this in South London. Earlier, I'd woken at Headingley Lodge, in a room named after some cricketer that overlooks the famous Test-match ground, having covered the 2016 rugby league World Club Challenge the previous evening.

Making my way down to breakfast in the on-site café, I encountered Amanda Murray — the wife of the late, great coach Graham 'Muzz' Murray, and their daughter Kara. Muzz — whom I considered a friend despite occasional reporter-coach fallouts — had helmed both clubs involved in the WCC, the North Queensland Cowboys and the Leeds Rhinos, and the Rhinos had flown his family in for the week.

52 GAMES ... 52 GIGS

GAME 1 (FEBRUARY 21): World Club Challenge, North Queensland 38 Leeds 4 at Headingley, Leeds
Johnathan Thurston jumps the fence and gives his headgear to a kid at the back of the famous South Stand. I stay inside the ground, at the Headingley Lodge, filing error-filled copy from bed. This fixture becomes more of a mismatch as the disparity of the salary caps increase.

GIG 1 (FEBRUARY 22): Steel Panther at 100 Club, London
Back in the capital after a week of real work covering the World Club Series, this is a hoot. Steel Panther claim to be making fun of misogyny — but they still get girls to flash their boobs every night. As far as I can tell, they're not parody boobs.

Lining up to pay for my eggs, I engaged an Aussie couple in conversation. Turns out this Aussie couple runs rugby league in the Czech Republic and the fellow was Facebook friends with my partner. 'I'm following that book project of yours,' the stranger said. Of course, right?

Back at the Murrays' table we were soon joined by the former Great Britain enforcer (that's a kinda stale word now, isn't it?) Barrie McDermott, who related hilarious stories about boys being too scared to visit his daughters at home because of his fearsome reputation. I'd be scared too.

Following a train journey to London, I visited the Royal College of Communications at Elephant and Castle at the invitation of an old friend, Huw Richards, to address sports journalism students. I covered ethics, the role of the journalist within sports and writing. I tried to impress on these students who will enter a workforce scarcely recognisable from the one that welcomed me in 1989 that for every 100 days of beer and skittles, there'll be one where you will have to ruin a friendship, pursue a cheat or cover a tragedy.

I briefly shed a tear at the mention of Alex McKinnon.

My favourite cadet lecture allegory is about the journalist who walks past a fish shop bearing the sign 'Fresh Fish Sold Here' every day. Each day he removes a redundant word from the sign until there is no sign at all. Journalists should apply this test to every sentence they write. 'Good writing is like maths, with beautiful simplicity,' I tell about a dozen kids, 'and unless you can do basic addition, you are not ready for algebra.'

My day ended with an intimate showcase performance at the 100 Club on Oxford Street of the parody hair metal band Steel Panther. In the '80s, they would have been massively successful. To get a foothold now, they must resort to using lyrics such as those from *If You Really Really Love Me*, which has lines ending with 'Melanie', 'felony', 'this kind of infidelity' and 'Tiger Woods and me'. They 'ironically' get girls to flash their breasts like it's a Mötley Crüe video.

This all sounds like a fantastic way to live, right? My girlfriend and I were added to the guest list because I emailed Steel Panther's singer. I know people you've only heard of. What's to complain about?

Yet in recent times I have been reminded of Fox Mulder's rumination in the rebooted *X-Files:* 'I am a middle-aged man.

Maybe it's time to leave behind childish things.' Our Fox also believes he has been manipulated most of his life.

A little while ago, after an early season Super League game in England's north, I got a lift back to Salford Quays with the competition's digital whiz Adam Treeby and we found ourselves stuck behind a Stobart truck ('lorry' if you're from this part of the world). Stobart, infamously, signed a no-cash sponsorship deal in 2014 with Super League — the English rugby league competition that also includes a French team and, perhaps soon, one from Canada — in which the main benefit to the sport was artwork on the side of said trucks.

Now, Stobart has fans. Yes, seriously. People sit outside Stobart depots and write down the time the trucks arrive and leave — as a hobby. I began to say how tragic this is ... and then it hit me.

My own love of sport and music is really no different — a largely involuntary reaction to familiar stimuli — colours, logos, faces, even smells and sensations. The whiff of liniment, the thump of a bass drum. The opening riff of *Highway to Hell*, the sound from the sideline as bodies collide. Scientists call this the reminiscence bump. Whatever you were exposed to between 16 and 25 is hardwired into your melon because those are the years you established an adult identity. Love, apparently, is merely the memory of a positive chemical reaction.

Do sport and music have any more intrinsic, independently verifiable worth than a Stobart truck? Or am I just a hamster on a wheel, wearing a black t-shirt and a striped scarf?

Settle back friends. That's what I plan to find out over the next 52 weeks.

CHAPTER 1

FACETIME

I wander, half-drunkenly, out of the Head of Steam bar, down the stone steps of Huddersfield train station, and out into the Yorkshire drizzle. It's June 11, 2016, and it's my bucks party, my bachelor party, my stag do; whatever you call it where you're from. I'm on my fourth pint. Into St George's Square now, veering to the left, I come to a pause in front of a building that loomed like Valhalla in my childhood imagination.

Given a choice at 12 years old between visiting Disneyland and the George Hotel, I would undoubtedly have chosen the Industrial Revolution over the Magic Kingdom.

Where I stand, fumbling with my mobile phone, is roughly where — on August 29, 1895 — 22 clubs voted to break away from rugby union and form what would become known as rugby league. While other kids were obsessing over Batman *and* Charlie's Angels, *I was trying to memorise the names of these long-dead men and the exact order of their actions. In suburban Wollongong during the early 1980s, watching* Seven's Big League *starring Rex Mossop and Barry Ross, memorising Malcolm Andrews'* The A to Z of Rugby League *as if it was the New Testament and I was planning a life in the clergy, I devoured everything I could dust off about the game.*

52 GAMES ... 52 GIGS

GAME 2 (FEBRUARY 28): Lock Lane 37 Oxford 22 at Braywick Park, Maidenhead
The first time I've been to a game where you can order a bacon and egg roll and when it's ready, they come to find you in the grandstand to give it to you.

GIG 2 (MARCH 4): Clutch at Metro Theatre, Sydney
Jetlag + six beers + pizza + one Jack and Coke = covering three NRL games from the floor of the Fairfax news room the next day between projectile vomits. If it comes through the nose, is it still classed as vomit? I only woke up at 9pm and went to straight to the Metro, so technically I had the six beers for breakfast. Much respect, Lemmy.

Now, at the birthplace of rugby league, I am speaking to fellow journalist Melinda Farrell via video link. They call it FaceTime. Even Star Trek couldn't foresee it.

My stag do is about to unfold at half-a-dozen train stations that snake across the Pennines. Two days ago, I saw Angus Young bunny-hop along a vanity ramp at Etihad Stadium, Manchester, accompanied by guest singer Axl Rose.

I am 47 years old, on the opposite side of the world from where I was born and raised, standing among the touchstones of my youth.

But, but ...

Geoffrey Moorhouse, in his 1989 tome At The George and Other Essays on Rugby League, *artfully rendered the architecture here as 'late classical from quoin to pediment', describing a 'pastel shaded dining room where long mirrors are ranged along the walls and deep windows are curtained heavily in chintz'.*

I'll have to take his word for it because the George Hotel is boarded up and for sale.

In the circumstances, I'd almost prefer the blue plinth marking it as the birthplace of rugby league was not there at all. It's a sad indictment on what a short distance rugby league has come in these years, that its birthplace sits lifeless and useless.

Even in the beery and cheery haze of one of the most memorable (or pleasantly forgettable) days of my life, I must at least consider the possibility that the George Hotel is just a building, that the great and good of British rugby league journalism waiting for me back in the Head of Steam are just 'work colleagues' and that a sport is just a bunch of fellows chasing a ball for the entertainment of others.

That the magic which has mesmerised me since my youth is entirely of my own creation.

And yet …

WINDSWEPT SUNDAY AFTERNOONS AT Wollongong Showground remain untouched in my memory by such bitter realism. Lining up for the gates to open, dressed head to toe in the Illawarra Steelers' scarlet and white with a flag for good measure, watching Ian Russell's offload, John Dorahy's jink, Kevin Kelly's chip-and-chase, Mark Broadhurst's backstreet brutality …

Recalling the circa 1986 *Slippery When Wet* promo poster above my childhood bed, the *Kerrang!* centrespread of a svelte Axl Rose standing on the seat of a convertible next to my teak desk …

Is it possible that Jon Bon Jovi and Axl are no more than lucky men with looks and a voice?

Recent pictures of puffy 54-year-old Axl surrounded by fame-hungry 29-year-old models, those albums of ballads Jon's band now releases ... do they mar those memories, render them inaccurate and unreliable? Do the off-field misadventures of Andrew Johns and Andrew Ettingshausen and Craig Field and Jason Smith ruin your memories of them as players forever? And whatever your answer to these esoteric questions ...

Why? Or why not?

I set myself a demanding schedule in search of answers: attend a heavy metal rock gig and a rugby league game each week, absorb life lessons from practitioners, endure and enjoy trans-hemisphere travel and deep contemplation, and write about my quest. I had to be careful this did not turn into a treatise on logistics: how does one get from point A to point B? How much is the toll on that motorway? Is there a toilet on this train?

Take week two, for example. Initially, I planned for the gig to be old indie-rockers-turned-metallers The Cult at London's Brixton Academy on Sunday, February 28, and the match to be a few days later, on the other side of the world, when the 2016 NRL season opened. The opening premiership game was scheduled for the Thursday at Pirtek Stadium: Parramatta hosting Brisbane.

First problem: The Cult were not playing Brixton on Sunday night. I had misread the gig guide and in fact the show was Saturday night. Saturday night was *last week*, not *this week*, see. A stark reality soon revealed itself: that this year I was going to go to a number of gigs which I knew in advance I would not enjoy. In all likelihood, I would pay scalpers/touts astronomical fees for entry to shows which I did not want to see.

I had already witnessed the Maryland fuzz rock band Clutch and didn't like them. While they had the House of Blues in Boston transfixed that night and were spoken about in reverential terms by many of my friends, I just didn't get them. But the parameters of my book dictated that, instead of going — for work or pleasure — to Manly-Canterbury on the second night of the new NRL season, I would spend 70 dollars seeing Clutch play once again at Sydney's Metro Theatre.

Then, another problem: an alternative for my rugby league game in week two, for which I had travelled to Oxford (first visit; lovely place), a Sunday afternoon Challenge Cup tie, was not at Iffley Road, Oxford, at all! I'd misread the playing schedule. So, from a football point of view, the overnight stay had been pointless.

I'd not been to a Challenge Cup game from any earlier round than the final since 1990, my very first day in Old Blighty when Warrington beat Oldham at Central Park. This one was between Oxford and Lock Lane, a club from Castleford in West Yorkshire. When I finally arrived at Maidenhead Rugby Club, an AstroTurf rectangle amid a patchwork of playing fields — there was a spot of archery taking place on one — I found a quaint clubhouse, a game of rugby league and very, very few spectators. Maidenhead is in Berkshire, about 50 kilometres west of London, 60 kilometres south-east of Oxford.

'Congratulations,' said Roger, a southerner in an Oxford Rugby League hoodie. An anorak in a hoodie, how about that? 'This will be the smallest crowd in the history of professional rugby league in Britain. I just stood opposite the grandstand and counted 51 — and they were mostly officials.'

My friend Howard Scott countered, 'No, Lock Lane are not a professional side. So this is not a professional game as such.'

Good point Howard. (Yes, I can go to a rugby league game in Maidenhead, at which there are only a few dozen paying spectators, and have a friend there by complete coincidence. That's what a lifetime of obsessive behaviour will do …)

The raffle prize was a bottle of whiskey. I bought a ticket. The total takings would not even pay for the whiskey. I suspected a number would be drawn that belonged to someone who cannot be reached …

As for the match itself, I was surprised at how clean it was — Cas lads are normally so tough they sleep with each other's wives for a lark — and how structured this game, which pits amateurs against part-timers — seemed to be. Because I'd not heard of any of the players, I could focus on shape and skill. The main difference between these guys and the pros was the speed of the play-the-ball and finesse late in the tackle count. For them, that meant slow and very little, respectively.

At one stage, I spied a lanky back-rower bring down a rumbling opposing forward with a copybook 'legs' tackle in mid-field. A legs tackle is a rarity these days — and a thing of beauty. But when he made the exact same tackle in the next ruck, there were two team-mates already holding the Lock Lane attacker. The results were dangerous, with the offending player forced off. The legs tackle became a 'prowler' or 'cannonball' because of the involvement of the other two.

The amateurs beat the professionals 37–22. It transpired that another friend, Matt Rossleigh, was one of the touch judges. In a gathering of less than 100 people, 17,000 kilometres from where

I was raised, I knew two people who were there independent of me, and of each other, all because of a shared interest sparked, in my case, by swapping footy cards in the playground.

Something to be proud of? Or the opposite?

Roger is definitely of the proud persuasion. 'I go to most of the games around here — Skolars, Oxford, Hemel, Broncos,' he said. 'I used to go to a lot of away games and still go to some. I've seen parts of the country I would never otherwise go to and made some great friends. My girlfriend is into it now too. We normally make a weekend of it — go see some historical site or place of interest one day and head to the game the next. We'd not have done that if it wasn't for rugby league.'

I understood what Roger was saying. The world's a big place, and it's often hard to figure out where to go. It's usually been league or music that has made the decision for me. Sometimes, the actual quality of the sport and music is inconsequential.

It doesn't matter what leads me here. It's the fact I'm here.

UNFORCED ENTRY I

RUGBY LEAGUE

IF you're annoyed by Phil Gould's, 'No, no, no, no, no!', angry at Denny Solomona's defection to rugby union and excited about the Toronto Wolfpack, I invite you to skip ahead a few pages.

If you find that sentence almost completely incomprehensible, by all means read on.

You see, it's my sincere hope that someone out there will be reading this without any knowledge of the sporting references I've made so far, and will again make. Perhaps it was the promise of Marshall stacks, Spandex and Les Pauls that got you this far. Maybe it's the sadistic anticipation of a middle-aged man making a spectacle of himself, whinging pathetically about being adopted and struggling to find an identity like an emotional cripple.

It strikes me that if you write about the NFL and grunge, that is not going to be too jarring. Millions love both. Likewise, if it's male alienation and Britpop, there is something of a burgeoning market there and not a little crossover, and writers have made a living out of the combination; not many, but a few. But rugby league and heavy metal?

For roughly 40 of my first 45 years on the planet, league was central to my existence. I could not have dreamed that I would one day attempt to communicate with people who don't know what it is. But I also liked science fiction. I understood instinctively that people felt similarly obsessive about that. Or maybe motor cars. Or sex. Well, I didn't understand at the same age that I wanted a Lego Millennium Falcon that some people were similarly drawn to prostitutes. Thank God. That would be fucked up.

Anyways, rugby league is merely a character here; one with which some readers will be more familiar than others. I hope those who don't know about it will see the constant it's provided to me in terms of whatever pop-culture obsession, sphere of art, piece of technology or variety of bordello has helped them mark the passage of time.

So let's introduce the character to which I was introduced by being taken away from my mother and adopted out to a loving couple in suburban Wollongong in the winter of 1969.

Rugby football was born in 1823 when William Webb Ellis picked up the ball and ran with it at Rugby School in England … not. This almost certainly did not happen; the sport which involved holding the ball and running at the opposing team more likely evolved from games that were played between entire towns over non-distinct playing surfaces measuring miles in width and diameter.

They eventually managed to whittle down the size of the field to roughly 100 metres and a team from several thousand to 15, no doubt following the introduction of a salary cap (that was a joke). Rugby union became a major sport in England and spread throughout the British Empire.

Yet it wasn't long before there were increasing tensions between England's entitled south and the workaday north. Clubs in Yorkshire and Lancashire, where the players usually worked in a mill or down t' pit when they weren't chasing a pig's bladder around a muddied pitch, wanted to pay their men a few shillings if they missed work because of their rugby commitments. Clubs in the vicinity of London's Twickenham, where players could afford to do without a few shillings, were unsympathetic. So, in August 1895, the Northern Union, which would morph into rugby league, was formed when 22 clubs broke away from their southern counterparts. Initially, the Northern Union was just another rugby union competition — the rules were more or less the same.

Far away in New Zealand, a young rugby player named Albert Baskerville saw an opportunity to make more than a few shillings. He secretly signed up a host of All Blacks (maybe you've heard of *them*) and sailed to Britain via Australia for a professional tour, ending 12 years of isolation for the vulgarians of England's north. The Australians picked up the game too — it was a relatively unionised (as in, trade unions) society, after all, and players disliked being out of pocket when injured while the rugby union authorities snaffled the gate takings. At the behest of the Australians, the game changed its name to rugby league and several rule changes were introduced to make it more open, to attract more spectators and pay the players more money. And that's pretty much it, really …

The next interesting thing to happen was in 1995, when Rupert Murdoch was launching pay television in Australia and decided to start a breakaway competition he could screen on his new channel. This seemed like Armageddon at the time but wasn't. Around then, rugby union became openly professional which meant the original reasons for there being two kinds of rugby no longer existed.

Except, rugby league is still about money; rugby union continues to have close connections to private schools, diplomacy and commerce after it pruned a branch it considered rotten a century and a quarter ago. As a result, union is played in many more places than league, which has only recently begun to overcome its historical disadvantage of being a meal ticket for those of limited means.

In recent years, rugby league officials have shown themselves capable of breathtaking parochialism on an almost daily basis. Few seem to have their forebears' sense of adventure. The game remains dominant only in eastern Australia, parts of Auckland and Papua New Guinea. In England, it struggles to stay afloat, as soccer's Premier League grows while mainstream media and the corporate sponsorship budgets that once supported league shrink.

League's belated expansion — the 2025 World Cup is scheduled to be in America — could be seen as a metaphor for the breaking down of the old order and the ability to organise people at little expense with the help of social media. Although at the time of writing rugby league was not recognised by SportAccord (the association of international sports federations) or the International Olympic Committee, it can legitimately pilfer the IP of its main rival — with whom it shares half a name — in new territory.

This annoys rugby union authorities in places where their code is still small. A man trying to start league in Dubai was locked up for 13 nights in 2015.

None of which mattered to me when I started at Windang Primary School aged seven in 1976. The flickering *Seven's Big League* on the colour TV and pink bubblegum-infused swap card packets were just more fun to think about than whether I was going to be beaten up today on the way home from school.

Nostalgia is a Powerful Thing

On the surface, it's hard to see any problem with the proposal to resuscitate the North Sydney Bears on the Gold Coast.

My colleague Chris Garry, of *The Courier-Mail*, explained to me during the World Club Series that Hollywood now has a 25-year rotational policy for franchises like superhero movies. Basically, after 25 years, people get nostalgic for familiar things — and they generally have more money than they did a quarter-century ago — so unless you do a particularly crappy job of reviving said cultural icon, you're going to make a motza.

The Bears have been gone as a top-flight side now for just under 20 years.

Nostalgia is a powerful thing and the trademarks of the past in rugby league probably aren't being utilised as well as they could be, with a few notable exceptions such as Newtown. One of the 'whole of game' strategy's major considerations should have been to bring back, and leverage, old brands. How do you get city dwellers interested in the 'Platinum League'? You put the Balmain Tigers, Illawarra Steelers, Western Suburbs Magpies, etc, in it. Some diehards would suddenly be more interested in the Platinum League than the NRL (perhaps including me).

Again, there seems to be an insecurity at play, a concern that the trusted old brands will out-perform the new ones. Certainly, the makers of throwback jerseys and memorabilia understand the subconscious triggers that Kerry Boustead dressed as Bruce Springsteen on the cover of *Rugby League Week* can set off.

But back to the Gold Coast Bears. How many fans feel emotionally attached to the light blue and gold to the extent they would not support the tourist-strip franchise if it was red and black? No reason, then, the big black Bears should not be back on the road again.

A quick word on the World Club Series.

Rugby league in Australia is not perfect. Rugby league in England is even less perfect. History and money are responsible for most of the imperfections. The money in rugby league is in Sydney. It gobbled up Newcastle, Canberra and Wollongong, then Brisbane, the Gold Coast and North Queensland, then New Zealand. Eventually — maybe it will take advanced air travel, maybe it won't — the money in Sydney will gobble up England, too.

In the meantime, just look upon the World Club Series as interstate football, pre-State of Origin. It's what we have until natural evolution of the rugby league business gives us something better.

From **theroar.com.au,** *February 26, 2016.*

CHAPTER 2

INTRODUCING ANDREW JOHN LANGLEY

Most people, at some stage of their lives, ponder the question: if I wasn't me, who would I be? If one or two small things in my life had changed, what would that have made me? I've pondered and I have a simple three-word answer: Andrew John Langley.

That's the name under which I was born, with a completely different life ahead of me than the one I am now at least halfway through. My mother, Elizabeth Langley, was a ballerina. Her father was a surgeon, her mother a socialite. The Langleys came to Australia from Ireland and South Africa. Our distant ancestor is Oliver Cromwell's right-hand man, Henry Charles 'Iron Hand' Langley (so called because he sported a metallic hand, not for his grouchy disposition).

As best I can tell, Elizabeth suffered a mental breakdown in London when her lover, a medical student, committed suicide in the early 1960s. She never fully recovered. By the time she had me, in Australia, she was institutionalised and had already miscarried a number of times. Under the law at the time, I became a ward of the state.

I don't need to look too far to discover how different my life would probably have been as Andrew John Langley. I have a biological cousin who stayed with her mother. Unlike my mother, her mum was able to resist the pressure applied by our grandmother to trim the family tree by giving her child up for adoption. Like Elizabeth, my cousin's mum had mental problems, which meant my cousin had to raise herself in some ways. She always had the poorest clothes in her class but she turned out pretty good. She's a talented artist and lives in an idyllic spot in rural New South Wales, with connections and business interests in the art world.

What she doesn't have is an affiliation with the Newtown Jets or Saigon Kick.

But we're not trying to discover here whether my life would have been better as Andrew John Langley. Being raised by a single mother with diagnosed mental illness would undoubtedly have had its challenges for me. What's at issue is whether my overwhelming pop culture obsessions were a result of environmental factors or were endemic — and if my life would be appreciably better without them.

Andrew John Langley, the poor bugger, looks almost exactly like me. His hair is cut more neatly, his beard is less ratty. He has never worn a black band t-shirt in his life. He never collected footy cards; perhaps he was raised by his grandmother on Sydney's north shore, as another of my biological cousins was. If so, he went to a private school and played rugby union and was caned by a tyrannical principal a few times. Maybe he likes indie rock and AFL.

While attending my 52 games and gigs, I'll be taking Andrew John Langley on a tour of my life. I'm going to introduce him to newsrooms, dressing-rooms and band rooms. I'm going to get him drunk, sneak him onto planes, introduce him to my friends. Most importantly, I'm going to invite him to pass judgment on what I've done since our paths diverged at the age of three months — when my biological mother Elizabeth Langley kept him but was forced to give me up and never see me again.

And then, at the end of our journey together, I'm going to let Andrew decide where I go from there, which parts of my life I leave behind and which I hold onto.

Being a journalist has trained me well for this task; it helps me achieve the required objectivity, question everything I am. I really do feel I am capable of looking at myself, and my life, as if from above, because that's the way my training has taught me to see the rest of the world.

Maybe I don't need to be a slave to my circumstances any more. There is still time for me to weed out things that circumstance foisted upon me, even if they are things I think I love. If I want to, I can start again.

There is still time for me to be Andrew John Langley.

CHAPTER 3

EMERALD CITY

'All Day Breakfast Until 2pm ... Bacon and Egg Roll and Coffee Only $16.50.'

Only in Sydney could these boasts be in 50-point type on a chalkboard outside a coffee shop, rather than dirty little secrets hidden at the bottom of a menu.

I've lived in Sydney since I was 21 but have never completely fallen for the place. If you've met me, you've probably heard me say, 'Sydney is a dumb blonde and Melbourne a brunette who speaks four languages.' Sydney has an over-supply of the vacuous and of venal bullies. Somehow, they take credit for the city's natural beauty and glorious climate — as if when Cook landed it was a pock-marked Martian wasteland that has since been painstakingly moulded into paradise by obnoxious shock jocks, leathery real estate agents and foul-mouthed restaurateurs.

Sydney sees itself as the home of rugby league, even though the sport was invented in the north of England and — it could be argued — brought to Australia by a Kiwi, Albert Baskerville. Yes, the city does have eight-and-a-half NRL clubs (not nine — Wollongong is a separate city, folks!), but these days, Brisbane has

52 GAMES ... 52 GIGS

GAME 3 (MARCH 10): Canterbury 18 Penrith 16 at Pepper Stadium, Penrith
Sport is repetitive and spontaneous, all at once. Penrith mark their 50th anniversary in this match — that's a lot of games against Canterbury of which most are forgotten. But then Bulldogs debutant Kerrod Holland wins the match with a conversion on fulltime. If that bores you, you're probably done with sports.

GIG 3 (MARCH 11): Buzzcocks at Factory Theatre, Sydney
A gig I would never have attended had I not been writing this book — and I'd be much the poorer. Music genres are so arbitrary and without a true aural underpinning, right? Tonight's support band plays so fast as to be almost unlistenable. Meanwhile, the Buzzcocks perform singalong gems such as *Ever Fallen in Love (With Someone You Shouldn't've)*. I ran into some friends I've not seen in a decade.

bigger crowds at Broncos matches and Queensland beats NSW in Origin every year.

Sydney — specifically, Burwood — did, however, give us AC/DC. Back home from England, I walked past the room in which they were formed (above a video store that must be close to foreclosure) on the way to the gym. It's anonymous, vacant. The Emerald City, with its gluten-free sourdough and skim macchiatos, is far too cool to celebrate the world-beating 'bogan' rock band it begat. The Ackadacka (that's Australian for AC/DC; AC/DC is also Australian for AC/DC, you Scottish upstarts) statues and lanes are in, respectively, Fremantle and Melbourne.

But Sydney's bluntness, its naked competitiveness, its preponderance of the uncouth, is well-represented by the sport it loves.

IT'S HERE THAT I returned to the grind of being a rugby league writer at the beginning of March 2016, dropped into shimmering heat and cascading sweat straight off the plane from London. I lost my media pass on the way to the first game of the season.

My pass was a lanyard (I'm surprised lanyards don't come with driver's licences these days) and a plastic card with a hole through the top. Walking from Parramatta train station to Pirtek Stadium, I removed a bag from over my shoulder and the pass came with it. I walked off and, unbeknown to me, left it lying on Parramatta's main thoroughfare, Church Street, where rugby league fan Scotty West found it. Scotty tweeted me and at half-time I walked to the other side of Pirtek Stadium and collected it from him. He could have got into the footy free with it all year — no one ever looks at the photos on the front of these things. 'It's not mine,' he shrugged when I mentioned this to him. Not everyone in Sydney observes the city's convict heritage.

Parramatta official Josh Drayton agreed to get me some tickets for Scotty and his girlfriend for the following week … but by then, Parramatta was embroiled in a salary-cap scandal and Josh had other things on his mind.

My weekly routine during the 2016 NRL season looked a little like this: on Sunday, I go to a game wearing three hats: *The Sydney*

Morning Herald, Sydney FM radio station Triple M and *Rugby League Week*. (Actually, the radio station was the only one that actually issued me with a hat.) For the *SMH*, my assignment is to file a 'Set of Six' column (all ideas in mainstream newspaper coverage of sport right now are hackneyed; everyone is too busy trying to keep their jobs to be imaginative). For *Rugby League Week*, I try to speak to one player from each of the competing teams in the hope of getting a decent news story. This is rather unlikely at the best of times and the magazine's new editor, Shayne Bugden, is picky in this regard. For Triple M, it's 'around the grounds' at the 2pm game — if there is one. Later in the year, when *The Australian*'s Brent Read is at the Rio Olympics, I'm told I'll be back on the sidelines on Sunday.

On Sunday night, I have a column to file for the Super League website about Englishmen playing in the NRL. On Monday, I bash out whatever I have for *RLW* from the weekend. I try to get some exercise. I then need to be at the Monday Night Football venue by 4.45pm for pre-match coach interviews for Triple M, for whom I am touchline commentator or — as they are now officially known in Australian rugby league (it says so on my pass) — 'sideline eye'. Starting this book, and deciding that I am only back in Sydney to make money, made me better in this role. I grew up listening to Frank Hyde and Alan Marks and all those 'callers' and for years I was obsessed with the idea of being on the radio. The first time I did 'around the grounds' for 2UE, I froze live on air. It took weeks to get over the embarrassment but as ex-Australia captain Brad Fittler once said, stuffing up in public is '15 seconds in someone else's life' so there's no point being scared of it.

Nowadays, I'm not concerned about embarrassing myself. I don't see my future as being a rugby league radio commentator. So I just try to get the message across as best I can.

For the next 12 months, Tuesday will be book day — working on what you are now reading. Wednesday is for the *Herald*'s 'Discord' column and any features I can conjure up for *RLW*. On Thursdays, I write the *Far & Wide* column for *RLW* and a comment piece for *The Roar* website, along with doing matches in the evening for Triple M. *Far & Wide* is what my Australian colleagues would call a 'trainspotter' column — it's about the game outside the NRL and Super League. In Australia, most fans and media are about as interested in this as the *USA Today*'s NFL correspondent would be about American football in Brisbane. (I once met that correspondent at a Guns N' Roses show in Vegas, and it is the only time I have ever asked a random person what they do for a living and they replied, 'Sportswriter.') Friday is another game and Saturday is a marathon 10-hour live blog of the afternoon and evening NRL games, usually from Fairfax's Pyrmont, Sydney, office.

I have no days off, but what I was doing was infinitely more enjoyable than the grind of being a beat reporter scrabbling for hard news each day. In addition to making dozens and dozens of calls trying to pin down a back-page lead, for these unfortunate sods there are team announcements on Tuesday, judiciary on Wednesday, interminable previews and injury updates.

But it was still hard to maintain perspective, living off the selective glow of a professional sports league for eight months a year. Sitting there at Fairfax for the second Saturday night of the season, embedding screen captures and tweets and instagram photos in a blog that examines three games in microscopic detail for 10 or 12 hours, I looked around a near-deserted newsroom and saw an AFL game on a distant screen. And a soccer game on another. And a rugby union match on another.

It dawned on me that someone, somewhere, was live blogging these games too. And that those blogs might have a bigger audience than mine, with more people who cared about the results of those games than mine did. But I didn't care about *those* results. Did I really even care about *these* results, and *these* men running up and down with an inflated synthetic bladder? And if I did, why *these* men and not *those*?

The answer scared me. I only cared about these men and that ball with the word 'Steeden' on the side because, as an adopted kid in suburban Wollongong, I craved an identity. I instinctively did not fit in at home and at school got beaten up occasionally. Rugby league was popular at school and I found the iconography of it, the colours, the logos, the football cards, television and magazines, completely seductive. Rugby league quickly became who I was. Thirty-five years later, I know who my biological mother was. I at least have a name for my father.

I no longer craved a personality crutch, I no longer needed to tether myself to something on television. I was tied to it nonetheless — most of my friends come from rugby league and journalism (which I only entered out of an interest in rugby league) and without it I'd have been broke.

Yet as I sat there in early March 2016, I was thinking, *Maybe I'm ready to file for divorce from rugby league … has it provided me with anything but a psychological escape as a child?* I followed my obsession as far as it would take me, to a career, but now, fortunately, my existence is so peripatetic that I should be able to let it go pretty easily. Pay off a few credit cards and I'm outta here. *Do I need it any more?* Everything was on the table. There were almost infinite paths before me.

The movie *Concussion* does its best to flesh out a paradox — the beauty and brutality of body contact sport. 'It's a brutal game — and the next minute it's Shakespeare.' The final scene leaves the contradiction unresolved. If one over-emphasises the Shakespeare for the first half of one's life, is he condemned to focus on the brutality for the second half? Had the first few months of my life been different, would I even have any interest in sport?

What? The Cowboys are in again? Better do a screen capture of Johnathan Thurston and see if the NRL has posted the try on Twitter.

Is someone doing a Thai food run tonight?

ANDREW JOHN LANGLEY SAYS: Great way to sell a bunch of books, Stephen. Slag off the city which is home to most of your potential readers; the rest of the world swoons over; one of the only places your sport is popular; and has a climate like paradise. What on Earth were you thinking when you wrote this chapter? It is going to cause you SO MUCH grief, you won't believe it.

CHAPTER 4

COWSVILLE

Some day, I'd like to write a book that sums up the soul of each team in Australasia's National Rugby League. Not the history. Not the players. Not the fans or officials. The soul.

I've been around Sydney premiership clubs since 1982. Back then, when the Illawarra Steelers from my home town of Wollongong joined the competition, I went to their first training session. I attended almost all home and away games. I knew the time keeper, the doorman, the ball boys. The soul of the Steelers? Something that would gladly have been exchanged for the funds to pay the next bill.

Seven years later, as a professional journalist, I got to know other clubs almost as intimately. Back then, reporters would wander to training on a Tuesday or Thursday night at Belmore or Leichhardt or Kogarah and speak to whomever they liked. Although, as an over-worked cadet at Australian Associated Press (AAP), I rarely had the time.

As the years passed, the tone in most football clubs has increasingly been set by the all-powerful head coach. If not, it's the CEO — in which case the coach either eventually challenges him for power or gets sacked. But no matter how powerful a coach or chief executive becomes, some things stay — as Jack Gibson used to say — in the woodwork.

I probably couldn't attempt to do a similar book on British clubs because, despite my Anglophile tendencies that started young with three-month old copies of *Open Rugby*, I simply don't have the same depth of knowledge. It's not knowledge, exactly — it's experience and instinct. I can't tell what kind of club Wigan is by looking at photos of Brett Kenny or Henderson Gill. You have to watch people behave, preferably interact with them.

What do I mean? I mean how Parramatta's spirit was realised in 1981 with Ray Price and Brett Kenny and Peter Sterling and Steve Ella and how it has loomed over, and intimidated, everyone there since. I know this partially by watching the Eels on TV but I also know it by being inside their dressing-rooms in 1982, seeing Price wrapped in a blanket, motionless on the floor, and Ron Massey walking around with a water bottle. And I know it from dealing with them ever since.

You can adapt this to whatever sport it is with which you are familiar. Sports clubs, even if we call them 'franchises', are groups of people. And groups of people develop a character over time, and that character is passed down. They call it 'culture' now. That's a cliché. Clichés, by definition, have little or no meaning. But this one comes from somewhere.

If there's one club aside from the Steelers into which I feel I have an insight — by virtue of being there at the start, if nothing else — it's the North Queensland Cowboys. That had absolutely nothing to do with me travelling to Townsville for a week in March, but in retrospect it was a handy co-incidence

52 GAMES ... 52 GIGS

GIG 4: (MARCH 15): Buckcherry and The Poor at Max Watts, Brisbane

This is the life — catching a plane, catching a cab, quickly getting changed into your rock clobber and walking to a show involving two of your favourite bands. I'm on the way to Townsville for football and despite my parlous financial state, I can't resist seeing The Poor and Buckcherry in BrisVegas. Love West End with its strip of bars and restaurants — didn't discover the area until my mid-40s. And The Poor's Skenie must be at least as old as me but looks 35.

GAME 4: (MARCH 17): North Queensland 40 Sydney Roosters 0 at 1300SMILES Stadium, Townsville

My only foray to the far north this year, combined with a few interviews for *Rugby League Week*. Sydney Roosters had won three minor premierships in a row; they aren't about to make it four going by this evening's proceedings.

in terms of this book. In 1994, the year before they entered the NRL, I was flown north to cover the unveiling of their jersey at a function. I won one of the first Cowboys jerseys in a raffle at that function, during which — no doubt at all, even though I am only surmising — I drank too much.

I attended their first trial game, in Mackay, in early 1995. On match eve, Illawarra CEO Bob Millward teased the Cowboys' star signing, Martin 'Munster' Bella, about dropping the ball from the kick-off when playing for Canterbury in the previous year's grand final. I can't quite recall Munster's response but it was something along the lines of 'at least I was *in* the grand final'.

Early one morning that week, the hefty Test prop came to my sister's house in Mackay, a little more than 300 kilometres south of Townsville, where I was staying, and took me out to his cattle farm to show me how things were done. Despite the temptations of weighing and delousing steer, I stayed in journalism. (I also remember how, when I told a local cabbie I'd flown in from Los Angeles, he commented: 'We're happy to keep those places where they belong — on television.')

And I attended the Cowboys' first competition game, on Saturday, March 11, 1995 — part of a chartered flight that took reporters and sponsors to Auckland on Friday night, Brisbane on Saturday afternoon, Townsville on Saturday night and Perth on Sunday.

When Melbourne was stripped of two premierships in 2010, I watched the news at Cowboys coach Graham Murray's house, in the shadows of Castle Hill, Townsville. I was sitting next to Muzz on the plane that arrived back in Townsville at the start of grand final week, 2005, with the local team having qualified for the first time. He joked that the crowd at the airport would be chanting my name. (I've never felt particularly bad about watching the Cowboys' first premiership win in 2015 from an office 15 kilometres away from Stadium Australia at Homebush until … um, now actually.)

In 1997, the World Nines were held at the Cowboys' home ground. I recall the PA announcer demanding a retraction from a columnist for claiming he, the announcer, had introduced Rugby League International Federation chief executive Maurice Lindsay as 'Boris' Lindsay the day before. He demanded this retraction *over the PA*. 'TO THE CORRESPONDENT FROM

52 GAMES ... 52 GIGS

GIG 5 (MARCH 22): Songhoy Blues, City Recital Hall, Sydney

Who better to speak to about why music upsets fundamentalists so much than a band kicked out of their home country by fundamentalists? Who better to speak to about travel than a band from Timbuktu? Guitarist Garba Touré and some musician friends formed Songhoy Blues in part to boost the morale of other refugees from northern Mali. But I don't have any quotes from them. Not really my type of gig but extremely illuminating after being dragged along by fellow rugby league trainspotter Joanna Lester.

GAME 5 (MARCH 26): Manly 22 Sydney Roosters 20 at Allianz Stadium, Moore Park

Anything worth doing is worth overdoing, Gene Simmons once said. On Saturdays, I do the *stupidsaturday* blog for Fairfax. It sounds easy, watching three NRL games and typing a bit of smart-arse commentary. But I make it hard, inserting tweets, instagrams, audio, video and more. Tonight, I blog the early game, Canberra v Gold Coast in Canberra, off the tele in the Allianz Stadium press box, and do this one live.

THE COURIER-MAIL ...' he boomed, to the bemusement of 20,000 spectators.

During the same tournament, colleague Tony Adams asked me if porn films were part of the in-house entertainment at my down-at-heel hotel. 'No,' I said, 'but I think they make them there.'

I digress. My visit to Townsville in March 2016 allowed me to run the sideline for *Triple M* at a match, the Cowboys' 28–4 belting of Sydney Roosters, and knock over a couple of *A-List* profiles for *Rugby League Week*. In between, I sat in my hotel room and worked, went to the gym and tried to stay away from the Flinders Street and Palmer Street nightclub-and-bar precincts. These areas have created as many hurdles as most opposition teams for the Cowboys — bored players' careers have self-immolated in Townsville, where the army and the local footy team are community focal points. One former club CEO told me the Cowboys had an account with local hotspots that allowed them to send players home and bill the club for the cost of the taxi.

Luckily, the temptations of Townsville are even bigger diversions for visiting teams. Even touch judges have tales about the local girls treating them like Beatles.

My partner, Sarah Ryan, who is Irish, finds the mere name of Townsville a paean to Australian illiteracy. 'It's called Towns-town?' she'll say, pretending to be French. Well, no. The settlement was founded by a Robert Towns in 1865. Towns was considered a decent man at the time but his love of kidnapping Pacific Islanders for use as labour — a practice called blackbirding — would no doubt see him judged far more harshly now. It was blackbirding that brought the ancestors of the current Australian coach, Mal Meninga, to Queensland.

My interview subjects out at the Cowboys' Kirwan headquarters were the utility back, Michael Morgan, and the second rower Jason Taumalolo. These interviews normally go one of two ways: the guy's guard is up or it is down. Former Queensland lock Ashley Harrison once gave me an *A-List* interview that was so stilted and reticent I could not use any of it. Luckily, these two were quite the opposite.

We sat outside the Cowboys' gym, finding some shade in heat that isn't quite 'blazing', as much as I want to use that word. Morgan, 25, had the sparkle in his eye you subconsciously associate with intelligence. I put it to him that he will be trading for the rest of his life on the try he set up to tie the 2015 grand final in the final minute. Johnathan Thurston missed the conversion from the sideline but then in extra-time kicked the field goal that won the premiership. Morgan seemed surprised at my suggestion. He seemed to think people would soon forget about it completely.

'I don't see it at all [that] I threw the pass to win the grand final,' he said. 'I genuinely believe that I got extremely lucky and there were other things in the game that I didn't do that I should've. So no, I don't think it's changed my life at all.'

Morgan went on to speak intelligently about a range of subjects, including the pressure he felt when he first came into the Cowboys side, playing alongside one of the great halfbacks of all time. Initially, he was more comfortable at fullback rather than his present position of five-eighth. 'The year at fullback just allowed me to see the game from a different angle and pop up where I could,' he explained. 'It was a bit more of a free reign without having to organise and talk. I could worry about myself more than anything and my own role.'

I cautiously brought up the subject of the suicide of his friend and clubmate, Alex Elisala. 'Everything with Alex was extremely hard,' he replied. 'But when a lot of people talk about depression they only talk about suicide. Yes, it's awful, but there's a lot of different types of depression that people don't know about, so to learn more about the different types of it, knowing that there's not just one single form of depression [is important].

Morgan said he grew as a person, but it was an awful way to grow. 'I'm just glad I can be in a position where I can help, maybe, one person,' he said.

If you or I lose interest in sport or music, we can. I'd probably have to keep writing about it until I found another job, mind, but generally speaking it's what most of us do with our weekends. We could just decide to sleep in, or have a barbecue. However, what if the best player in the game lost interest at the peak of his powers? It's not a hypothetical question. As it turns out, it happened — to Jason Taumalolo. He had changed countries — not just cities — for football at the age of 12. After a decade of being groomed as a superstar, he felt washed up, past-it, unmotivated.

'Coming from New Zealand at a young age and moving here, not because of anything else but football, it was pretty scary thinking about it,' the New Zealand international, gritting that gold tooth, said. 'It's one of those jobs where everyone thinks you're living the life and stuff. They don't fully know what you have to do and the sacrifices you have to make to get there. I knew everyone was on the same page but me. I obviously knew I was letting the team down. It's the last thing you would expect from a 12, 13-year-old to be coming over here just for football. Mum and Dad were big on me trying to be an A-plus student in New Zealand. Like every good student, when they play a sport and become good at it, they don't really concentrate that much on school work. The last thing a 12-year-old or 13-year-old needs if he's playing good footy is to put pressure on them.'

While we sit around worrying if we spend too much time in front of the television watching sports, while twats like me dissect the relevance in adulthood of our childhood obsessions, we don't pause to think of the toll taken by those who keep ungrateful proles like us pleasantly diverted. We don't think about the casualties of the industries that feed our — perhaps irrational, yes — fascinations.

'There was pressure on me and a lot of wraps. I couldn't cope, especially at a young age,' Taumalolo continued. 'I've seen players come here at a young age. I've played Australian 15s, made rep teams with them, they get that wrap where they talk them up as the next big thing. I look at them now and they're not even playing NRL. Some of them don't even have jobs.'

ANDREW JOHN LANGLEY SAYS: You write about football clubs having souls as if they are people. It's nice you got to make a career out of this stuff you grew up around but I think you're taking it all a tad seriously. But it's a family trait, after all: finding a narrative from random events. At least you've put it to good use.

A City in Name Only

My media career began when I was at high school, as a casual reporter at AAP. But I still lived mainly for Sunday afternoons, when footballers like the late, great Greg Mackey would take to Wollongong Showground and throw outrageous cut-out passes, chip and chase from their own quarter and upend much bigger men. I remember Mackey and his teammates as footy heroes, not league identities I must have interviewed.

Today, I rarely recall such memories when commenting on the game. But when only four St George Illawarra games were scheduled for Wollongong in 2016, as part of a policy to play more games at Sydney's major venues, I couldn't help myself ...

If St George Illawarra are being forced to play more games at one of three Sydney stadiums, why aren't the Newcastle Knights?

The people of Wollongong are an agreeable, placid bunch. It's a nice place to live. What's to get worked up about? Even if you live in the 'western suburbs' you're 15 minutes from the beach.

The Steelers have now been gone longer than they were actually around.

Wollongong people have not endured the natural disasters of their Steel City cousins up north. They don't have an extra hour of road between them and the big smoke. Sydney casts as big a shadow as Mount Kiera. If we keep quiet and get on with things, maybe the property prices won't go up so quickly. *Shhhh.*

But even though the Dragons are based in Wollongong, the city's right — yeah, I'll use that word because they're a 'joint venture' — to host games has been steadily eroded since the club's formation in 1999. The extent to which the NRL values the custom of Australia's 10th largest city has to be questioned. There seem to be absolutely no minimum number of games the governing body wants played there each year.

And when it comes to finals matches, the Dragons are unequivocally deemed a Sydney team — a slap in the face to a region that gave us some of the greatest players of all time, including two Immortals. The NRL seems to take Wollongong for granted.

No doubt one day 'Illawarra' as a suffix will go the same way as 'Warringah' and 'Bankstown'. The reasons for it will fade into history. For some, that happened almost immediately the merger occurred.

But will this process be accelerated by the team no longer playing there?

For those of us still breathing who remember Owen Saunders, Scott Greenland and Chris Macklin-Shaw, maybe it's time to put down our beers, get up off our beach towels, leave the hang glider in the garage and kick up a bit of a stink.

From **The Sydney Morning Herald,** *March 25, 2016.*

STEVE MASCORD'S LOST AND NEVER FOUND EMPORIUM

Almost everyone I know worries about my financial situation more than I do.

I estimate I've earned between $1.5 and $2 million since 1986 covering rugby league. Yet on the most recent occasion I came to visit all I have to show for it, at the place I call my Lost and Never Found Emporium, I walked 50 minutes to save myself the $13.80 cab fare. Behind me, I dragged a bag with a binder full of *Big League* magazines and another full of *Classic Rock*.

In a $260-per-month storage room at Moore Park, Sydney, lies the detritus of more than 30 years on the road chasing footballs, guitar plectrums and teenage dreams. Sold at auction, it's doubtful the contents would pay for more than two months' rent for the room.

There are more copies of *Rugby League Week* from all the years since 1970 on the right-hand shelving than there are missing. *Big League* goes back to 1980 with few absent editions. (I once had a water main burst and the drains were blocked by rugby league magazines, resulting in neighbouring flats being flooded. Inconveniently, it was the morning of the grand final breakfast. I still went.)

Against the back wall are about 500 CDs, arranged in alphabetical order. I used to acquire CDs free at *On The Street* magazine and when everything went digital, I felt compelled to get every single CD in digital form, even though I did not even like many of them. I compiled endless lists and even now have a 'missing songs' file on Google Drive.

The left wall is dominated by shelving up to the grilled ceiling full of pre-recorded VHS, home-recorded VHS, DVDs and cassette tapes. I have more than 40 hours of music video, compiled by sitting down with my finger on the pause button watching the likes of *Rage* and *MTV* and *Sounds* and *Countdown* ready to tape a song at a moment's notice for the best part of a decade. You want Stryper interviewed at the Hard Rock Café on their first Australian tour? Got it. When I went to England, I would rent a VCR and do likewise; the same in the US. Some of the pre-recorded VHS tapes includes *Ratt: The Video, Europe In America, Winfield Cup Grand Final 1988*. Even the recent DVD boxed sets betray me as an arch geek: *Lost, Heroes, X-Files.* Cassettes have only been kept for titles I've not yet digitised.

Below the 'recorded media' are rugby league programs going back to the 1950s, and entire sets from the 2000, 2008 and 2013 World Cups. There are Illawarra Steelers annual reports from the early 1990s, mint copies of *Hot Metal* magazine with the original poster of Axl Rose used to promote issue one and other music magazines I worked for including *Juke, On The Street* and *Kerrang!*.

And in the spaces between the shelving are records, singles, my original Scanlens football-card locker, a cardboard footy ladder with all 12 clubs intact, a five-panelled 2000 World Cup ball, a Russian Rugby League pendant from the 1990s, a *Rank Arena Big Game* sticker lying on the floor, a St George Supporters' Club kit still in the envelope addressed to Steve Mascord, 44 Waratah Street, Windang, NSW 2503, with contents in mint condition. There is a giant cardboard box of rugby league jerseys. I have a 1991 Australian jersey worn in Papua New Guinea by Chris Johns, a 2008 Centenary Test blue and maroon hooped Australia shirt autographed by the team, a 2007 All Golds jersey autographed by the whole side. (I got the Aussie shirt at a jersey presentation to which I was invited and the Kiwi one when photographer Andrew Varley won it at a rugby league media dinner in Leeds but didn't want it — I ran out to the nearest ATM, got some cash and paid for it immediately.) I could have so many more of these but I only ever asked for one item to be autographed in my entire career, that was for my friend Jim Savage. Asking for autographs or photographs, I always believed, was demeaning for my profession. How can you profess to be holding someone to account when you also simperingly want a selfie with them?

Everyone has an attic with memories in it. I don't have an attic, I don't have a house. I just have the memories. And this storage room. I can hear Andrew John Langley tsk-tsking, saying how pathetic I am. He says this stuff is nothing but junk, a tragic reminder of a fortune wasted on teenage fantasies. Given that when I downsized my storage room, I paid someone $800 just to take my couch away, it's difficult to argue with him right now.

I consider myself a sensible person. I deplore gambling and have turned down several offers from betting companies to sponsor my meagre online assets. And yet running up credit-card debt that would take a decade to clear was some sort of intellectual blindspot.

For this I blame two things: *erm* … rugby league (journalism) and heavy metal.

Because covering rugby league is seasonal work, it's always going to be feast and famine. You tell yourself that no matter how much money you spend in summer, you get it back in winter. For years, I did … almost. Each year, I paid off a little less. Then the traditional media started to collapse and the debt became a problem.

Heavy metal was more of an influence in the early years, when I had a Diners Club card, an American Express card, a Visa card and a MasterCard and liked to tear down Hollywood's Sunset Strip in rental cars and fly from Sydney to London for the weekend. These predilections derived purely from magazines that depicted Mötley Crüe lead singer Vince Neil doing the same thing. My rationale was: work like a demon for eight months a year so for four months I can be … Vince Neil.

I'm sure most of the guys upon whom I modelled myself are better off financially than me. At the start of this book's compilation I had around $40,000 in credit-card debt. It had been as high as $56,000. My ambition is, by the time this book is completed, to have it down below $20,000. But, strangely enough, although in my mid- to late-40s I have grown used to seeing the words 'insufficient' and 'funds' juxtaposed on an ATM screen, it has only rarely got me down. And I never – *never* – wished I had a nice house and a fast car.

Never.

What Andrew John Langley will probably never understand is that, for Steve Mascord, finding money to fly to Pittsburgh for an AC/DC show is actually no more or less fun than coming up with the cash to pay this week's rent. These are just little intellectual challenges that keep us occupied. As Israeli historian and author Yuval Noah Harari has written, money is a fiction created by *homo sapiens*. Money feels no suffering, no pain. Unless we are starving, having enough money is just a game we play with ourselves, a way we trick ourselves or others trick us into doing things — many of which we don't want to do. Dollars are just numbers. You can talk about quality of life, about not being able to afford a holiday or a night out, but what is your quality of life when you are doing something you hate for 40 hours a week?

Sorry Andrew, I'd rather live on a shoestring and never go anywhere than waste a second more of my remaining time on this planet than I have to. I do realise that once you have children relying on you, things change. But I don't, so they haven't.

All of which doesn't negate the fact that I could have spent my money on something else or that the contents of my storage room represent obsessions gone absolutely bat-shit crazy.

Lango, you might have a point there.

CHAPTER 5

A COMPLETE BOOFHEAD

One of my first stories after transferring from AAP to *The Sydney Morning Herald* in 1994 involved making a call to another fellow who had made a recent transfer. New Zealand utility back Darrell Williams had moved from Manly to Parramatta and the sides were about to play each other. How did he feel about his former club?

'As far as I am concerned,' observed Williams, 'Manly can get fucked.'

On the record.

I quoted him.

The Sea Eagles didn't know whether to be angry or to just laugh.

As preview angles go, it took some beating, although I did once read in a Dubai newspaper during a fuel stop there that the coach of the Iranian soccer team, in the event of defeat, had vowed to kill himself. Pens down, sportswriters. There's no point trying to find a 'newsy preview angle' ever again. We have a winner.

Williams' move to Parramatta was ill-fated (in the non-Iranian sense of the term): he played only five games there before retiring.

52 GAMES ... 52 GIGS

GAME 6 (MARCH 28): Parramatta 8 Wests Tigers 0 at ANZ Stadium, Sydney Olympic Park
Parked on the sideline as the Eels grind down the joint-venture team. Junior Paulo scores a try that would not have been a try in the pre-television era. Happy Easter!

GIG 6: (MARCH 31): Vintage Trouble at Factory Theatre, Sydney
If you've not seen Vintage Trouble ... when you do so, you'll walk out incredulous that the mainstream media hasn't told you about them. Technically, they're a rhythm and blues band but really, it's a rock'n'roll revival show. Ty Taylor, the singer, is like James Brown on speed. He climbs the balcony, he invades the audience and gets the entire pit down on all fours. They opened for Aerosmith's Joe Perry at the Sunset Strip House of Blues once and I was standing at the bar. My friend tapped me on the shoulder. Slash was up on stage with them, playing *Gimme Shelter*.

The Canberra club secretary (before they were chief executives) John McIntyre once answered my query about the Raiders' interest in rugby union international David Campese by saying, 'You'd have to be a complete boofhead not to be interested in David Campese.' McIntyre was highly entertained to see the word 'boofhead' in his *Canberra Times* over breakfast the next day. The Green Machine eventually snared Campo's nephew, Terry.

As I watched Parramatta take on Wests Tigers in round four, 2016, I was reminded of the time I arrived late at a post-match media conference (they were stand-up huddles until roughly

52 GAMES ... 52 GIGS

GAME 7 (APRIL 3): Warriors 32 Sydney Roosters 28 at Central Coast Stadium, Gosford
The positive about going to the 2pm game in 2016 is that I can do around-the-grounds for Triple M and get some post-match stuff into *Set of Six* for *The Sydney Morning Herald*. Yet another casualty of the shrinking newspaper industry is the copy deadline — covering events that occurred the day before may seem non-negotiable... but now there is pressure for my column to be filed *before* Sunday's games finish.

GIG 7 (APRIL 8): Dragon at Terrey Hills Tavern
'Where's the gig?' I ask an employee after a 35-minute bus journey from Wynyard. It is half an hour before show time. She points back into the dining area. 'We'll move the tables and chairs ... $25 please.' Things get even sillier when Dragon starts and plays 10 covers as their own support band. The show improves — but not enough for me to contemplate missing the 11.15pm bus back to the city.

1997) to hear Eels coach Mick Cronin lament, 'Eric's got a bad knee injury and could be out for the year.' At least that's what I thought he said.

Eric Grothe missing the remainder of the season was indeed big news and, after I wrote my piece for AAP, the story led most radio sports bulletins the next morning. But Cronin had actually said 'Erickson', as in 'Michael Erickson', a handy player but one who would not be missed to the same extent. Ever the gentleman, 'The Crow' simply asked *The Daily Telegraph*'s Les Muir to correct my error.

Another late arrival to a coach's huddle almost resulted in me having my lights punched out — by young fellow reporter Paul Kent. Because at AAP we had to file for radio before heading downstairs to the dressing-rooms, our correspondents usually were last on the scene. On this occasion, I jostled the other reporters to get close enough to hear what Canterbury coach Chris Anderson was saying in the tunnel at Belmore Sports Ground.

A week later, I walked into the anteroom adjoining the main home sheds at Leichhardt Oval — which is pretty much unchanged today — and Kent grabbed me by the scruff of the neck. 'If you ever do again what you did last weekend, I'll knock you out,' he growled. Then he explained what my offence had been. Jostling was just not on. Kent was a recently retired footballer – with a boxing pedigree, too — and threatening to 'posh' (a common phrase among league writers of the '80s and '90s) people was clearly the way you got things done at a footy club.

Paul and I walked into the same room in mid-2014 and I remarked, 'Isn't this where we met?'

There were times early in my career when it looked like it wouldn't be a career at all. A few beers before a Panasonic Cup match in Bathurst in 1988 resulted in 19-year-old me making a goose of myself in front of NSWRL general manager John Quayle, being barely able to type at the game and throwing up in colleague Mike Gandon's car on the way back to Wollongong. 'I gave you a reference to get your job,' Illawarra secretary Bob Millward admonished, when told of my misadventure.

On one occasion, I called Western Suburbs hooker Joe Thomas to interview him for AAP. Joe told me he believed I was writing too many beat-ups. 'Players talk, you know,' he chided.

Being an 'around the grounds' reporter for radio is easily the most stressful duty I've undertaken. My basic maths is abysmal, which means that if someone crosses to me as a try is being scored by Parramatta, which had been leading Gold Coast 10–4, I need a good 30 seconds to figure out that Parra now leads 14–4.

Most of what you see after hours is ineffably funny. One morning, an Australian player who had been up all night was sighted standing at the hotel bar wearing only Glad Wrap (cling film to UK readers). After the 2004 World Club Challenge between Bradford and Penrith, veteran props Joe Vagana and Martin Lang got talking about how much they enjoyed playing against each other. Before long, they were winding up and running headlong at each other in a crowded bar. The 1994 Kangaroos kicked off each night's festivities in the Roundhay Bar of what is now the Leeds Crowne Plaza by singing, '(Antagonistic player who did not make the team) is a cunt, do-dah, do-dah.' Three years later, a footballer's 'indiscreet' party trick in front of the families of the Australian cricket team that was touring England got him an early flight home.

Despite my shaky start as a brash and jostling young drunkard, I've had a good run over the years. Only two players have blocked me on Twitter: Newcastle fullback Robbie O'Davis, to whom I broke the news that his positive drug test was about to become public, and former Bradford hooker Matt Diskin (I have no idea). The only permanent falling out I can recall is with the dual international Mat Rogers, which happened when he was playing with the Gold Coast Titans. In retrospect, he was right and I was wrong. I asked David Gallop if Rogers' wife working for Titans club sponsor Sea FM was a contravention of salary-cap rules. Gallop said he would investigate and that was the story. For years, I justified my actions to myself but they were cynical at best. It's sad, because a few years earlier, late one night at the 2000 World Cup, Rogers asked me to write his biography. He's the only player ever to do so.

Curiously, the coaches and players with whom you have the biggest arguments tend to be the ones with whom you form the best relationships, while those you know are upset with you but say *nada* end up always staying at arm's length.

I have had stinks with both the Smith coaching brothers, Brian and Tony. I've known Brian since I ran the Illawarra Steelers Junior Supporters Club, and can still remember leaning over the fence at the Sydney Cricket Ground and shaking his hand in 1983 when he coached James Cook High there in a semi-final curtain-raiser. He was the Steelers coach the next year.

With Brian, it was the old Sports Ears controversy. During a Parramatta-Brisbane game in 2002, Parra coach Smith heard, via his little green box that tunes into what's happening on the field, Broncos captain Gorden Tallis talking to referee Tim Mander, and then relayed what Tallis was saying to the referee back to his own troops, with instructions to highlight the disrespect. Brian was upset about how this was covered, though I was far from the only recipient of his wrath. He was also disappointed with my coverage of a game the previous year when his halfback, Jason Taylor, was replaced in a match in Melbourne when just short of a point-scoring record. I suggested it might be advantageous for the Eels club for Taylor to break that record at their home ground and that's why his match in Melbourne was cut short.

Today, I consider Brian a friend. In both cases, I maintain I was within my rights as an independent journalist but I did make concessions about how I had carried out my duties.

With Warrington coach Tony Smith, the dispute arose in a more esoteric setting: an Emerging Nations World Cup game in Hull, when he was coaching Japan. One of his players appeared to protest being interchanged by storming to the sheds. When I raised the issue in his post-game meeting with the press, Tony insisted that is not how things played out at all. I wrote what I saw, in the process applying the same rules to covering essentially amateur sport as I would to professionals. I argued that this is what my contribution should be to a game of that stature, just as Tony was offering his professional services as a coach. I cannot apologise for that.

What I can apologise for was trying too hard to prove a point on this issue. If there was a reasonable excuse for similar behaviour in an NRL game, the player storming off would not lead your story. But because I was trying real hard to prove how 'big city' I was, I took the most aggressive route. I later acknowledged this to Tony.

I now have a very good relationship with Tony Smith, as well. The secret is that regardless of how personal your adversary gets in an argument, keep your responses to the issues at hand. I'm a bit unusual in this regard. On Twitter, I re-tweet abuse but never compliments.

In truth, I have a bit of a martyr complex. I see myself as an outsider, even a crusader, and abuse and personal insults help reinforce my self-image. I am always happy to do things the hard way, to wait until everyone else has got off the plane before

I leave my seat, to stop dead and let a distracted pedestrian walk into me on the street and to chip away at projects that will never be finished, because I see myself as someone who finds his way around obstacles rather than charging through them.

I was considered too young to be the chief rugby league writer at AAP straight out of school in the late 1980s (I was also too young to be the first editor of *Hot Metal*, despite coming up with the name). Instead, at AAP I worked under a slightly older fellow named Trevor Marshallsea, who had a razor-sharp memory for amusing anecdotes and the peculiar and ridiculous lexicon of leaguelish. ('Who should walk into Leichhardt Oval but one P. Pot,' he once joked, talking like a cross between Ray Warren and Geoff Prenter.)

Trevor woke in a sweat one night and realised he had been covering the game for too long. In one horrible hour, he dreamed that he was saved from a mugger in Brisbane's Queen Street Mall by Paul Sironen and that Ken Arthurson had kissed him on the lips at a function.

One morning, a daily newspaper had a story: 'Simon Poidevin to join Balmain'. Poidevin was a rugby union Wallaby and his switching codes was quite a big deal. To authenticate the article, Trevor called the Tigers' club secretary, Keith Barnes, who told him in the Welsh brogue made famous in commentary of mid-week Amco Cup matches: 'Feck me did, Triv. I've never iven met the bloke.' So, being close friends with the author of the scoop, Trevor called his print colleague and asked a question reporters only pose if they are extremely, extremely close: 'Where'd you get it from?'

The response? 'Made it up.'

ANDREW JOHN LANGLEY SAYS: What is the actual point of being a sportswriter? Writing and journalism have a purpose if you are uncovering universal truths. If you are keeping tabs on corrupt presidents or reflecting on man's disregard for the environment and each other, you are performing a worthwhile role in society (even if the money's bad). But sports journalism, writing endlessly about an event that could be summed up in one line — Blue Team 4, Red Team 2 — is a profession that deserved to be gobbled up by the death of traditional media. The sports coverage is, by far, the least important thing in any newspaper.

CHAPTER 6

HELL'S BELLS

It was the school uniform that got me. It just didn't seem right.

For a Saturday night in early April I reserved a room at Indio in the California desert on *booking.com*. It had just been announced that Guns N' Roses were to make their comeback at Coachella music festival. (Which iteration, I did not know, but Axl Rose and Slash would be playing together for the first time in 23 years.)

I'd gone to Coachella in 2015, saw the first AC/DC show in six years and — as things turned out, 'in related news' — the beginning of the final tour with singer Brian Johnson. Andrew Johns and Simon Moran, the 'rock impresario' who owns the Warrington Wolves, helped me get press credentials.

In 2015, I had to stay 90 minutes' drive from the Coachella site. Every rich kid in LA goes to Coachella to pretend to be wasted in hippy threads that actually cost a semester's worth of parental allowance. Rooms in Indio on either of the festival's weekends are hard to come by; in 2016, mine was more than 300 bucks for one night, but still cheap by comparison to others on offer.

When my credit card was declined, the room was quickly on-sold to some Hollywood director's spoilt boat-shoe wearing brat

(I'd imagine …), but that was OK because it was announced that Guns — who were doing no interviews and wouldn't even confirm their line-up — were playing Vegas first. I'd have been filthy if I'd wasted money on Coachella, only to find there was an earlier show elsewhere. Had I got tickets to *Vegas*, in turn, I would no doubt have felt a little gypped that they played the Troubadour in West Hollywood before *that*.

I remained in Sydney.

As things stand … Axl didn't stand. He broke a foot (journo and author Malcolm Andrews taught me to never say 'broke *his* foot unless he only has one) in the first warm-up show in front of 300 people with golden tickets and performed the next six megabuck-making concerts seated on Dave Grohl's 'rock throne'. (In 2015, Grohl broke a leg when he fell off the stage during a show in Sweden, and while recovering performed in a gigantic metal chair.) At the first of these Coachella shows, 54-year-old Rose admitted he felt guilty at not being able to snake-dance around the stage and introduced 'a friend of ours' — AC/DC guitarist Angus Young, who I had seen on the same stage 12 months earlier. I've already got an idea for another book: *A Year in the Death of Rock'n'roll*. And this is its natural starting point.

Now, taken at face value, Axl and Angus together was beyond the point of being a stellar guest spot. On my very first night in America, back in 1990, I saw Tom Petty and the Heartbreakers at the LA Forum. For the encore, Bruce Springsteen and Bob Dylan got up. *That* was a stellar guest spot.

Angus in full school uniform (when he guested with the Stones one night at the Enmore in 2003, he wore jeans, as he would in

52 GAMES ... 52 GIGS

GAME 8 (APRIL 10): Cronulla 25 Gold Coast 20 at Southern Cross Stadium, Woolooware

A group of Cronulla players are lifting a dune buggy at the southern end of the pitch, like three Incredible Hulks. Seriously. Three-year-old Rocco Heighington, son of Chris, has been run over when a corner post thrown into the buggy caused it to take off without its driver. Amazing, right?

GIG 8 (APRIL 15) Sarah McLeod at The Vanguard, Newtown

'I've just been in New York writing a new album,' says the erstwhile Superjesus front woman at this intimate King Street venue. It strikes me that creativity requires focus. It also strikes me that this is why writing this book is hard — because I have to earn a living at the same time. Sarah's new stuff sounds good, by the way. A special mention to the *No Life 'Til Leather* rock club, where I venture afterwards.

early 2017 with G N' R in Sydney) next to Slash in top hat and leathers would be like a hole ripped in space-time on a sultry desert night. Like Area 51, suddenly open to the public.

Warning: here's that word again. These were the touchstones of my childhood, iconic images even in silhouette, but they were just never meant to be in the same place. It was like seeing Columbo next to Aqua Man, or Abraham Lincoln and Martin Luther King playing tennis (one in tights, the other in top hat). On a very basic level, it appeared to disobey the laws of nature. And it felt like a betrayal of teenaged Steve Mascord.

And, as things turned out, Young seemed to have forgotten how to play *Riff Raff*, a Bon Scott classic. Latter-day Guns-slinger Richard Fortus has played it far more regularly in recent times.

But there was an underlying adult reason for my cynicism, too, about this gig I never attended. Earlier in the evening, it was announced that Axl would be fronting AC/DC in Europe and the US following the sudden departure of the aforementioned Johnson, confirming a rumour that millions had steadfastly refused to believe.

As a result, the velvet school uniform Angus wore on stage at Coachella in 2016 appeared wrong to me because it seemed calculated, a crass attempt to promote upcoming shows that themselves had a strangely unseemly quality to them.

AC/DC had protected their trademarks zealously for 40 years. While most people assume drummer Phil Rudd was kicked out of the band for trying to have someone killed, I wouldn't be surprised if his biggest crime was doing a solo album.

But now there were tickets to postponed shows which needed selling and refunds that needed avoiding so let's put the old uniform on and duckwalk around G N' R's stage with the help of their singer — who we have just hired. Yes, I am guilty of over-thinking almost everything. But a moment that should have been transcendent was badly tainted.

But how would I know? I wasn't actually there.

When Guns' *Appetite for Destruction* first came out in 1987, I was well-entrenched as an ignorant 18-year-old rock critic at Sydney's *On the Street* newspaper. I taped side one of *Appetite* onto a C-60 cassette, walked up to the Windang sand dunes and listened to it repeatedly. And I decided it was rubbish. In happy serendipity,

52 GAMES ... 52 GIGS

GAME 9 (APRIL 18): Penrith 20 Sydney Roosters 16 at Allianz Stadium, Moore Park
I'm going to miss *Monday Night Football* when it's gone. Tonight, on Triple M, I interview Penrith prop Leilani Latu at fulltime. He immediately starts talking about God. The God Squad are taking over the NRL, but he seems like a nice guy.

GIG 9 (APRIL 19): Black Sabbath at Rod Laver Arena, Melbourne
I leave early. Sabbath are a band I am supposed to like and, honestly, I do. But being weaned on KISS means we are spoiled when it comes to onstage activity. Ozzy saying 'Go crazy' and 'Are you louder than Perth and Adelaide?' only takes you so far. I think I like Dio-era Sabbath more. Plus, I get to Cherry Bar in AC/DC Lane early. Soon, there is a line around the corner. My friend is in the line. So I leave and never get to have a night out at Cherry Bar. Because the line is too long, see.

Appetite for Destruction had already been reviewed by someone else at *OTS* so my catastrophically ill-informed opinion would not immediately see the light of day.

Alas, I was determined to share my stupidity. I had previously not had anything published in *RAM* — *Rock Australia Magazine* — which seemed at the time too snobby for any music that was any good. It was the *Guardian* to *JUKE*'s *Daily Mail*.

So I optimistically sent off the review to *RAM*, sharing my wisdom about this new record by an unkempt LA glam band. If you were the editor of *RAM* at the time and are reading this, you have free beer from me for life. (Actually, I recently did come into contact with a former editor when he vaguely threatened me with legal action for starting up a *RAM* Facebook page. I'd rather just give him a beer but you can't choose these things.)

In this blessedly mislaid piece of prose, I reasoned that if Guns N' Roses kept working on it, they *may one day be as good as Poison* ...

Appetite is now regarded by me, and maybe millions of others, as one of the greatest albums of all time.

When I called Slash for an *OTS* interview in 1988 (long before mobile phones) a girl named Kimberley answered and told me she was his girlfriend. Slash was leaving tomorrow for Japan and she was a bit upset. Are you planning a big farewell? 'No, just a private one (giggles).'

Saul Hudson (AKA Slash) later became available and confided he had been 'urinating with my pet spider'.

'You keep doing what you're doing and be good at it 'til people aren't interested in it any more,' he said, then aged just 23. 'And then you're out. People who think they're going to be the next biggest thing for the next 10 years and try to make a lot of big comments and stuff ... I really think you should just go out and do what you're good at for as long as people are interested.'

Of course, they're still interested. Stadium-sized interest.

The day after *G N' R Lies* came out, in November 1988, Axl Rose gave me one of my best after-dinner stories.

The place: the newly christened, and now demolished, Sydney Entertainment Centre. You know you're getting old when you remember public buildings being opened — and being demolished.

This was a snarling, drunken, anarchic G N' R at the Ent Cent, yet to receive the royalty cheques from their debut

52 GAMES ... 52 GIGS

GIG 10 (APRIL 24): Rival Sons at Frankie's, Sydney
Frankie's Pizza is an ineffably fantastic rock club in Sydney's CBD. Down stairs off Hunter Street, you encounter a pizza parlour with obligatory checked table cloths. Behind that is a huge performance space serving craft beers. And through a staircase at the back is an unmarked, candle-lit, cool-as-fuck cocktail bar. Rival Sons frontman Jay Buchanan seems charmingly vulnerable and un-rock. 'I've got a young son and I miss him, being a touring musician,' he says halfway through this chaotic, triumphant gig by rock's best new band. The pain of that separation is part of his performance. There's nothing new about how Rival Sons sound, but there is about how they feel.

GAME 10 (APRIL 28): Wests Tigers 30 South Sydney 22 at ANZ Stadium, Sydney Olympic Park
During an after-match interview on the wireless, Wests Tigers' coach Jason Taylor says he enjoyed the preceding week despite being under intense pressure to keep his job, even though that might sound 'sadistic'. When I say to him off-air that he probably meant 'masochistic', Taylor is unimpressed. 'You're the only person out of the whole audience who would pick that up.'

album that would soon ignite their own collective appetite for destruction. Steven Adler played without a drum riser, the only prop was the electric fan behind him, and it was rumoured Duff McKagan was performing with a broken hand deadened only by Jack Daniels — particularly impressive to a sports writer.

Second on the bill after opening act Kings of the Sun were The Angels, the Oz rock band with cult status among an LA long-hair community basking in global sunlight never so intense before or since. Another of these influential Australian bands was Rose Tattoo, whom G N' R covered via the song *Nice Boys (Don't Play Rock'n'Roll)*. In the lead-up to the Entertainment Centre show, Kings of the Sun told me in an interview they had been forced to decamp to the US because Australian apathy had destroyed so many bands. 'Rose Tattoo should have been one of the biggest,' said singer Jeff Hoad. His today-estranged brother, drummer Cliff, added a comment that was similarly supportive of Rose Tattoo and was also critical of Guns N' Roses and Mötley Crüe. I quoted him word for word.

After the first song of G N' R's set, Axl Rose told the swirling, restless audience: 'We've been reading this article backstage. (My article!) I want to apologise for having a puny-ass band like Kings of the Sun open for us. We love Rose Tattoo.'

My date laughed at Axl's wackiness. I sank deeper into my seat. Later that night on *MTV* — then just a show on network television — Cliff and Jeff revealed my story had prompted Axl's henchmen to pull their PA support before the show and the laminates from around their necks afterwards. 'Misquoted in a magazine?' *MTV*'s host, Richard Wilkins, asked the boys. I've always resented Wilkins for asking that question. 'Just sensitive Americans,' Jeff replied.

Twenty-three years later, I met Cliff on the Gold Coast as part of my attempt to reanimate my rock journalism career. He stood by his comments in the original story. 'History has shown anything that comes out of [Axl Rose's] mouth can be taken with a grain of salt,' said Cliff, a whirling, ebullient performer who put out a wonderful KOTS comeback album, *Rock Til Ya Die*, in 2013. 'Whatever he said about me, or Kings of the Sun, is just water off a duck's back. I never thought anything of it. When I said those things, I meant them. It wasn't necessarily aimed at Guns N' Roses. It was aimed at the Australian press and public. OK, make a fuss over Guns N' Roses but at least know that Rose Tattoo exists.'

Rose Tattoo have lost pretty much every member to cancer. Surviving singer Angry Anderson has become a right-wing politician. Like AC/DC's drummer, Rose Tattoo's skinsman Paul DeMarco has been in trouble with the law. He was arrested on firearms offences in 2014 and admitted to them in 2016.

Nice boys, it would seem, actually do not play rock'n'roll. Perhaps that's the most important thing rock'n'roll has in common with rugby league: criminality.

ANDREW JOHN LANGLEY: Finally, something I agree with. Rugby league and heavy metal are beacons for bogans. People who piss in their own mouths and, if they're rich enough, hire prostitutes to hang out in various rooms in their house, and hire hit-men to knock off the boyfriends of said prostitutes when they aren't paid. Stephen, you would never have got into this shit if you'd stayed on the north shore with me.

HARD ROCK

It's about time I answered this: why hard rock and hair metal?

Last year, I had someone on Twitter say my love of Spandex and Aqua Net (I don't wear either, and haven't since ... oh, the first half of 2011) was damaging my credibility as a serious sports pundit. But I never set out to be a 'serious sports pundit' and certainly wouldn't pretend not to love something I do to convince people I'm something I never set out to be.

A generation after I began writing about music, what I like to call my 'Sunset Strip halcyon days', it is now acceptable to analyse the era in a scholarly, earnest way. Writers like Chuck Klosterman (*Fargo Rock City*) and Seb Hunter (*Hellbent for Leather*) have sold many books by name-checking the brief stint in KISS of guitarist Mark St John or recounting the yarn about Slash auditioning for Poison.

I suspect the story of what drew me to cock rock, and still holds me there, is like that of Klosterman and Hunter and millions of others. And I wonder if disaffected teenage males today have anything — be it a musical genre, a television show, a pastime or an exotic fruit — that can perform the same function for them.

Growing up, I liked my parents' — specifically my mother's — music, which was pretty much Elvis Presley and ... well, Elvis Presley. After watching *The Partridge Family*, I remember taking a bizarre interest in David Cassidy and asking Mum and Dad for some of his LPs. It was the lamest beginning to any campaign of teen rebellion.

Perhaps the start of it all was asking to see KISS at Sydney Sports Ground, home of the Eastern Suburbs Roosters, in 1980. At this point, KISS had become a pop act and merchandising entity rather than a band, and I didn't want to go that much because I had no friends to go with (and hardly any to not go with). But after my mother conferred with my aunties, I was denied on the rather reasonable basis that I was just 12. Consequently, I became a KISS fan.

When I say 'disaffected male', I mean: I was unpopular at school, riddled with zits, regularly mocked and even attacked on the way home from the bus stop. I lived largely in a Walter Mitty-like fantasy world. I didn't want out of my fantasy world — still there, folks — but I wanted a cooler one than Dr Who's, notwithstanding his hot female assistants.

KISS was a perfect bridge from my childhood obsession with science fiction and fantasy to the adolescent pursuit of sex and sex. They encompassed both. By 1980, Gene Simmons, who wore gargoyles for boots, spat blood and breathed fire, had only slept with about 2000 women, a figure he has now comfortably doubled (actually, he's slowed down). Trevor Marshallsea once remarked, 'For him, it must be like sneezing.' I subsequently purchased every magazine carrying even the slightest reference to the New York glam kings, blissfully ignorant that they were commercially floundering with their best days — back in the '70s when I followed popular music by taping songs off *Countdown* but had hardly been aware of them — seemingly behind them.

I was the archetypal KISS drone: the sort of person who today unquestioningly accepts two stand-ins dressing as Ace Frehley and Peter Criss. I liked every single thing they released (with the sole exception, much later, of Peter Criss' *I Finally Found My Way*, off *Psycho Circus. Blrgh!*)

There were other bands in American magazines such as *Circus*, *Hit Parader* (a friend at school pronounced it 'Hit *Parahda*' — we knew about the magazine before we even heard the term 'hit paradc') and *Faces Rocks*: Mötley Crüe and Ratt and the Scorpions. But I can't remember being hooked by any of them until I heard the single — or, more specifically, saw the video — from another act whose purist fans had recently abandoned them following the departure of a singer.

Van Halen's *Why Can't This Be Love* (why is there no question mark in this title?) was driven by synthesiser and, in truth, was most notable for its live video. The lighting and staging reminded me of what was not only my favourite band at the time but my only band, KISS. (It was 30 years before I learned that there were rooms under that stage where Sammy Hagar and Eddie Van Halen would screw multiple groupies during instrumental breaks, hence Sammy re-emerging in a dressing gown.)

The next non-KISS song I remember being impressed by was *She Don't Know Me* by a then unknown New Jersey act called Bon Jovi. Bon Jovi's self-titled debut, backed with Dokken's *Under Lock and Key*, was one of the first things I had taped by a friend onto a TDK D-90. (Remember when one of the most important things you needed to know about a new record was whether it fit on a D-90 or a D-60? Then there were the rare and special D-45s ...) From here, an entirely new world opened up: Kix, Keel, Y&T, Whitesnake, Disneyland After Dark (or D-A-D), W.A.S.P. and much bigger names such as Poison, Iron Maiden and Def Leppard. My own cousin, I learned, had choreographed the video for *Dancin' Queen* by local metallers Boss.

This period, the second half of the 1980s, was the only time in my life the zeitgeist and I even remotely shared the same real estate. The bands I raved about, almost inevitably, became huge. After leaving high school, I wrote news stories about Poison having a groupie computer; it was mentioned in Queensland parliament and made them the biggest story in Australia when they came to town. In 1988, working as a cadet on AAP Sydney's general news desk, I asked fundamentalist Christian minister Fred Nile what he thought of a touring Christian metal band called Stryper. He slammed them, saying churches who had been sent promotional copies of their records should send them straight back. Suddenly, Stryper were big news.

In fact, in both cases, the bands were fringe acts before my stories for AAP were sent to every media outlet in the country. Suddenly, the bands were on every current affairs program, and I ponder how successful I could have been as a PR man, and about how enthusiasm for a subject really can be infectious with commercial rewards if you maintain enough perspective to appeal to the reference points of others, something most people are unable to do.

But there is a question at hand: what is it that I liked about hair metal and hard rock?

The biggest misunderstanding about '80s hard rock and heavy metal is that it was almost entirely misogynistic. There have been some glaring exceptions — Skid Row's *Get the Fuck Out* comes to mind — but heavy metal lyricists generally liked women more than those in any other genre.

You might argue that metal lyrics of that time objectified women but popular culture generally objectified women in the '80s. Metal was obsessed with women and sex, with goblins and dragons a fair way back in third and fourth place respectively. If I was a girl, I would have been a groupie, and I would not have seen it as demeaning.

But that's not what I liked about it. The things that parents and much of the media overlooked were that hard rock and heavy metal in the '80s was aspirational and individualistic. The hits were normally love songs or party songs, but the album tracks preached positive re- enforcement and ambition. I'm talking about Van Halen's *Best of Both Worlds*, KISS's *I*, Keel's *Right to Rock* and dozens and dozens more. When you are used to being marginalised socially, a long-haired guy in leather pants giving the short-haired no-eyeliner world the finger is incredibly empowering.

There was also a blueprint of the way life could be, welcome assistance for someone looking for ideas. You didn't have to marry your childhood sweetheart and have kids by the time you were 25. You didn't even have to be accepted by the other members of your geography class. 'Here I go again on my own,' David Coverdale crooned. L.A. Guns' Phil Lewis told us he didn't need anyone to tell him to settle down. The 'fast lane', he insisted, suited him to the ground.

(The greatest anecdote in rock history surrounds the former's song, *Here I Go Again*, which most famously appeared on Whitesnake's eponymous platinum album in 1987, but had previously appeared on *Saints and Sinners* in 1982. The line after the one quoted above originally went, *'Like a hobo, I was born to walk alone.'* When time came to re-record it, the American producer insisted on a change to 'like a drifter ...' Why? He thought most Americans would mistake the original lyric for 'like a homo I was born to walk alone'.)

If you were captain of the football team and banging the prettiest girl in school, you probably didn't need heavy metal the way I did. But I wasn't, and I did.

Hard rock and heavy metal were responsible for me ringing newspapers and magazines and hassling them for work. These preening rock gods taught me anything was possible, that there was an alternative to toiling at the steelworks. At Port Kembla High School, the most precocious ambition any of my fellow students had was to be an engineer, and that was considered borderline elitist. When, in *Higher Ground*, Thunder sang that they didn't want to spend their 'whole life' in their hometown, how that town was driving them away, they could have been singing for me.

While I can't sing and the market for triangle players is limited, I heeded these lessons to such an extent that rock'n'roll filled the role religion plays in the lives of others. And as Lemmy said, rock'n'roll is a religion that gives much and takes little, particularly if you download illegally.

One more quote, though, from the sublime Drive-By Truckers (Sublime, however, are not drive-by truckers): 'Rock'n'roll means well, but it can't help telling young boys lies.'

These lies take years to reveal themselves. One is, you cannot spend your entire life approaching love as 'EZ Come EZ Go'. You will not live long if you rock'n'roll all night and party every day. If I am sleeping my day away, I am not making any money. You will not always be the youth gone wild. Discovering these things does not make me a rock'n'roll atheist. It just makes me less of a fundamentalist rock'n'roller. Age hasn't caused me to lose my religion.

Anyway, it's time to stop writing this unforced entry. You can't be king of the world if you're slave to the grind.

The Adolescence of International Rugby League

W e will one day look back on this period in the development of international rugby league as an adolescence, with all the excitement, awkwardness and pain that implies.

Today, we have had the announcement of the 2016 Four Nations dates, with Anfield to host the final on November 20, 2016. That was a venue for the memorable World Club Challenge final of 1991 — an amphitheatre from which we have been absent as a sport for way too long.

Rugby league is also back at London's Olympic Stadium, we visit the Ricoh Arena in Coventry for the first time and the tournament also goes to Hull, Huddersfield and Workington.

But at the same time as these bright, optimistic developments there have been growing pains, most notably over the question of player eligibility for upcoming Tests. These pains even manifested themselves in the unlikely location of Lucerne, Switzerland. There, league hoped to be accepted this weekend into the SportAccord union of global sporting bodies. Funding in countries such as Thailand, Italy, Germany, Poland and Latvia would have been forthcoming from governments as a result. But the applications of rugby league, arm wrestling and poker have been delayed because SportAccord is looking for a new president. They will be examined again in November.

A sports politics news site set the cat amongst the pigeons on Thursday by reporting World Rugby had asked that rugby league not be admitted. SportAccord has said nothing official about what happened at this week's meeting.

Rugby league officials believe any obstruction can be solved by diplomacy and at the time of writing have neither confirmed or denied that report. But there's no doubt acceptance by SportAccord and the International Olympic Committee would be a huge boost to rugby league, as it would open up government funding streams around the globe.

The three theatres — Four Nations, international eligibility and government recognition — are intertwined. At the top, rugby league seeks to engage sponsors, broadcasters and fans with its biggest name fulltime professionals. In the middle, through workable eligibility criteria, it hopes to soon turn 'the Big Three' of New Zealand, Australia and England into 'the Big Four' or 'Big Five'. And for smaller countries like Serbia, Burundi and the Philippines, it aims to make it easier to access venues, insurance and the other benefits afforded to recognised sport.

When adolescence is over, rugby league can really go to work.

From **rugby-league.com** *on April 22, 2016.*

CHAPTER 6-6-6

NUMBER OF THE BEAST

Is it the domain of middle-aged men to boycott things in protest? I feel like I am on the verge of making a living from boycotting things, and then writing about it.

One of the things I was looking forward to most during the first half of the 2016 league season was the Anzac Test between Australia and New Zealand in Newcastle on May 6. Maybe a few days in a city that looks and feels like the Australia of my youth– all weatherboard houses and milk bars — would have been good for the soul. But then Australia picked Semi Radradra, a Fijian who only qualified because he had lived in Australia for three years. I became infinitely less interested.

Australia has 15 of the only 32 full-time professional rugby league clubs in the world. Half the world's pros have to go to Australia to earn a living. If Australia and England pick players on residency (which England has already done a couple of times, with Rangi Chase and Maurie Fa'asavalu), they can have anyone from anywhere … and we don't have an international game.

My lack of interest only became a boycott, however, when the Warriors club side from New Zealand brazenly claimed they

52 GAMES ... 52 GIGS

GIG 11 (MAY 6): Iron Maiden at Qudos Bank Arena, Sydney Olympic Park
A wonderful reminder of how much heavy metal means to people and a clue as to why. Thousands of smiling faces and a sort of rock opera/morality tale kicking off with hooded singer Bruce Dickinson over a steaming cauldron. I finally 'get' Iron Maiden, even if they're still very hard to explain to someone who doesn't.

GAME 11 (MAY 7): Pacific Tests at Pirtek Stadium, Parramatta
Samoa coach Matt Parish rails against the unfairness of it all — his players not getting paid, Anthony Milford and Joey Leilua failing to gain a release from their clubs to play. Outside, a 15,000 crowd disperses. The NRL lose an estimated $400,000 on this game — but if it's part of the TV deal, then it's worth millions. This is what the crossroads looks like for international rugby league.

could decide who was in the Kiwis' national team and who was not — and then did so. The players 'banned from selection' were Manu Vatuvei, Ben Matulino and Bodene Thompson, who were reported to have enjoyed a night out that reputedly didn't end until 3am. Three more Warriors players — Sam Lisone, Albert Vete and Konrad Hurrell — were 'stood down' from the Tonga-Samoa international the same weekend.

The mistake that rugby league fans make in analysing the arguments surrounding these decisions is that they play the man. I don't care about the individuals; my arguments have nothing to do with them.

For as long as I have followed rugby league, international football has sat *above* club football. Players were 'chosen' by national team selectors, their clubs had no say in the matter. At one point recently, we almost went back to making players show up at medicals if they felt they were unfit — even if it meant a wasted flight.

And right up until the week preceding the representative round of 2016, clubs had to come up with crappy excuses if they wanted to pull a player out of a game. Mitchell Pearce, who had only played one game *all year*, apparently could not play for City Origin in Tamworth because he was suffering 'soreness' (tell that to the dog, right?).

But Andrew McFadden, the Warriors coach, and Jim Doyle, the chief executive, don't remember Les Boyd lying on a bench in his jocks being looked over by Dr Bill Monaghan. They weren't around then. Wayne Bennett was — which is why he pre-empted the reaction to his own decision that week to ban Anthony Milford from playing for Samoa by saying: 'I don't care what anyone thinks.'

Arguably, Australian Rugby League Commission chairman John Grant was most culpable in all of this. He played on the wing for Australia. He probably once met Dr Monaghan while only wearing his Reg Grundies. Instead of standing up to the clubs, here's what he said when I asked him at a media conference about the mass withdrawals from the representative weekend: 'We'd like a better turnout. There's not a lot of players who are not going to play for Country, because they want to play for Country. I think that reflects on City.' You read that right. Given the chance to show leadership, Grant instead decided to throw a churlish barb at City coach Brad Fittler, who had spent the week attacking the NRL for a lack of … well, leadership.

Grant described all clubs releasing players for representative games as 'a journey'. Better get in the DeLorean — the 'journey' involves only going back about five years.[1]

So despite having a gig on the sideline for Triple M at Hunter Stadium for the Test, I passed … didn't even watch it on television. What did I do instead?

I went to see Iron Maiden, of course.

The previous June, I had been escorted by a publicist from Stockholm to a backstage area at Sweden Rock in Sölvesborg (the best *thing* I have ever been to, that festival) for an interview with The Darkness's hirsute bass player Frankie Poullain (it's pronounced 'Pool-on', he informed me). On the way, the publicist explained the Scandinavian love of heavy metal thus: 'Look at us. Do we look like we are hip hop fans? We are Vikings. This music is in our blood.' She had never met an Australian journalist and was going to visit the country for

---

1. *Of course, things only got worse. As this book was going to press in early May 2017, the lead-up to the final City-Country game descended into farce when some clubs decided not to release their players for the fixture. This is part of how I summed up the situation for the* Sydney Morning Herald:

It's fitting that City-Country is dying at the same time as the quaint notion about the primacy of representative football.

In one corner, we have a commercially-driven pro sports league with clubs who think they pay the players' wages, when in fact they are just the second middle-man between the athletes and their real employers, TV networks. In the other is the Victorian era concept of 'representation', 'caps' and 'tours'; ideas from a world where players were merely paid 'broken time' for missing work and when the only income the game had was gate takings.

Under international rules, players who are not released for a Test can be stood down from a club game the following week. No one expects the NRL or the

the first time to coincide with the upcoming tour by her close friends, Iron Maiden.

Eleven months later, we met in a Sydney hotel. Our backstage passes, she explained, had been left by singer Bruce Dickinson in the business centre of the band's own — much more salubrious — digs and that business centre was now closed. We would still have passes — they just wouldn't be as good. Who cared, right? After the train ride to the Qudos Bank Arena at Homebush Bay, we met by coincidence at the ticket office a pair of kids best described as Europe's answer to Wayne and Garth. There was a Swedish guy with long blond hair and a hilariously mangled Scando-Australian accent alongside his tall, short-haired German friend.

The four of us were given 'band hospitality' laminates. The Swede ('Garth') knew Iron Maiden because his aunty worked on one of their videos once. Or something. The two of them lived in a tiny town in South Australia, where they worked for minimum wage and slept in the back of an office. They weren't allowed to use the Wi-Fi because their boss thought they would surf porn.

Rugby League International Federation to try to do that in 2017 — the clubs are far too powerful, the commercial realities too stark. It is perhaps even more ridiculous that Super League teams missing England players next weekend will be taking on opposition that refused to release their own Pacific Islands players for the same fixtures in which England are taking part!

Time to call that situation what it is: a joke and an embarrassment.

Everyone involved in representative football treads warily around clubs, trying to get things done by goodwill and consensus. And as a result, less gets done with each passing year.

The representative weekend should have become the sport's FIFA window — no games in either of our two major professional competitions and everyone playing rep matches. Instead it is a ghoulish reminder of the game's dysfunction, with players held out of matches on the whim of a coach and clubs releasing players to some teams and not others.

I kid you not, these kids really exist.

Even though they were half my age, we bonded over black t-shirts. My industry friend felt less enamoured with a pair of lads whom, if you saw a picture of them under a headline containing the words 'glue' and 'sniffing', you'd be less than startled. We were directed to what is basically a giant sports dressing-room in the bowels of the venue, where there was a fridge full of beer and that's pretty much it. Apparently, band members often drop into this area to check on their personal guests. None tonight. My companion regaled me with some inner-band gossip that I dare not repeat here and we hoarded our beers before walking out onto the arena floor for the headliners.

Maiden themselves were astoundingly sprightly for men approaching their 70s. Dickinson ran from side to side of a Mayan-themed set, the playing was exemplary and the tribute to Robin Williams, *Tears of a Clown*, rather moving. I'd seen Iron Maiden before in Sydney, and at Rock in Rio in 2001. While *Number of the Beast* is an album that evokes my high-school memories better than just about any other, the subject matter always seemed far too ridiculous to take them seriously. Cowboys and Indians, 17th-century voyages, execution. The band itself is named after a mediaeval torture device.

But when Bruce Dickinson started the show wearing a shroud, holding his hands over what looked like a boiling pot, I finally got it. This was opera — and despite a bout of tongue cancer, Dickinson has the voice for it. While much of metal from my era is sexual schmaltz, Iron Maiden trade in morality tales. This was good, evil, human flaws and honour. While KISS's Paul Stanley spends the time between songs using the old line about being welcomed with 'open arms and legs'; Dickinson told of an Australian rifleman shooting down the Red Baron.

Iron Maiden played a lot of new material without apology and nor should there have been any because *Book of Souls* is a quality release. I was getting on well with my hostess, exchanging national generalisations and twee slang expressions as one does in such situations. With the show almost over, I was looking forward to taking her to Frankie's. She received a text. Then she told me, 'I have some bad news.'

'You're dumping me?'

'Yes. The band says to meet them at the hotel and "just you". I'm sorry.'

In my world, I can pretend that people are equal. Rugby league players can be evasive and even hostile to the press but if they are caught dismissing members of the public, there is shame. What I don't like about the music industry is the complete suspension of that notion of equality. If you are summoned by the lead singer of a multi-platinum rock band, it is a given that you will ditch whoever you are with. If they are in any way put out by this, they just don't understand.

Perhaps the death of rock'n'roll isn't all bad. There is less room now for rock gods whose gravity draws everything and everyone towards them and creates chaos wherever they go. I have a mantra: if you try to tell me who my friends (or companions) should be, you're not my friend. Doesn't matter how long I've known you, if you try to exclude someone I'll go off with that someone and ditch you.

I saw a fellow back stage I had encountered repeatedly overseas. He had hair down to his arse and wore designer rock clobber. In the past, at the Rainbow on Sunset Boulevard or the Monsters of Rock Cruise, he gave me only cursory attention.

I used to have long hair. May do again. Don't now.

But now, having come across me in the ... *erm* ... outer sanctum, he instinctively showed great deference. I was more important than he thought. As Axl once crooned, 'It's that prejudiced illusion that pumps the blood to the heart of the biz.'

Sometimes I wish I'd spent the last 25 years in the 'biz'. As I went home alone on the train that night, I thanked God I hadn't.

ANDREW JOHN LANGLEY SAYS: I kind of admire the principles being upheld here, even if the subject itself is not worth getting riled up about. But, I mean, Iron Maiden? Seriously? Maybe you do take all this moral stuff seriously. Maybe that's one thing we have in common that you didn't learn in Windang.

CHAPTER 7

THE SIDELINE

'A plastic bottle.'

A ground official at Belmore Sports Ground uttered these words, nodded to the object he had just described which lay at our feet, then gave me a funny look. A look that said, 'There's more to what I'm saying than I'm saying.'

Standing there in light rain, four metres in from a raging NRL game and holding a wireless radio microphone, I was confused. Perhaps, I thought, the guard's Curly-from-The-Three-Stooges scowl was related to the fact that a year and a week earlier, at another Canterbury Bulldogs game, a hail of said plastic bottles had descended upon the match officials as they left the field.

I fast-walked my way back to my seat on the sideline, next to tech Phil Agnew, and reported the news to the commentary team of Dan Ginnane, Peter Sterling and Jamie Soward. 'A plastic bottle's been thrown at the Canberra bench,' I said. 'It didn't hit anyone. Security are looking for the perpetrator.'

I do this about 50 times a year — sit on the sideline and tell an east coast Australia radio audience what's going on at the football. Mostly, it's a lot of fun. I've had players put their hands

52 GAMES ... 52 GIGS

GIG 12 (MAY 9): Not Palace of the King, Frankie's, Sydney

I show up tonight expecting to see the southern (that is, Melbourne) rockers, Palace of the King. Former Manly star Darrell Williams is there and tells me his mates, the house band, are playing instead. Frankie's has got the internet listing wrong. The house band is good, this counts as a gig, I sleep until 2.30pm next day.

GAME 12 (MAY 12): St George Illawarra 16 Canberra 12 at Jubilee Oval, Kogarah

The Canberra PR, Ben Pollack, says he's never been to Kogarah Oval. That means I beat him by a clear 36 years. I remember dragging Mum there one Mother's Day and screaming at the referee, 'You're weak, Weekes!'

on my shoulder as they warm up, referees crack jokes, Melbourne Storm, Queensland and Australian captain Cameron Smith comment into a live mic about a hail storm as he walked past. But every three or four years, the role would expose a flaw in my make-up as a reporter — and as a person. It was about to happen again.

About 10 minutes later, there was another commotion near the players' race. Upon investigation, I saw a cleaner being instructed to sweep up a Wild Turkey bourbon bottle lying near the fence, again behind the opposition reserves bench. This, clearly, had been thrown from the crowd. Photographer Phil Hillyard of *The Daily Telegraph* was taking close-ups of it. 'Oh yeah,' said a belligerent fan. 'Is the *Daily Telegraph* gonna say what a disgrace Bulldogs fans are tomorrow? Well, I dropped it. It was me. I was drinking from it and I dropped it.'

Yeah right.

Again, I reported this second incident to the radio listeners. And all the talk afterwards was about the glass bottle, nothing about the plastic one. It was 24 hours before the likely truth descended: there was no plastic bottle incident. The one on the sideline had probably been discarded by a trainer … or even a sideline eye. When the ground official, whose name I didn't know even though we often spoke at games, gave me that funny look, he wasn't telling me the truth.

I am painfully naïve, a terrible trait for a reporter. I am an appalling judge of character; a failing that makes me an easy target for exploitation. The only saving grace is that I'm smart enough to know these things, which is why I always try to have quotes up very high in my stories. There have been times I've been onto massive stories but if I couldn't get a quote to go in the third paragraph I just didn't write it — because I have no faith at all in my own judgment. In print journalism, you can get by this way. Make sure you are always hanging stories on someone else, avoid going out on a limb.

On the sideline, however, the assumption is that everything you are told is off the record. When someone informs you a player who was carried off on a stretcher will be back in the second half, it's understood that you will not name the person who told you. It's just 'the Dragons bench'. So the onus is on you to judge whether that is indeed possible or whether they are peddling you a competitively motivated fabrication.

It's the wild west down there. People can and will tell you fibs because they know they are not going to be named. It's an environment in which I feel very uncomfortable and ill-equipped to work.

You can't have your wits about you if you have no wits.

My worst experience — which I hoped to learn from but clearly didn't — in this area came on March 24, 2014, at Melbourne's AAMI Park. I wasn't working the sideline that night but I was covering the Melbourne-Newcastle Monday Night Football game for a newspaper and Triple M.

I'm not sure I saw the three-man tackle on Knights second rower Alex McKinnon live. I may have been looking away. But I heard a gasp from the press box. Then I saw the replay. Grabbing my Sports Ears, I dashed downstairs because I knew the radio would want an update.

Now, I'm not sure if I was already on the sideline or still upstairs when I heard, over the ref's mic, McKinnon describe how he felt and what he was experiencing. He couldn't feel anything. He was panicking. It was never broadcast and it haunts me to this day.

In trying to find out how Alex was, I did what I would normally do with a minor injury. I was given reports by multiple staff that were too positive — they were trying to shield his family and friends from the fact that he had suffered a terrible injury — and while I thought I had taken this into account by mixing in some caution, my initial report on radio was still way too optimistic.

This was just like the plastic bottle — only obviously that was not in the same solar system of seriousness. I utterly failed to read the situation and in my report for the paper even included a quote from a Knights official saying, 'The signs are good.'

Few would have predicted that the Steve Mascord in the bow tie from May 1971 would one day be interviewing high-profile footballers such as Canterbury and Australian forward David Klemmer.

Led by Johnathan Thurston (right, and holding the trophy with Matt Scott above), the North Queensland Cowboys won the 2016 World Club Challenge.

Opposite page: Living in the '70s with parents Norm and Betty, sister Tammie and (in the middle left photograph) Aunty Gail.

Dave Gleeson, Screaming Jets

The Lazys

Above: The Angels'
John Brewster

Right: At Etihad
Stadium to see Axl
Rose front AC/DC.

Axl, in Dave Grohl's 'rock throne', alongside Slash at Coachella (above) and with Angus Young in Manchester.

State of Origin 2016 lacked nothing for passion and excitement.
Above: Queensland's Corey Oates scores at Suncorp Stadium.
Below: NSW's Aaron Woods is surrounded by Maroons.

Meanwood Road, Leeds

Nissan Stadium, Nashville

I vividly recall walking past the medical room with the game still in play, the door open and Alex lying there. It's likely someone else was in the room but they were out of sight. My job was to describe emotions but about how I felt this night, I cannot. Nightmares eventually fade; this one remains.[1]

Straight from AAMI Park, I travelled to Melbourne international airport and flew to New York via Hong Kong; got straight off the plane at JFK and went to a taping of *That Metal Show*. The entire first leg of the flight, I found myself going over the horrific events in my head repeatedly. Try as I might, I was unable to flick my brain onto anything else.

In Hong Kong, I learned Alex McKinnon had suffered a 'catastrophic spinal injury'. When, months later, McKinnon criticised Cameron Smith on *60 Minutes* for continuing to argue with the referee as he lay prone on the turf, I wrote this in *The Sydney Morning Herald:*

'In a manner of speaking, I have a small inkling of how Cameron Smith feels after Sunday night's *60 Minutes* program. I covered the game in which Alex McKinnon was injured, for radio and for the newspaper. Like Cameron, I misread the situation completely. When people told me Alex's treatment was "just precautionary" and that he reacted the way he did because he "got a fright", I foolishly believed them. Fox's Andy Raymond showed himself to be, frankly, a better journalist in the way he

---

1. In round 10, 2017, I was watching from Boston when Newcastle's Jacob Saifiti suffered a knock to the neck and play was held up for several minutes while he was fitted with a brace and then carried from the field. The sideline eye was none other than Knights great Danny Buderus, who had to walk the line of not worrying the youngster's family but also honestly reflecting the situation. As detailed in this chapter, it's a very difficult balance.

reported on the injury. Like Smith, I focused too much on the short term — in my case, trying to get a quote in the paper. I did that — but the quote was another well-intentioned smother. I am sorry for my performance and my decisions that night, which do not stand up to scrutiny. I wish I could change them. I'm sure Cameron feels the same.'

Generally speaking, I regard my naivety as a blessing. I find violent movies intensely unsettling and avoid them, I can't watch surgery on TV, I am mystified by almost all kinds of deceptive behaviour.

I can keep secrets on behalf of others but I have few myself. I don't need a reason to share. I need a reason not to. This gullibility allows me to react with genuine outrage in opinion pieces when people are caught out being less than truthful with me. But it makes me incapable of dealing with an essential part of modern life. I can't tell if someone is lying to me, or ripping me off. I find the devious mind impenetrable.

Capitalism relies on deception or at least the withholding of information. If everyone knew how much everything cost to make and how much everyone was being paid, we'd have socialism. And socialism, at its core, seems to overestimate the positive aspects of human nature — just as I do.

ANDREW JOHN LANGLEY SAYS: My alternative self seems to have deliberately deluded himself into thinking the world is a nice place in which everyone tells the truth. Then again, I'm not even sure he believes what he says he believes; he seems to be taking the high moral ground in a very disingenuous way to justify the more invasive and unpleasant aspects of his profession.

CHAPTER 8

GONE BUSH

How do you know you've been working too hard? When Van Halen and Aerosmith play on the same bill 15 kilometres from your front door and you go to Penrith to cover a Samoa versus Tonga rugby league match instead.

That was the nadir of my mental malaise in April 2013, when I was trying to juggle two full-time jobs (*The Sydney Morning Herald*, *Rugby League Week*) and four or five others on the side. The Stone Music Festival, at ANZ Stadium at Homebush, boasted those two behemoths (who perhaps had not played on the same bill since the 1970s) along with Jimmy Barnes, the all-star Kings of Chaos, Buckcherry, the reformed The Superjesus, The Choirboys and more.

If that situation arose today, I would take the day off and go to the gig and damn the consequences. But it's worth noting that just as easily as I can turn my back on rugby league and focus on rock as a true calling, I am equally capable of doing the opposite. Then, still only five years into being self-employed, I was burnt out. Somehow, in my polluted and muddled cranium, I decided I *could not* go to the show. The day after, I told myself,

52 GAMES ... 52 GIGS

GAME 13 (MAY 15): Cronulla 62 Newcastle 0 at Hunter Stadium, Newcastle

Nathan Brown offers a handshake — twice — after this lowlight in the history of the Newcastle Knights. You know how sometimes someone sticks out a hand the first time and you're not ready? Hard not to feel sorry for him ... not over the handshake, the score ...

GIG 13 (MAY 19): Palace of the King at Frankie's, Sydney

There's a girl in the front row blowing kisses at Palace of the King's guitarist and deliberately bashing into me to get attention. Her boyfriend is behind her. I arrive late because I've dashed from the South Sydney-St George Illawarra game to catch the set because, basically, I have to go to a gig a week for this book, don't I? Only get four songs but one of their best, *Black Heart*, stretches out to about 10 minutes. Pretty awesome.

City-Country was in Coffs Harbour on the NSW north coast and the flight to Coffs was so early I could not possibly enjoy myself at Homebush had I gone. The earlier finish at the football would give me the chance to drive at least part of the way to the Sunday game.

So mid-afternoon on the Saturday I chugged past Homebush Bay on the M4, close enough to hear the thud of someone's bass drum, and went to Samoa-Tonga instead. It ranks as one of the worst decisions I've ever made. The sense that I just shouldn't have been there at the foot of the Blue Mountains reporting on rugby league was only exacerbated by a story I wrote about the game that caused all sorts of dramas. Just before full-time, after a Mahe Fonua try, there was a pitch invasion that brought the international match to a premature and chaotic end. I quoted someone saying security guards had been allowed to go home early. That person was repeating a rumour. Sloppy from Mascord.

That night I drove on to the Ibis Budget in Wallsend, west of Newcastle, and early next morning continued to Coffs Harbour where my City-Country duties started at around 11am. The first leg of the journey took two hours, getting me there about 12.30am, and the second was four hours, necessitating a 7am start. I spent more money than the airfare would have cost me and earned very little more by going to the game at Penrith.

Who cares? Well, I do have a point here …

Which is: when we go to a gig or a game, ritual is a powerful factor. In my 2013 case the rugby league ritual was more powerful than the cock-rock ritual because it was one I had been observing more often. Rugby League Steve had subjugated and enslaved Rock Steve; out of the battle, my obsessive and compulsive behaviour had got worse. I wasn't making logical decisions based on the relative merits of the two competing events, as a sane person would. As noted in the opening chapter of this book, events are often just excuses to go somewhere, to stay on the move, and the journey becomes — to quote a tedious cliché — more important than the destination. This was my mania stripped bare.

I've done so many of these eccentric trips that I've lost count. In 2000, I saw Wales play South Africa in Pretoria in a rugby league international one day and the United States take on England at Walt Disney World in Florida the next, travelling overnight.

Two years later, it was Serbia v Italy in Belgrade then straight to the airport and overnight to Cardiff for a match on New Zealand's tour of the UK. I saw KISS at Budokan, Tokyo, one night and Skid Row at Manchester Club Academy the next, pretty much travelling door to door. I've tried to figure out why I did these things and the only answer I can come up with is … so I could sit here 15 years later and tell you I did them.

Susan Krauss Whitbourne, a professor of psychological and brain sciences at the University of Massachusetts Amherst, writes: 'Sports fans are particularly subject to the effect known as superstitious conditioning.' She cites a study in which pigeons were asked to perform certain tasks in order to be fed pellets. Without prompting, the birds would add rituals of their own, such as turning in a circle or jumping up and down, even though these things were not essential to them being fed. And they would keep performing them.

Since I didn't care if City or Country won that Sunday in Coffs Harbour, my superstitious conditioning was different. I didn't set off in my lucky underpants. Truth is, they were probably last week's underpants. My superstitious conditioning was merely being there in Coffs, making the trip. My identity was tied to being 'that guy' and if I told Triple M I wasn't going and the *SMH* I would do my column from home, I feared I would not be Steve Mascord any more.

In 2016, Van Halen and Aerosmith were otherwise occupied and since I am usually stuck in an office on a Saturday, the decision to go to the Fiji-Papua New Guinea and Samoa-Tonga double-header at Pirtek Stadium was an altogether wiser and healthier option than it had been three years previously.

Once more, it was an overnight drive to City-Country, which was in Lismore. My halfway house was Singleton rather than Wallsend; I arrived at 1.30am and I was up at 8am to continue the trip. But that was OK because Aerosmith and Van Halen were in America doing nothing. What was a bad choice in 2013 was the right call in 2016.

Right, doctor?

ANDREW JOHN LANGLEY SAYS: Hello! You go to the rugby league game and you get paid, you go to the hair metal concert and you don't. How is this a conflict? You chose the bloody job, now do it. My other self is off with the fairies.

SCREAMING DRAGON

It's doubtful anyone I encountered during the year covered by this book straddles the twin worlds of rugby league and rock music as thoroughly as the singer of the Screaming Jets, Dave Gleeson.

'My dad went to school with Les Johns [the great Newcastle, Canterbury and Australian fullback of the 1960s] and he was a mad Western Suburbs Newcastle fan,' Gleeson tells me, after I ask when he first encountered the sport. 'He'd take me along, me and my brothers. My sister used to come along as well. Everyone in the family played footy if they were boys, netball if they were girls.

'Both my brothers took out the most outstanding junior award at Cardiff rugby league club when they were kids.

'My career was cut short by a neck injury. I finished up when I was 12. Then I became a referee ...'

Hold on. Yes, you read that right. David Gleeson, rock'n'roll madman who sings "Fat Rich Cunts", was a referee.

'And a highly decorated touch judge,' he adds. 'I refereed with [future first-grade refs] Tony Archer and Paul McBlane. I've always had an affiliation with league. I love it.'

Today, Gleeson's brother Tony is a member of the Newcastle coaching staff, in charge of the Knights' Harold Matthews Cup (under-16s) team. But Dave is not a Newcastle fan; he supports St George Illawarra.

'I remember 1975, it was the first grand final I can kind of remember I was excited about. I was seven,' he explains. 'My brother Tony, he was a Dragons fan. My brother Gerard was a Roosters fan. I'd imagine I must have had a fight with Gerard or something in the week leading up to it, so I sided with the Dragons.

'And even though it was a 38–0 drubbing, I stuck by them. We got the wins in '77 and '79 and, of course, there were the lean years.

'I always carry Saints socks around with me in my bag — just in case. They might call up and say. "Dave, we need you." They're Anthony Mundine's socks. I got them in the dressing sheds. It was between '96 and '99, I think.

'There'd been a crackdown. They'd said to the players. "You can't keep giving jumpers away anymore, it's just costing too much money." Anthony took off his socks from the game and his shorts and said, "Here, put these in your jacket."

'I went out and showed the wife. She said, "You're an idiot."

'Every now and then, I put the shorts on and the socks and I feel a bit special.'

Gleeson never became disillusioned with the game — he says he wouldn't have been happy had St George joined Super League, which some reports suggested they nearly did in 1995 — and is grateful that being a musician has allowed him to meet many of rugby league's stars.

He also appreciates the perspective he now has for his years in rock'n'roll. Again, there is no disillusionment …

'Back in the day … you're full of bluster, living the dream, sleeping till four o'clock in the arvo and you're getting up and brushing your teeth with Jack (Daniels),' he chuckles.

'You're saying. "Check me out." It does change over the years. You realise it's your job. While it is still a huge amount of fun, you don't take yourself too seriously. That's the thing you learn.

'You get out there and you enjoy those two hours of performing or you enjoy the recording process … and then you get back on with life.'

Screaming Jets were in amazing form when I saw them at the Bridge Hotel at Rozelle on May 26, 2016. This interview took place early in 2017.

RULES FOR A CAREFREE LIFE

- Don't try to make anyone else do anything.
- Truth over loyalty — all the time.
- Anyone who tries to choose your friends for you is not your friend.
- Don't even allow what other people think of you to cross your mind.
- Discover what you like to do, then find a way to get paid for it.
- Be anyone's friend but nobody's ally.
- Don't covet things that expire.
- Minimise the number of things you do for money, maximise those you do for love.
- Don't become attached to objects; you'll only lose or break them.
- If you do lose something, don't let it affect your actions unless you can't continue without it. Make an effort to find it — but accept straight away that you won't.
- Be nice to people who hate you.

CHAPTER 9

STATE OF ORIGIN

Perhaps there are always clues that one will eventually encounter a crisis of identity. One such clue can be found in people who, even as they associate themselves with something mainstream, with 'the crowd', disavow themselves of the *most* mainstream aspect of that thing. They're the most 'out' part of the 'in-crowd'.

That's what it's like for me and State of Origin.

During the autumn internationals in the UK and France in 2012, I happened to amble past York racecourse. There, on a shoulder of the road, was a sign that explained why the site was chosen. Highwayman Dick Turpin was hanged there in 1739 and it was determined that if the racecourse was sufficiently close to the scaffold, the crowds already attracted by the latter would stay on for the former.

It was sport's inaugural double-header: one in the basket in the morning, followed by the first past the post in the afternoon.

The sign set in motion the squeaky wheels and gears of my melon: slowly, we are becoming more genteel in what we watch for entertainment. When it comes to what we digest for amusement, we are growing more capable of enjoying pursuits in which no one is actually quartered, drawn or hung. (Or perhaps we are just becoming more fearful of litigation.)

Each time a sport undergoes a change to make it more civilised, someone has a whinge. In rugby league, we allowed injured players to be replaced: 'Pussies!' We increased the number of replacements from two to four: 'Wusses!' We forced bleeding players to leave the field: 'Pansies!' Head Injury Assessment? I can't remember exactly what I thought about that …

In 2012 and 2013, we saw the death of the shoulder charge and then — in State of Origin and the NRL — of punching. One of the most common catch-cries of the bloodthirsty during this process was: 'They'll ban tackling eventually!'

Correct. They will.

In another 200 years, I'm willing to wager that body-contact sport will have all but died out. We'll look back on participants breaking bones and getting knocked out to the cheers of thousands with the same disgust we now reserve for ancient Romans who fed slaves to lions.

Yes, it is the death of rugby league — a very slow death that started long ago with the introduction of replacements. It's evolution, baby. Alex McKinnon's injury and the spate of suicides — the late Chad Robinson, a former NRL player, reportedly expressed concerns about the long-term impact of head knocks — will hasten us down this road.

So make the most of the next couple of centuries, OK? One day, there'll be a plaque (holographic, I'm tipping) at Homebush Bay that reads: 'On this spot, during the first game of the 2013 Origin series, NSW's Paul Gallen punched Queensland's Nate Myles in the head repeatedly and was not sent off.'

I agree with the process that will eventually make rugby league obsolete, strangely enough. I don't want it to disappear tomorrow, mind. But making the sport more acceptable to parents is sensible and, long after I'm dead, that acceptability will equal obsolescence. I'm comfortable with that. I won't be around and left with nothing to do on weekends.

The counter argument, which I have heard from more than one colleague is: what if we do all these things to win over parents and they don't come back anyway? But that's not the point, see? Blokes who are not wearing boxing gloves standing in the middle of a packed stadium punching the bejesus out of each other while drunken bloodthirsty hoons cheer is *uncivilised*. It's sub-human. If we saw it on the streets, we would be horrified.

The new Parramatta chief executive, Bernie Gurr, once took me to task for predicting on social media the death of body-contact sport. 'What good are you doing?' he demanded. It was an excellent question: why tell members of a rugby league audience that their favourite sport is on death row, albeit a row longer than Wagga Wagga's main drag?

The reason is to put things in perspective. I didn't play rugby league to any decent level (unless you rate Windang under-10s and the Illawarra High School knockout as a decent level). My role therefore must be to put things in context, explain the significance of events. Growing up with rugby league obsessive compulsive disorder helps in that regard, but so does the ability to step back from my own obsessions and comment on the subject at hand dispassionately.

Which brings me to State of Origin. I don't particularly like it.

If Super League is more endearing than the NRL because it's more friendly and accessible and French rugby league is more endearing than Super League for the same reason, all the way down to Jamaican under-16s, then State of Origin is positively unfriendly and inaccessible.

When all of rugby league looks up to the NRL, it's humiliating to see the NRL bend over and touch its toes in the prison shower of sports for seven weeks every year around Origin time. For a rugby league trainspotter, it feels vaguely like — here's that word again — betrayal.

I realise it's hard for a rank-and-file rugby league fan, much less a rank-and-file sports fan, to understand this perspective. If you're the latter, Origin is probably the only time you even watch rugby league. The best way I can explain it is this: you have a local band you follow around to pubs all over town. One day they release a record of cloying, catchy pop songs, sell millions and play the stadiums of the world. You don't like those songs and you don't like the band any more. That's how I feel at Origin time.

State of Origin is a cultural phenomenon. It's a television leviathan. It's the NRL's cash cow. It's also an unedifying, crass sell-out by the sport of rugby league. I always understood that at some level. About a decade ago, I criticised the NRL for ambush marketing at Origin games. They'd charge hundreds of dollars for tickets, and then flog a Hollywood blockbuster on the big screen and have Toyotas doing laps of the stadium while the PA blared, 'Oh what a feeling.' A former senior NRL executive was mortally offended. 'You *can't* over-commercialise Origin,' he said the next time he saw me. 'That's what it is. It's a commercial entity. That's what it's about.'

52 GAMES ... 52 GIGS

GAME 14 (MAY 22): Gold Coast 28 Penrith 24 at Pepper Stadium, Penrith

All year, I've been proud of not stuffing up a score doing around the grounds for the radio. Today, I stuff up the score once. Who cares, right? It's only football. The first time I ever dealt with Neil Henry, he called to blow up about something I'd said on television. He was very sensitive when he started at Canberra. I really like him now.

GIG 14 (MAY 26): Screaming Jets at Bridge Hotel, Rozelle

My gig of the year so far. My date is a guitarist in an AC/DC cover band. I put away a dozen beers. I harass David Gleeson backstage. I buy a t-shirt and a CD and lose the CD before I get home. I love every song. The Screaming Jets are a national treasure, with a repertoire so deep they could play three completely different sets and be no less spellbinding each time. When I was going through this book before it went to the printer, I removed the one-word sentence 'awesome' from this mini-review because it appeared in the previous one.

In mid-2016, as part of Fox Sports' panel show, *NRL 360* (on which I was an infrequent guest), it was put to Origin coaches Laurie Daley and Kevin Walters that the 22-minute half-time breaks — you read that right, 22 minutes — that allow TV to insert many advertisements, had the potential to change the course of matches. Daley and Walters cheerily agreed! 'Alf [Langer] fell asleep, it was that long,' Kevvie chortled. 'I ran out of things to say!' Loz chimed in. Did you hear that? Rugby league has so little regard for the very structures that surround the playing of matches, let alone its history and traditions, that we find commercial imperatives that impact on the actual game a simple fact of life. Integr-what?

Doesn't this seem to you like nothing is sacred; that everything's for sale? To underline the inequalities and expediency that Origin exposes every winter, let's go back to the 2016 series. New South Wales called up the Canterbury utility Josh Morris hours before a Bulldogs away match in Canberra. This meant a 19-year-old named Reimus Smith, who had played a whole game the day before, was forced to make his way to the Australian capital and play again as Morris's replacement.

Canterbury CEO Raelene Castle told me outside the Bulldogs sheds that day: 'The etiquette in place at the moment is that we have to release our players for Kangaroos and Origin. But, in reality, when you're running a professional competition, to expect us to do that on the morning of a game when we're 300 kilometres away and our NSW Cup team played yesterday is not very reasonable. If we played [Saturday], they would still have called J Moz up [on Sunday]. The three teams which have lost the most players [to Origin] all lost this weekend. The Broncos, the Cowboys and the Bulldogs — five, five and three (players), four for us on the morning — have all lost. So you've got to question: is this another form of salary capping? The teams that don't have many players involved in Origin end up with points they may not have otherwise got. Origin's amazing. Commercially, it's really beneficial. We all know that. But when you look at the actual integrity and credibility of the NRL competition over 26 weeks, you have to question whether this is the right outcome.'

52 GAMES ... 52 GIGS

GAME 15 (MAY 29): Canberra 30 Canterbury 22 at GIO Stadium, Canberra
I'm starting to fall for the Canberra Raiders. The winning try this afternoon is scored by one of my favourite players, Sia Soliola. They not only throw the ball around, they are incapable of shutting a game down — an infuriating trait from a coach's perspective but endearing if you're a semi-neutral fan.

GIG 15 (MAY 31): Karaoke at Frankie's, Sydney
Surely there is room to *be* the gig at least once during the compilation of this book? Sadly, I show up too late to get my name on the list. The best karaoke I've been to — and perhaps the only one.

Here's another contradiction: a club coach, Wayne Bennett, was able to say that a player (Anthony Milford) could not take part in a Test match for Samoa just a few weeks earlier, and he didn't even have to give a fair reason. But when a state team wants a player, it gets the player immediately regardless of whether he is just about to put his boots on to turn out for his club.

The difference? Money.

That's why I say State of Origin is a sell-out. Origin pays our bills and that is enough to justify to the rest of the sport almost any inconsistency, compromise or inconvenience. The clubs complain, but they are complicit. Everyone is still living hand to mouth, even though food became plentiful years ago. Our neighbourhood has been gentrified but we still think like street thugs.

We'll keep playing Origin on Wednesday night (where it was originally stationed to *avoid* interfering with club football) because they'll give us heaps of cash to keep it there. Des Hasler got it right that day in Canberra. Rugby league in Australia running two competitions at the same time, using some of the same players, is about as barmy as you can get. Three sheets to the wind.

The only sheet that matters to rugby league, though, is the balance sheet. Time to spell it out: the NRL *not* pausing while Origin is played is undiluted greed. Just like the old delayed Sunday telecasts, they won't get away with it forever. Common sense and justice will find a way — the inclusion of one weekend Origin in the TV deal that will come into effect in 2018 is evidence of that.

Having said all this, I am not immune to the sheer magnetism of a contest that stops a nation three times a year. I've covered rugby league games while battling tear gas in the Papua New Guinea highlands, electrical blackouts in Lebanon and hangovers in Keighley. I even once received a text from Canberra Raiders fullback Clinton Schifcofske as he was lining up a conversion from the western touchline at Suncorp Stadium. But until 2013, watching Origin from the sideline was one journalistic odyssey that had eluded me. The honour was finally bestowed thanks to Triple M securing the rights and was made even more enjoyable by the fact that during the game, I didn't have to say anything on air. No doubt, listeners were also grateful for this.

For Origins I and III in '13, both played in Sydney, I sat next to former NSW centre Ryan Girdler and a tech a few short metres from the whitewash and just watched (and tweeted and instagrammed). For the second match in Brisbane, my partner-in-crime was the hulking Ben Hannant, and Maroons prop from

2008 to 2012, and I was behind him, which meant I didn't see quite as much ...

I've got to admit, being so close to something that others hold in such reverence was energising and almost intoxicating. I could not fail to be transfixed as the teams ran out to such a cacophonous response and stood in front of me for the national anthem. Then the game began, and almost immediately I discovered something that I'd never sensed in the press box. I had always believed that Origin players knew, intellectually, that they had a licence to be more physical, more brutal, more violent, than in club matches. This behaviour was tacitly condoned by officials, who were raking in the cash from the public's expectation of fireworks. But, sitting on the sideline, I realised that committing mayhem was not just an intellectual decision. It was primal. It emanated from the 82,000 souped-up spectators who came not just expecting stiff-arms and fisticuffs but *demanding* them.

I came away thinking that it was a miracle of restraint on the part of the 34 players that an Origin series is not just one big 240-minute rolling brawl.

ANDREW JOHN LANGLEY SAYS: I heard you went on a high-rating rugby league TV show and said you didn't like the highest-rating rugby league games of the year. Are you insane? *No wonder your segment on that show was canned and you're broke. Don't you get it? This shit is just* entertainment. *It's the opiate of the poor, dumb masses. You're like the blonde with a plunging neckline on* Entertainment Tonight. *Get with the program, mate.*

The Origin Pantomime

The investigations, self-immolation and recriminations in NSW since Wednesday night's Origin II defeat create different impressions depending on your vantage point.

If you're a True Blue then the whole thing is quite gut-wrenching, I'd imagine. From a Queensland point of view, I am sure it is hilarious.

NSW shows what is different, what is wrong, about the entire state far more vividly after a defeat than during it. It's a convict state, Sydney is a city of bullies, gangsters and show ponies and nothing will ever be allowed to get in between these people and their egos. The lack of unity and community south of the Queensland-NSW border, the naked competitiveness and selfishness of everyday life in the Harbour City, is laid bare every time NSW loses a league match, when these self-absorbed hyenas tear each other apart.

Banana benders love it, like a gift of a cream pie being smashed on the face of Curly or Moe … over and over again.

To a neutral, the fallout since Wednesday is just stupid, more like school kids fighting over a bag of lollies. It's a football game between two Australian states. These people all care far too much. From a neutral perspective, it's also rather boring and hard to take seriously. Sporting team loses, fans and media want coach sacked, coach considers sacking players. It's a scenario repeated the world over every day. Nothing to see here. Just parochial rubbish. Tap us on the shoulder when there's another game to watch.

What's my point here?

That while Origin is no longer the pinnacle of rugby league because Australia aren't even the No.1 nation and a large proportion of NRL players are not eligible for it, its ability to push the buttons of New South Welshmen and Queenslanders is undiminished. Where once those south of the border refused to take Queensland seriously, the Maroons have got under the fingernails, and in the heads, of millions with their ten wins from 11 series.

But neutrals continue to be alienated. Rugby league fans outside NSW and Queensland grow less impressed with Origin with every passing year. The fact that rugby league isn't a big enough sport for its most celebrated competition to be seen in more reverential, stately and objective terms — rather than as an overblown pantomime seen through the prism of rampant and unchecked parochialism — is unfortunate.

The series is becoming ever more inward looking and self-obsessed. I am sure Ray Warren was joking when he said the Welsh community would be proud of Tyson Frizell, but still…

If Origin is disappearing up its own backside, it's a warm, lucrative, welcoming backside.

From **theroar.com.au**, *June 24, 2016.*

CHAPTER 10

FROM LAHORE TO LOS ANGELES: TOURING THE DREAM FACTORIES

When I tell people about my time hanging with rock stars on the Sunset Strip back in the day, there is one perennial sin of omission in the telling. It's not the fact that I never actually hung with rock stars, just saw them from a distance. It's the year. Nineteen-*mumble-mumble*.

What? *Er* … 1990.

The sad, shameful fact is, I didn't make it to the heart of '80s rock in the 1980s. I only managed to get a passport by the *end* of that storied decade and my first time outside Australia was not to Odsal Stadium or the Whisky a Go Go but … the men's hockey World Cup in Lahore, Pakistan.

The first time I ever heard of the Taliban, I was 21 and they were a few hours' drive away. On my first day in Lahore, a baby was (so I was told) stoned to death for being illegitimate. At the time, I'd barely even been to Brisbane. I'd never seen, let alone tasted, a curry. Suddenly, I needed a driver's licence with proof of my age to drink — my only regret is that it was kept at reception in my hotel and I therefore could not take it home and frame it. The westerners in town for the World Cup (to be held at the Gaddafi Stadium, Lahore) reckoned the local beer was made with industrial acetate.

I typed my copy with a typewriter, handed it to a person in the press centre and it was faxed to Sydney. Given the advances that have occurred since, I'm grateful to have had such a quaint experience. The Netherlands beat Pakistan in the final and West Germany, although a leading contender, was beaten by Australia in the play-off for third. I was suddenly in the middle of an adulation jamboree for athletes of whom I had never heard, like the Dutchman Floris Jan Bovelander.

Each day was full of colour, aromas and … fear. But that extra *frisson*, the one only aroused by the things that excited me (basically, hair metal and rugby league) was absent. When I was introduced to the Australian hockey team, one of the players asked if I was a fan of the sport or had just come for the trip. I *had* played hockey in school (I was a terrible goalie) but I told the truth — I was a cub reporter on my first junket. They never particularly liked me after that.

Between covering penalty strokes and bullys, I was forging ahead with my rock journalism career, faxing breathless Mötley Crüe stories to the London offices of *Kerrang!* My only companion in the hotel gym, most of the time, was an American military contractor.

The Australian journalist Michelangelo Rucci ('Mick Rucci' when the Brisbane *Sun* ran his stories across a single column)

52 GAMES ... 52 GIGS

GIG 16 (JUNE 9): AC/DC at Etihad Stadium, Manchester

A perfect day. Half the gig down the front soaking up a slew of Bon Scott classics crooned by perhaps the biggest rock star of the late 1980s, half of it in the posh seats thanks to Warrington owner Simon Moran, and alongside coach Tony Smith. We meet Cameron from Noosa — he works merch for Ackadacka, basing himself in Europe and travelling around selling plastic flashing sets of horns. He has many perfect days, I suspect.

GAME 16 (JUNE 10): Hull 19 Warrington 12 at Halliwell Jones Stadium, Warrington

There are so many mistakes that winning coach Lee Radford congratulates England boss Wayne Bennett for not being there. But five days after watching Canterbury-Cronulla at ANZ Stadium from the sideline, I enjoy it. At least they try to do things that NRL players don't dare.

was also in attendance and he couldn't have been more different to my lost-boy-abroad. He was making presentations to the International Hockey Federation. Twenty-seven years later, I find myself in a similar position with the Rugby League International Federation but at the time Rucci seemed impossibly important and worldly.

On the way back to Sydney, my senses singed, I had a few hours in New Delhi with a journalist I'd met at the World Cup — and that was it. As if it had all been a particularly awkward one-night stand, field hockey and Steve Mascord never darkened each other's door again and — I strongly suspect — never will, given that I can hardly front up to someone in 2017 and say 'Hey, it's Steve from the 1990 World Cup in Lahore! You know, the one from Windang. Give me a story!'

Your correspondent arrived back from Lahore and had one night at home in Wollongong — even my parents suggested that I stay in a hotel in Sydney but at the time distance was a hurdle I already saw myself in a brutal war against (plus I had a relatively new girlfriend in Wollongong).

Then it was my first trip to the United States. My hotel, the Mondrian on the Sunset Strip, had been organised by Mushroom Records with the blessing of its Svengali-like lead, Michael Gudinski. It was a rock star's room. When I was awoken from my first real jetlag stupor by an earthquake alert, I was able to comfortably cower under a majestic oak desk.

I soon set about interviewing every rock star I could track down. When the PR at Virgin Records asked me who I wanted to speak to, I said 'anyone' and since they thought this crassly expedient, they gave me no one. The names of most of the musicians I encountered have been lost in the mists of time — The Big F, Lord Tracy, Dirty White Boy, Rock City Angels. I visited Enigma Records to meet the punk band T.S.O.L., famous mainly for their t-shirt being worn by Steven Adler in Guns' *Sweet Child O' Mine* video. They were punks, making a pit stop in hair metal territory they'd probably rather forget.

Without Google maps or mobile phones, the entire process was often difficult. I was supposed to meet someone from Oingo Boingo somewhere up the Pacific Coast Highway but got lost, and was unable to call, resulting in me arriving two hours late and being sent packing. Hurricane's Kelly Hansen, now Lou Gramm's replacement in Foreigner, told me that pretty soon they would stop pressing records and albums would only be released on these new compact discs. I'll admit, I had trouble believing him.

I did, however, visit Poison's Bret Michaels at his Sherman Oaks home. The door was answered by Susie Hatton, his girlfriend of the time, who had starred in the *Fallen Angel* video. Bret and I played pool (me, very poorly) upstairs before settling in front of a fireplace much like the one in the *Every Rose Has Its Thorn* video (he kept his shirt on) for our interview, which was published in *Kerrang!*

Given that Michaels, a mid-western boy upon whom fame had just been foisted, was still only 27, it's not easy finding any transcendent insights in the interview. Even though fame has a way of accelerating the ageing process. *Wikipedia* lists 61 rock stars who died at the same age Bret was then — including Jimi Hendrix, Janis Joplin, Jim Morrison, Kurt Cobain and Brian Jones.

Bret had already glimpsed that doomed world. His bodyguard had died after mixing alcohol with insulin less than 18 months before and in the months preceding our chat, drummer Rikki Rockett and bassist Bobby Dall had suffered bereavements. Michaels was promoting *Flesh & Blood* at the time, an album in which he sang about his fears of going 'over the edge', of how he had to stop living at a 'pace that kills' or else he'd 'wake up dead'.

Michaels told my battered Sony Walkman: 'I went on stage at Madison Square Garden when I was shit-faced, off my brain, collapsed because my blood sugar level was low [Michaels is a diabetic], and we took shit for it. And we should have. We didn't mean to do it, it was just one of those things we felt like doing. I never became cynical about playing live. I just became cynical about some of the red tape that's involved in whether your song gets played on the radio, like whether you said hello to someone's daughter. Because you forgot to, maybe you were sick that night, in the next day's newspaper it's written that you're the worst band in the world. There's a lot of red tape that's involved between rock bands and the media. That's the truth.'

Michaels also reasoned that many of the reporters he encountered mistook his friendliness for weakness. The more convivial you were in interviews, the more licence the journalist felt he or she (let's face it, in 1990 it was mainly he) had to misquote him.

Misquoting a multi-platinum rock star simply would not have occurred to me. Dirty White Boy was a project of former David Bowie guitarist Earl Slick. I met them in a shopping precinct café and they were dressed in lace-up leather pants and sunglasses, speaking lasciviously about the waitresses behind their backs. Were they on the way to a photo shoot? No, they'd dressed that way for me. I, on the other hand, hadn't even listened to their album since I wasn't travelling with a record player, my Walkman was on the blink and MP3s were inconveniently still a decade and a half away. Their publicist wanted to call off the interview when I confessed this to him. It went ahead. I like their album to this day.

It was possible in 1990 to convince record companies to spend money, more or less on the spot, to fly you places. That's how I ended up in Portland, Oregon, interviewing L.A. Guns in a motel by the home court of the Portland Trail Blazers. Heavy metal records were flying out of shops; this was big business. PolyGram had warned me there would be a driver waiting for me at the airport — 'you know, a limo' but until a guy in a cap was holding the car door open for me, I refused to believe it. Dan Reed, whom you will read about elsewhere here, met me at my five-star hotel for my first interview and then it was L.A. Guns — Englishman Phil Lewis, Australian-born bassist Mick Cripps, drummer Steve Riley and guitarist Tracii Guns.

Their show was that night. I have tried hard to find the name of the venue but the entire evening seems lost in the mists of hair spray. The support was Shark Island, whose singer Richard Black allegedly invented the 'snake dance' later made famous by one W. Axl Rose. Another thing I can recall is that one minute there was a young girl ogling the stage, the next she was *back*stage. At 21, as I was then, it was easy to be jealous of these rock gods.

Next (and this probably sounds like the dumbest sentence ever written in a book that purports to be serious), it was off to see Mötley Crüe in Minneapolis. Do you want me to type that again? Next, it was off to see Mötley Crüe in Minneapolis. Just as ridiculous the second time, right?

Little could prepare me for moving into the orbit of a bona fide rock circus.

I stayed in the same hotel as the band (they were 'satelliting', which means basing yourself in a regional capital and commuting to shows, rather than living on a tour bus) and was given time with each member. Basically, I found them to be two nice guys and two aliens. Excitable, buzzing Tommy Lee, revelling in his new-found sobriety, chose to do his interview after a show, around midnight. He advised me to get a tattoo at Sunset Tattoo, the

West Hollywood shop then owned by Ed Hardy, who would go on to found a global fashion label. (As I said earlier, you know you're getting old when you remember businesses that stood on the site of something that has since been constructed and itself knocked down. Sunset Tattoo was replaced by the much-missed House of Blues, which was in turn superseded by a residential tower.)

Mick Mars was playing guitar, fully kitted out in rock regalia, when I enter his room. 'Do you play?' he asks. Er, no. But if there were any affectations from Mars, they were minor. He was then the oldest in the band at 36 and the most mature. 'I had this guy from a guitar magazine do an interview the other day and he says, "My editor asked why do you want to interview Mick Mars? He's a shitty guitarist." 'I felt like going, "Fuck you."'

Vince Neil and Nikki Sixx, on the other hand … In Nikki's room, we watched MTV (back when it showed music) and KISS's *Forever* came on. 'This song blows,' Sixx declared. I was a kid from Wollongong. I didn't know if it was good or bad to 'blow'. I just smiled and nodded.

Mötley Crüe was always a delightful soap opera for a reporter. In the resulting story that first appeared in *JUKE*, I was able to juxtapose the following paragraphs:

'Sixx will marry his girlfriend, Bandi Brandt, a model he started dating before travelling to Vancouver to record *Dr Feelgood*, after the Australian tour in May. "It's cool but I'd rather not say too much about it," Sixx says coyly. "Who told you about it anyway?"'

It was Vince Neil. During our interview the day before, Neil had mentioned that, 'Nikki is getting married in May.'

Twenty years later, in 2011, Mick Mars told me his bandmates didn't appreciate that they were now 50 years old and not 16, and that if they wanted longevity they would have to start doing things like rehearsing. Clearly, he was out-voted. Instead, Mötley Crüe embarked on a giant farewell tour and then tossed it in.

I began a feature on the band with Neil saying, 'I really don't understand what Mick's talking about. Maybe he took the wrong pill that day.'

Back to 1990 and the show was at Met Center in Bloomington, Minnesota — now an Ikea. In my review for *Kerrang!*, there is much that makes me cringe, particularly like my rather personal disparagement of Taime Downe, the lead singer of support band Faster Pussycat. On the night, they had made me wait so long outside their dressing-room for an interview that I just gave up and left to watch the Mötley Crüe show. It was not above 21-year-old me to be vindictive but the fact is I just didn't understand music that didn't at least have an element of KISS back then. Faster Pussycat referenced such bands as Aerosmith and Hanoi Rocks. In 1990, my Aerosmith knowledge didn't go back more than two years and I didn't know who Hanoi Rocks were.

My assessment of Mötley Crüe is more complex and, perhaps, more in keeping with how I view them now. I described them as 'a pop metal band with a yearning for immortality'.

Twenty-one-year-old me wrote, 'Neil is singing a stirring song, the pyro is ready, the staging is perfect, I love the music. So why am I not moved? Why does Neil not even seem to be in the same country as me? Why do I think listening to the Crüe on my Walkman would be more enjoyable? Perhaps because it's all too much for my finite senses. Perhaps because I sense that, underneath everything, there isn't very much at all.'

You need balls to be a good music journalist — to be out there on the road living off a band's largesse and to be slagging them off to the wider world as you do it.

Next it was back to Los Angeles to interview more bands who would amount to very little. In the evenings, I went to record launches — I remember seeing KISS's Bruce Kulick and members of Slaughter at the shindig for Hurricane's *Slave to the Thrill* and being stunned — and to the infamous Rainbow Bar and Grill. How did I afford all this? I've no idea. Another time I went to a David Cassidy album launch and picked up a girl about whom I remember not a thing. By then I had moved out of the Mondrian and into the Park Sunset, which was much cheaper. Today, it's the Grafton on Sunset; in some rooms, you can pick up the Wi-Fi from the Mondrian's pool bar. One night I saw a rock star walk into the Rainbow, sit down, meet five girls and leave with them without ordering so much as a Budweiser.

Believe it or not, I managed to convince my main employer at the time, AAP, to pay for a trans-continental airfare so I could cover a world title fight in Atlantic City. I've never liked boxing. Jeff Harding, an Australian who would later show up at my next-door neighbours' place in Annandale every Saturday, was trying to punch the life out of Nestor Giovannini. The fight's on *YouTube* … he was reasonably successful, winning by TKO to retain the world light-heavyweight title. My visit to Atlantic City was also the first time I encountered Harding's trainer Johnny Lewis, who would be involved in rugby league over the next decade. Lewis is a man with a deep belief in the redemptive qualities of boxing, his gentle temperament completely at odds with a violent pastime.

You know how random things people say to you stick in your mind forever, for reasons that never become clear? Someone in Harding's camp pointed out that America was full of out-dated infrastructure compared to Australia, using fire hydrants as an example. They were inefficient compared to modern technology, this fellow said, waving to the street below. 'You have to shut down a whole street to fight a fire.' It's an example I've used dozens of times since when asked to compare the countries.

After the fight, the beaten Argentinian claimed he went into the bout injured and that Harding had not improved since the previous time they'd fought. Harding wouldn't respond but, as I remember, resented me using the quote. It was one of my first experiences where an Australian abroad expected you, as an Australian reporter, to be on their side. Maybe that is natural to most people but it has never been to me. If I was a reporter, I was objective and the nationality of the person I was interviewing or the people reading had no impact on what I wrote.

Next it was up to New York for the first time. I stayed in a hotel on East 51st Street called the Pickwick Arms, so cheap that you had to put a chain from one door to the other on the shared bathroom between the rooms to stop your neighbour entering. One night, lying in a tiny bed, my bathroom door started to open from the inside. I shouted and there was no answer so I ran to the door, shoved it closed and locked it. I never found out who was trying to come into my room; they never said a word.

During the day, I hustled for rock interviews — my ultimate objective was New York natives KISS — and in the evening,

I would take my electric typewriter to a nearby pub, such as the Black Sheep on Third Avenue, and write my music features to be faxed to London or Sydney. At the Black Sheep, I met Irish-American Jim McDonald, who is still a good friend. In what will become a life-long habit, I left my tape recorder in a cab I shared with Kyf Brewer, the lead singer of a band called Company of Wolves, whom I'd just interviewed. I got it back.

Then on to England. I arrived on the doorstep of my long-time pen pal and eventual best man, Jim Savage, the day his Warrington side were to play Oldham at Wigan's Central Park for a berth in the Challenge Cup final. I look at the video now — referee John Holdsworth in his black strip with white collar, Mike Gregory with his shorts pulled up too high — and can remember my excitement at attending my first match in England. Anally, I called AAP at half-time to file a radio report as I would if it had been a Sydney premiership game. AAP was not impressed. Warrington won 10–6 in front of 15,636 — Jim and I were off to Wembley — but it's worth recording that the other semi-final, between St Helens and Wigan, was played at Old Trafford in front of 26,489. Old Trafford for a semi-final! The 2016 Challenge Cup semi-finals were played in Doncaster and Leigh. How far we have fallen?

I had managed to convince AAP to let me work in the London office for a month. I stayed with a friend of a friend at Beckton E6. AAP's offices were in the Reuters building in Fleet Street, an area that now is dominated by the finance industry but then was packed with newsstands, litter and fried chicken shops. The local watering hole was called The City Golf Club. There was no golf played there but before the 1990 Challenge Cup final, I watched esteemed

English rugby league writer Dave Hadfield down 10 pints and then say, 'I have to meet a friend now for some real drinking.'

The final was such an eagerly anticipated experience for me that I taped the crowd on a C-90. Still got the tape.

The music interviews continued. There was Love/Hate, mentioned elsewhere in this book, and European journalists who seemed to think I was important because my name was sometimes in *Kerrang!*.

In the meantime, I had become aware that my favourite band, KISS, were about to start a World Tour in Lubbock, Texas, the birthplace of Buddy Holly. This was my chance. Going through PolyGram in Sydney, I sought an interview. I even promised to file on the opening night for Reuters — which I don't think I did. But the request was granted; KISS had taken off their make-up seven years earlier and they weren't mainstream news any more. Having an overseas reporter fly in would at least be a reassurance to Paul Stanley and Gene Simmons against their own burgeoning irrelevance. So, a week after my first Challenge Cup final, I was going to my first KISS show.

On May 3, 1990, 22-year-old Steve Mascord of Windang was given a guided tour of a concert stage by Gene Simmons.

Even at that age, I had a keen sense of a reporter's place and the dignity and objectivity to which one should aspire. I was in the presence of the most giant of giants from my adolescence and childhood yet it was important to me to represent my profession honourably and to be critical where necessary. As a result, Gene Simmons and Paul Stanley didn't like me much.

At one point during the tour of the Egyptian-themed stage in front of an empty arena, Simmons challenged me to ascend one of the catwalks. 'You'll need a run-up,' he said. Like an obedient dog, I took a step back, hurtled up the grating and stood there looking back at him. At first, I had a dumb grin on my face … and then I realised that as an independent reporter I had made a fool of myself. He looked back at me with the gaze of false god.

I asked Stanley how he felt about contemporaries Aerosmith being on the front of *Rolling Stone* (an honour that would elude KISS until the members were at retirement age). 'I don't give a fuck,' Stanley said. 'The truth of it is that we've secured our place, and what people choose to write will be unbiased — which I prefer — or based on their own insecurities.'

Never before or since has my childhood imagination and my adult life collided like it did that weekend in Lubbock. It never occurred to me to be a simpering fan in the presence of KISS; I wasn't there as an acolyte, I was there as a journalist and therefore I had to behave like one. It's only when I misbehave — I was drunk at an Ozzy Osbourne listening party once in his and Sharon's presence and am haunted by the memory whenever I hear Ozzy's music — that my enjoyment of the art is spoiled.

Like me, American comedian Don Jamieson grew up on KISS. He had the *Destroyer* poster on his wall. Much more recently than me, in his role as a co-host of the now-defunct TV program *That Metal Show,* he got himself on the wrong side of Simmons and Stanley. The show's principle DJ, Eddie Trunk, had roundly criticised the starman and the demon for putting other musicians in the make-up of Peter Criss and Paul Stanley, and Jamieson was caught up in the argument. 'At the end of the day, I go home and I still put on KISS' *Destroyer,*' he told me as part of a feature

I wrote for *Classic Rock presents AOR*. When he talked about the falling-out, I knew exactly what he was saying.

'It doesn't bleed into my love for that music. When he starts singing *Detroit Rock City*, I'm 10 years old again. I'm not thinking about the feud with KISS, is this KISS the real version, who's wearing whose makeup? I'm just thinking that I'm 10 again and I'm rocking out to KISS.'

ANDREW JOHN LANGLEY SAYS: One question Stephen: how much friggin' money did you blow on this brain-dead trip? I've heard that one night in the days before things were computerised, you walked into an American Express office and made up an account number to get a cash advance. This was the beginning of your illness, you realise. This trip ruined the next 20 years for you but you talk about it like a pilgrimage.

A pilgrimage to the poor house, that's what it was.

CHAPTER 11

DAN REED ON FAME

On New Year's Eve in 2012, I found myself in Portland, Oregon, for the first time since that 1990 trip when I had interviewed L.A. Guns and Dan Reed.

It was Reed — 'Prince Meets Bon Jovi', they used to say back in the '80s — who brought me back to Portland. The Dan Reed Network were playing a reunion show at the Waterfront Marriott and to me that was the most interesting thing happening on Planet Earth that New Year's Eve.

Portland is now the headquarters of US geek chic. In 1990, I'm guessing it was more about loggers than bloggers. Back then, Dan Reed was on the cover of Kerrang! *with Jon Bon Jovi. In 2012, there were people at the gig who didn't even know who Dan Reed Network were ... but I digress.*

After just six hours of rehearsals, the funk rock of DRN (not to be confused with DRI — Dirty Rotten Imbeciles) was reassuringly celebratory and upbeat. Dated? Yes, a little bit. But where I come from, dated is good. As is the case with many of the bands from my salad days (as opposed to the current epoch, which I call 'my kebab days'), only one or two members of DRN were still working in music full-time. Drummer Dan Pred is now a film-maker, for instance.

But it was a good show.

52 GAMES ... 52 GIGS

GAME 17 (JUNE 12): Wakefield 10 Huddersfield 2 at John Smith's Stadium, Huddersfield
One of the most turgid spectacles I've ever had the misfortune to witness. What makes it worse is that Brendan Crabb, a friend from Wollongong, is with me. He has never seen a Super League game. I'll be surprised if Brendan is sighted at another.

GIG 17 (JUNE 15): Dan Reed Network at the 100 Club, London
Back where the year began, a dingy club on Oxford Street, in the shadows of my Irish wedding, this is another spellbinding performance from the man who features in chapter 11 and his cohorts. Spiritual and muscular at the same time, simultaneously celebratory and reflective. Fantastic stuff.

I was writing rock'n'roll stories again after a two-decade break, which meant I was back on guest lists and being invited to parties. At about 10pm, I met some music industry types at the hotel bar and by 2am I was at a soiree in the hotel's penthouse suite. How long I was there, I could not tell you. Judging by my head the next day, it was a while.

I remember lots of people, lots of alcohol, a balcony I didn't venture onto and … that's about it. I remain grateful to the kind folks at the Marriott for letting me stew in my own juices all day and vacate my room of my own volition at 3.30pm.

That was only four years ago. I would say that at the time I had no higher ambition than earning enough to stay on the road — permanently. 'I used to be like that,' Dan Reed told me in a London hotel in June 2016, before flashing a snapshot from his wallet: 'But then I had my son …

'WHEN I'M LOOKING at time passing in my life,' Reed continued, 'I go back through these very different memories I have — from hanging out with John Gotti [the infamous New York mobster], being in these underground drug dens, not being high, just being an observer, to going to northern India in the early '90s and meeting the Dalai Lama. That was the same time-period as I was in New York hanging out with the other guys.'

Like me with Andrew Langley, Dan wonders about sliding doors, about being Daniel Reed, perhaps ...

'To see the different paths ... I always think about what I would have done if I'd taken this choice or that choice. I wonder about the creativity of that ... where would life have taken me? ... just for fun. I have no regrets and no hopes with that. The conclusion I've come to with that is because we're here for this short amount of time, it takes so much energy to emit jealousy or negativity. You see something on the TV or hear it on the radio and think, *I don't really like that.* And you judge it. "That One Direction crap," I heard someone say. "They're taking over the radio." You know, when I was a kid, it was the Archies, it was the Partridge Family, the Monkees. I'm sure our parents, who were Frank Sinatra fans, were going, "What's with the Partridge Family?" I've decided not to judge stuff any more. The time has come to sit back and enjoy the ride. That's the main thing.'

Dan, a young-looking 50-ish new ager who shaved off all his hair (my story in *Kerrang!* was headlined 'To Baldy Go') in 1990 to distance himself from the glam metal scene, revealed he still kept in touch with Bon Jovi keyboard player David Bryan. 'Bon Jovi's playing Hyde Park here in July. I saw it on the side of a bus yesterday,' he said, gently. 'There's pros and cons to that whole lifestyle. I read an article where he [Jon Bon Jovi] has got a child [who's] dealing with some [substance] abuse issues. It doesn't matter how much money you have and how much success and how many houses you have, you're still going to be dealing with human drama and dilemmas in life — the same stuff I deal with. I have less stress in a lot of ways because I don't own a car, I don't own a house and I kind of live month-to-month and I enjoy that.' (Yes folks, I seem to be interviewing myself!)

'The best thing right now is I'm doing these house concerts for people and I've never had a bigger blessing in my life than to be able to go into people's homes and take music back to the way it was before there was a music business. People would have a piano or a harpsichord in their house and you'd have an artist come over and entertain you. I'm doing a lot of those shows now. Everyone there knows each other, you share a meal with them, it's a totally different experience to playing in clubs. I wouldn't trade that for anything, I wouldn't trade that for playing for 20,000 people a day. Would the money be great? Yeah. Would I have more studios and more equipment? Yes. Would I get picked up from the airport? Probably.'

I finish by asking Dan Reed, the fellow I first met in a hotel café in Portland in the first half of 1990, how his life would have changed if he had become as big as we all thought back then he was going to. His answer surprises me.

'I think it would have been a complete nightmare for me. I think I would have made a lot of poor choices with the money I had, the ego it would have put inside of me. I would have had to try to sustain that level. Once you make that level, you start buying properties and you've got to try to sustain that, to keep the machine fed. There are some very humble musicians out there, like Charlie

Watts, who still lives in a small residence in the country. I know there's a place where Robert Plant lives and he still goes to his local pub and has beers and sits down and talks to the locals, the people he lives around. He's like a normal guy. [But] those stories are few and far between and I would never presume that I would have been that balanced in my mind. The Dan Reed Network and where we were at in that time period, I was pretty full of my ego. I was trying to talk about spiritual stuff … I still wanted to be a rock star. I'm kind of glad I walked away when I did.'

So Reed doesn't long for the late '80s and early '90s the way some of his contemporaries — and many of my friends — do.

His return to music is a fantastic story. It was sparked when a Tibetan monk asked him, 'What is this song? Ch-ch (clap), ch-ch (clap)?' Reed was a backpacking tourist at the time. He'd dropped out of western life. Confused, he asked the monk, who had never owned a TV or radio, 'Er, do you mean Queen's *We Will Rock You?*'

The monk said, 'Can you teach it to me?'

'I don't feel any older than I did when I was 29,' Reed said. 'I know when I look in the mirror, I look older but my spirit doesn't feel older.'

Portland's a nice place. When I was there in 2012–13, I went into a shopping mall on New Year's Eve and saw a sign that said it had opened in 1990. Portland's changed a lot since then.

Change has come much more gradually, and begrudgingly, for me.

ANDREW JOHN LANGLEY SAYS: Dan who?

CHAPTER 12

ENGLAND

In early 2014, my girlfriend and I braved annoyingly persistent rain to seek out an address in Kensington, London. It wasn't far off the High Street, up Kensington Church Street, a thoroughfare through which I had lugged my washing to a laundry several times on the 1994 Kangaroo tour and during the 1995 World Cup.

Little did I know that each time I went to that laundry I had walked past the apartment where my biological mother, Elizabeth, spent the first three years of her life.

Born into a Bohemian family when her father was in London studying surgery, the mother I never met would have been wheeled along these streets in post-war London as life was breathed once more into the capital. I imagine horns and shouts in thick cockney accents above the mostly dignified silence of pedestrians, some carrying umbrellas.

In the three years in which I've come to know my biological relatives, I've discovered that finding a narrative thread in random events is a family talent. My uncle — who died in late 2016 — could unfurl a gripping yarn about crossing the street.

I'm the same. When I went to Africa, I convinced myself I felt blood memory tugging at my emotions. 'This is where we came down out of the trees,' I told myself.

For the first 45 years of my life, I did not know my biological mother had been born in Britain. Yet the UK always had a strange pull for me. I travelled there as soon as I could, at age 21, but from the age of 12 I had an English pen pal, Jim Savage, who was to become my best man. In *Notes from a Small Island,* Bill Bryson wondered at tractor drivers who could recite Shakespeare; the latent learnedness of the English. I have a maxim: if 18th century Britain had been populated by Australians, they would never have discovered Australia.

Empire building is a nasty business. But can commerce alone motivate the building of an Empire upon which the sun never sets? Surely, in order to mobilise the masses, an insatiable, ingrained curiosity is another essential ingredient. I admire stoicism. My own attitude to social interaction is that I am quite happy for someone else to think they put one over me — as long as I got out of the encounter what I wanted, too. My pride does not require the nurturing of superficial victories.

Spend enough time in the UK and you recognise the trait as very English. The Brits almost revel in their status as a former world power that once oppressed multiple races and now absorbs them. Public racism will see you star in a viral *YouTube* video in Australia. In Britain — even post-Brexit — it will get you arrested.

It might be argued that rugby league is the most British of sports because it's a double underdog. The dog isn't just 'under', it's subterranean. An outsider sport in a country that for years

52 GAMES ... 52 GIGS

GAME 18 (JUNE 19): London Broncos 56 Oldham 16 at Trailfinders Sports Ground, West Ealing
London Broncos have one of the best hamburgers in the rugby league world. Aside from that, this is a pleasant enough afternoon. I see this in my retirement — a London Broncos game every second week and a few beers. Not that I'll ever be able to afford to retire ...

GIG 18 (JUNE 22): Vintage Trouble at Kentish Town Forum
Second visit to this venue (but first for this book), second time seeing VT. I've never been at a gig before where my date puts her hand over her mouth in shock, but such is the case when Ty Taylor climbs the balcony and lets himself fall into the crowd below. If you see a pin-striped grey suit jacket, I left it over the barrier at the front. There's a concert ticket in the pocket with the name 'Steve Mascord'.

(not any more) seemed resigned to be a sporting outsider despite having invented most of the sports at which it was being beaten. This imbues English rugby league people with a world view that completely mystifies Australians, a sort of cheery defeatism mixed with knockabout reverence. League Down Under has big guns to fight off the effects of globalisation — a $2 billion television contract, major corporate support, blanket media coverage. In Britain, it basically just has people; people determined to stand on the same terrace that their fathers, and their grandfathers, stood upon. People who refuse point-blank to be engulfed by London culture.

I try to go to the Challenge Cup final every year. In 1999, I attempted to partially fund the journey by selling a story to *Inside Sport* magazine. In it, I used a metaphor I have since run into the ground — that going to the Challenge Cup final is like renewing your vows to the game. Even then, at the age of 30, elements of the game at home had begun to leave me cold. 'What have I got in common with these players I interview each week?' I wrote.

The *Inside Sport* editor did not run the story. He said that being so critical of the essence of rugby league was not a good idea and could damage my career. Seventeen years on, I'm writing a *book* on the same theme. So much for my career.

The British did not invent rock'n'roll but they did create heavy metal. Like rugby league, it sprang forth in surroundings that could fairly be described as bleak. Birmingham, which we have to thank for Judas Priest and Black Sabbath, is no more tropical and exotic than Huddersfield. A sociologist would tell you hardship begets crude pastimes. There are frustrations to exorcise, anger to release.

Guns N' Roses, Metallica and the rest found an audience in Britain before they were accepted in America and many other US acts are far more successful in Europe than at home. The likes of Dave Meniketti's Y&T cross the Atlantic at least a couple of times a year. 'I think they keep coming because they like the songs and they know the band is a real thing and we don't have that mentality where we phone it in every night,' Meniketti told me in early 2016. Good spruiking. But somehow, there's more to it than that.

And yet my romanticised Britain — integrated, outward looking, humble — went missing when I returned there in June 2016 ahead of my wedding in Ireland. The Brexit vote, which left many of my liberal friends inconsolable, was taken on June 23, a week before I was to marry Sarah. To liberals in Britain, Brexit, which saw Great Britain elect to exit the European Union, felt like a sort of reverse visit by Santa Claus. You went to bed in a world that seemed to give a shit, and woke up in one that didn't.

And here lies the dichotomy: one of the hotbeds of the 'out' vote was Wigan, a royal seat in rugby league terms. The Aston area of Birmingham where Ozzy Osbourne was born voted to remain, although just over 50 per cent of the city of Birmingham wanted to leave.

My friends, as I said, were bewildered and dismayed. To some, the Brexit vote was like a death in the family, a realisation that the Britain I described in the first half of this chapter did not — to a significant extent — exist. Kids of immigrant families wept when their schoolmates told them they were being 'sent home'.

I became interested in rugby league and rock'n'roll before I got involved in journalism. I was raised by a working-class family. Yet I was horrified by Brexit. I abhor Donald Trump. Is being a 'leftie' inherited?

Perhaps what I inherited were traits that shaped my experiences and — here's the kicker — experience plays a much bigger role in our political leanings than we are willing to admit. The curiosity and confidence I inherited from my birth parents meant I didn't fall into the local paradigm (wanky word, I know) of working at the steel works, of settling down early, of making political choices based on the circumstances of myself and my family rather than principles and ideals.

I have rarely done anything just for money but have survived comfortably most of the time. I have travelled extensively. When

I was married, there were 10 different accents at the barbecue the next day and kids from three continents playing together. I have no kids of my own. My wife and I still, according to many definitions, 'live' on opposite sides of the world. How could I be fearful of the foreign? How could I obsess about 'protecting jobs'? I can afford to love the very technology which endangers my industry because, in effect, I have very little to lose.

We talk about 'right' and 'left' as if they are choices made by people with identical experiences. But speaking as the subject in an unintentional experiment — like one of the ant lions I used to put in an ice-cream bucket menagerie — they are not. I was transplanted from a well-to-do family into a suburban environment, clung to a couple of the cherished tropes of that environment, and still ended up more or less like my biological family with the likely political views of that family.

A friend of mine believes that world wars reinforce the powerful by sending to fight and therefore culling those who might vote them out of power. But if we gave more people better lives, maybe they'd have less to rail against and the turbulence we now see in society around the globe would not be so poisonous.

Then again, if people were enlightened and happy, we probably wouldn't have rugby league or rock'n'roll.

ANDREW JOHN LANGLEY SAYS: There's still a bit of me in there, Stephen. Trump is a pillock and Brexit is the product of scared, uneducated northerners. You're not going to say you like northerners, are you?

Dark Days

U nless you live under a rock or follow rugby union (give me a rock any day), you'll be aware that there's a match-fixing 'scandal' taking place in Sydney right now.

Two matches last year are alleged to have been manipulated by players involved being paid A$50,000 a man.

Now, the way this has played out is a reflection of two things: the changing face of the media and journalism and the way authorities in Australia seem to behave out of political expediency.

Many fans have drawn a comparison between the so-called 'Darkest Day in Australian Sport' a couple of years ago, when we were told organised crime had infiltrated out dearest institutions and doping was rife.

Since then, we have had sanctions levelled at Cronulla and the Essendon AFL club but the scale of the cheating was nowhere near what was initially touted.

From a fan's point of view, this smacks of something similar.

Even as a professional journalist I can appreciate the cynicism and that's because politicians and law enforcement in Australia seem to like to use the media to 'smoke out' offenders.

Apparently, many of my colleagues were aware of these match fixing claims for some time but couldn't get the story 'up' — that is, no one would be quoted. This changed when *The Daily Telegraph*'s Michael Carayannis managed to get a line from a police spokesperson at the end of May.

Again, for whatever reason but perhaps as some kind of deterrent, further high-ranking police officers have been quoted since. In other parts of the world, I would imagine police would be far more reticent to talk but there is a 'Wild West' feel to the way things are done Down Under.

As for the change in journalistic practices, that is reflected in the way the story has been covered since it broke.

In the old days, naming groups of people — such as football teams — or individuals would have been considered actionable and therefore ill-advised. But today, decisions are made based on what a news organisation can get away with. One former News Corporation executive used to say, 'Don't start a fight with anyone who buys newsprint (ink) by the tonne.'

The question asked is not 'can they sue?' but 'are they likely to' and 'does that person have a good reputation that can be sullied anyway?' Increasingly we see lines in stories like '*The Daily Bugle* does not suggest the players named in this story are guilty of any wrongdoing' when the rest of the story suggests exactly that.

As a result, we have seen detailed allegations of exactly who is supposed to have done what and which games and clubs are allegedly involved, when such stories would never have been printed in the past ...

From the July issue of **Rugby League World.**

CHAPTER 13

ADOPTOXIA

I realise it would be entirely possible to execute the narrative arc of this book without further side-trips into my personal life. It would certainly be possible to avoid anything that could be accused of being schmaltzy or corny.

But it would have been equally believable had I left out the bit about being adopted. I could have just waffled about being a misfit with imaginary friends who became unhealthily obsessed with the Dapto Canaries and Roxus. Then I could go about detailing these obsessions, questioning the deservedness of the Dapto Canaries vis-à-vis my devotion and deconstructed the song craft of Juno Roxas. I would presumably reach a conclusion towards the back of this book about whether I had wasted my entire life until now ... and typed the words 'The' and 'End'.

But that book would have to go in the fiction section of the shop. Because the degree of self-awareness required to contemplate these matters did not come from a particularly perspiratory half-hour on the treadmill, where many of my better ideas dawn. I did not suddenly 'grow up' the requisite amount to consider them. It came from a person, a person I married.

At this point you're probably sighing and considering turning off the nightlight and maybe popping this book in the neighbourhood fence-mounted wooden library in the morning. Give me a couple more paragraphs, please.

Consider the following …

One day in 2013, Sarah, my on-again, off-again girlfriend of almost a decade, told me over lunch in Brighton, England, that, through a work colleague, she knew about my entire biological family. As you know, I had first learned about my birth family back in 2006. However, in the intervening years, beyond conversations with Stephany, I had taken the matter little further. Sarah's conversation with her friend, which she recounted to me that day, went like this:

Sarah: 'Steve is writing a book. If it's crap, he can write the next one under his birth name.'

Colleague: 'What's his birth name?'

Sarah: 'Andrew John Langley.

Colleague: (silence) (more silence) 'His mother was a ballerina.'

Seriously.

The writing I was doing then has evolved into this book. Because of the project, I wrote about the conversation and its ramifications. I've not read for some time what I wrote then. Let's see if I can find it …

'YESTERDAY, OVER LUNCH AT Brighton, England, my girlfriend told me a friend of hers knew my birth family, had met my grandfather and grandmother and wanted to introduce me to my cousins. I have never met this friend. My girlfriend is

Irish and was raised a long way from Mosman, Gladesville and Windang.

Without warning, the jigsaw pieces of my life presented themselves next to my spaghetti marinara. Elizabeth was a ballerina. My grandmother was English. An auntie came to England to marry a lord. I had an uncle on the Gold Coast. A cousin in Hong Kong. All this, and there were prawns and oysters to spare.

It was one of those days.

Being told that the light shining through the crack in the door leading to the earliest months of my life was about to get much brighter reminded me of how I felt when Stephany contacted me. Most people never experience it. It's not anger, or happiness or wonder or confusion. It is just as likely to make you cry as laugh. There is no word in the English language for it … so I am going to invent one: *adoptoxia.*

Adoptoxia puts you in a daze. An entire dimension of your existence — I don't know if it was there before and dormant or if it was new — is opened. Concepts taken for granted, such as family similarities and inherited traits, suddenly apply. You have a bloodline after resigning yourself to living your entire life without one.

High on adoptoxia, I walked through the gardens around Brighton Pavilion as a Jamaican drummer and gnarled white jazz trumpeter played haunting music that belonged in an art house movie. I felt like I was in the movie myself, the camera following my every expression as I mulled over a plot twist that tested the viewer's ability to suspend belief. Whether my feet were touching the ground with each step, I cannot say for sure.'

WAIT, THERE'S MORE.

The Langleys moved to Australia from Ireland. Not just any part of Ireland. From Tipperary, the exact same part of Ireland my wife is from. By the time we decided to get married, we were able to arrange the ceremony for the biggest church in Sarah's home town of Fethard. It's a church in which a female ancestor of mine was interred right next to the pulpit in the 1600s. She was the best behaved relative you've ever seen at a wedding. There was no reason any of this should have happened: I met a girl from the town my ancestors — whom I did not know *were* my ancestors — sprung from and she then discovering by sheer chance details about my family I did not know myself.

Before that day in Brighton, I was adrift in my own head, lost in rugby league and rock. My touchstones threatened to be my headstones. Almost immediately, I began questioning things. I was no longer alone, no longer immaculate, no longer self-made. 'The book project' went from being some sort of C-grade *I Hope They Serve Beer in Hell* tome to something completely different.

If a life wasted is a life never experienced, then Sarah saved my life. And, when you look at it, even though it didn't yet exist, this book saved my life.

ANDREW JOHN LANGLEY SAYS: So you really do care. For the first 44 years of our life, you've basically ignored me — and I always thought it was because you preferred to wallow in hamstring injuries and drum solos. But now you know that love is a lot more than just a word that goes before 'youse all' … maybe you're not the man you used to be. I like that. I'm sticking closer than ever for the next few months, to see where all this takes us.

UNFORCED ENTRY V

LUCKY MAN

I'm sitting in The Raven on Wallgate in Wigan at 4pm on a Monday. The lady next to me is counting her change to see if she can afford another pint. For the last two hours, she has stared into the distance with her previous pint, oblivious to Sky Sports in the distance. They're playing what could best be described as 'classic rock and pop' on the pub's sound system.

Then it comes on. *Lucky Man*. The Verve, Wiganers and world-beaters. I remember going for a jog around central London on the morning of the 1999 Challenge Cup Final at Wembley, feeling chills as I passed the Houses of Parliament while Richard Ashcroft crooned lyrics that will always stay with me. The song fits with my attitude that life is a journey that comes with any number of corners to turn and things to learn. 'I'm a lucky man with fire in my hands,' he sings.

I was the luckiest man on earth that morning. Still am. But so many others who I've sat next to in pubs like this over the years are not. Why? She's gone to the bar. Now they're playing *Stuck in the Middle With You*.

CHAPTER 14

HIGHWAY TO PARADISE CITY

You've already read about me listening to Side G of *Appetite for Destruction* in the sand dunes of Windang. You know all about how 18-year-old me was completely ignorant of punk rock, smitten by the pop metal production sheen of Mutt Lange, Bruce Fairbairn and Ron Nevison and deaf to the raw barbarism of what I now regard as probably the greatest record of all time.

I have never met, or spoken to, Axl Rose but he has been almost omnipresent in my life since that afternoon I shared with my Sony Walkman. In 1988, as you've read, Rose cited from the stage a story I'd written when he told the crowd how he'd ejected support band Kings of the Sun from the Sydney Entertainment Centre.

Five years later, I was front and centre at 'Sydney's Woodstock', the sprawling and often anarchic Eastern Creek show featuring Skid Row, Rose Tattoo and the otherwise forgettable Pearls and Swine.

In 2001, I saw the band relaunch with 100,000 of my closest friends at Rock in Rio. My bus arrived back in Copacabana at sunrise.

In 2010, I was detained by Canadian customs on suspicion of planning to work illegally as a roadie for Axl — because of the number of plugs and cables in my luggage. It was true I planned to see G N' R five times, but I was paying for the honour. (In the end, to get out of the jam, I had to pull the old 'Russell Crowe based a character on me, Google it' card).[1] So it was probably wholly appropriate that around another significant life milestone, getting married, in Ireland on June 30, 2016, I would frame the sacrament with separate encounters with Axl, on opposite sides of the Atlantic. Twenty-one days before the wedding, in the company of my fiancée, I witnessed Rose front AC/DC at Manchester's Etihad Stadium. And nine days later, on the way back to Sydney, I saw G N' R alone, Nashville's Nissan Stadium.

My impressions of each of the shows were more or less what you'd expect. But they were reversed. I walked away from a patched-together and widely unpopular iteration of AC/DC feeling the way you may have fairly anticipated I might feel after witnessing the 'triumphantly' reformed Guns N' Roses, and vice versa.

Outside the home of Man City, we met a kid from Noosa selling official, flashing AC/DC horns for five pounds. He said he lived in Germany and toured with Ackadacka. I can't be sure but I think he overcharged us by 100 per cent.

I want to say that the thing about not being on the guest list, not being in the posh seats, is the people you meet. But that would be disingenuous … because I *was* on the guest list, with a ticket to a posh seat. This show was being promoted by Simon Moran, the owner of Warrington Wolves. I asked to interview him for this

---

1. Alternatively, you can see page 296 of this book.

52 GAMES ... 52 GIGS

GAME 19 (JUNE 24): Warrington 20 Widnes 18 at Halliwell Jones Stadium, Warrington
Around my wedding, I kind of cheated. No, not *that* sort of cheating! I was married in Ireland and afterwards went home via the United States so it was impossible to find a match. I therefore stockpiled the previous week. There were four matches in the week from June 19 to 25, although the last was in the following week if you're using Australian time zones. I don't remember a thing about this Challenge Cup quarter-final at Warrington. I hope I was there.

GAME 20 (JUNE 25): Wigan 26 Castleford 12 at DW Stadium, Wigan
A classic of the Mascord genre. Stuff around with live streaming, pack up and leave, stop at coffee shop in Manchester, discover I walked out of the stadium without my new Macbook Air. It would be delivered to me at my wedding by colleague Phil Wilkinson.

GIG 19 (JUNE 30): Our Wedding
I did due diligence before booking the local Tipperary wedding band Never Heard of 'Em. I mean, I tried to get The Angels, The Answer, Ricky Warwick and Jon English. This was not 1350 euro I was relishing spending. But they are great, even if we break with a few traditions and don't get the full repertoire of Irish dance tunes because it's 'a foreign wedding'.

GIG 20 (JULY 9): Guns N' Roses at Nissan Stadium, Nashville
An unforgettable experience but not an unforgettable gig. My first US stadium show, down the front in front of Slash, but I've seen other G N' R line-ups do it better.

book, and he instead offered me tickets to the show. When they arrived in the mail, they were, as I feared — seated tickets.

I don't mind seeing Warrington's Stefan Ratchford from 100 metres away. But Cliff Williams? Not if I can avoid it. So despite having the most expensive seats in the house, I bought standing tickets. Which brings us back to the people you meet. Two 17-year-old girls from the Midlands. A couple happy to stand at the very lip of the ramp, with the entire stage obscured, just so they can see Axl or Angus's nasal hairs once or twice.

Whereas shows in many Australian states have become suffocatingly rule-heavy, that night everyone had a smile on their face and — it seems — a beer in their hands. It was a rock crowd, so no one was going to step out of your way if you couldn't see or tell you to *shoosh* — but it's an *old* rock crowd so there was no unseemly aggression either. (My favourite trick when alone at shows is to buy two beers and walk back to the front as if you are carrying one for someone else.)

For all that, Sarah suggested that if the seats Simon gave me were *really* good seats, I may be missed and thought ungrateful. It was wise counsel — when we ascended to the box, we were next to Wolves coach, and my old adversary and friend, Tony Smith.

AC/DC's opening video acknowledged Australia heavily, something they have not always done over the past 30 years. Being a northern summer, it was still light when they came on, starting with *Rock or Bust* from the album of the same name, an album I thought was godawful.

Yet this is exciting.

AC/DC can go 100 shows without changing their set list. Brian Johnson once argued this was because the special effects in their production made doing so problematic. Yet Rose, with only a little less pyro and fancy lighting, would play an Elton John cover or a tribute to Doc Neeson without warning.

And so it was that Axl Rose made AC/DC learn one of their own songs, *Touch Too Much* off *Highway to Hell*, and play it live for the first time on this tour. When the Bon Scott classics began being peeled off during the night, I felt tears welling. *Hell Ain't a Bad Place to Be, Dirty Deeds (Done Dirt Cheap), Rock 'n' (fucking) Roll Damnation, If You Want Blood, Sin City, Shot Down in Flames.*

Sure, there seemed an intangible ... flimsiness to the delivery. Rose was having the time of his life, Angus was almost athletic but Cliff Williams would announce his retirement at the end of the tour because the band had become 'something else', with only one original member.

The reason I was so enraptured with this temporary version of AC/DC may have been that I am not as big an AC/DC fan as I like to think I am. The previous year at Coachella, I felt something approaching boredom tap me on the shoulder during the second half of their set. 'How many times have you seen AC/DC?' an unimpressed friend in Las Vegas asked when I told him I was going to that performance.

'But this is their first show in six years!' I responded, a la Jimmy Olsen. With Rose up front, I was rarely less than transfixed. Before *Let There Be Rock*, he had solemnly declared, 'Now, a reading from the book of Bon.' The show finished with *For Those About to Rock* but for me, penultimate *Riff Raff* was the *piece de resistance*.

Flying to Nashville to see a rock band may seem grandiose and money-wasting to you, but for me it's a normality I have sadly missed in recent months as I focused on writing this book and working to pay some bills. I've twice travelled to Denmark solely to see a little-known band called Disneyland After Dark (or D-A-D), you've already seen references to Sweden Rock and Rock in Rio, and I went to Japan in 2013 because I'd seen KISS at Budokan on TV when I was 10.

Going somewhere on your own a week after getting married? OK, I accept that's weird …

While delayed in Chicago, I learned there had been a shooting in Dallas in which police had been targeted. Walking through an otherwise deserted Nashville Airport, the newsreader on a flickering terminal monitor broke the news there had been five fatalities.

In Nashville, a day after the end of my quarter-century wait to see southern rockers Drivin N Cryin live, I set off for Guns N' Roses on foot from my hotel on West End Avenue, which is located outside the city centre. I endured an hour and 15-minute walk in searing heat that took me past Vanderbilt University, over the 66 freeway, into downtown and onto Broadway, which runs through the city's famous entertainment district.

This was the America of motion pictures, the 'hi-ways and bi-ways' immortalised (for me, anyway) in the kids' TV show *Shazam!*, which is about a superhero who lives in a motor-home. Crossing another bridge as I approached Union Station, now an upscale hotel, a freight train chugged below an endless sky and there was time to imagine its journey across the epic topography of the American south. The similarity between some of the carriages and the alien train from the *X-Files* only served to further fire a fervent imagination.

Nashville's Broadway was like Brisbane's Caxton Street on Origin night, times 20. The sidewalks heaved to such an extent you wanted to walk on the road, dance music blared from rooftop parties and the line for Jack's Bar-B-Que snaked down an alley. The John Seigenthaler Pedestrian Bridge over the Cumberland River impressed me as impractical in the way so many things in American cities seem to be (to me, at least) — you have to walk a block backwards from the waterfront to cross it.

Tonight was a meat-and-potatoes middle American jamboree with the added *frisson* of a host city populated by music professionals, a refuge for '80s hair metal stars who couldn't afford the rent in LA any more. Nissan Stadium, where Guns were playing, is the home of the Tennessee Titans football team and when I walked into the tiny GA area at the foot of the stage with a beer in each hand (aha — *gotcha!*), and looked back at the 69,143 seats, I *wanted* to have the time of my life. I wanted this to be the gig to end all gigs.

My wristband allowed me to stand in front of where Richard Fortus would be playing, but I slipped through the metre-wide passage between the stage ramp and the fence separating us from the seated area on the field and I was on Slash's side. When the area filled up, the passageway filled with people and it was there where I stayed. The agreeable stewards even gave me a second wrist band so I could not be sent back to Richard.

This was the only arena or stadium gig I have ever been to where the security in the pit was on such good terms with the people in the front row that when a drunk forced his way into their midst and obscured their view, he was ejected. After support from country singer Chris Stapleton (OK … but, you know, not my thing … the young girls down the front knew the words to his *every* song), G N' R came on to the *Looney Tunes* theme. I've learned that Axl likes 'soft' entry music — of flexible length — so that instruments can be tuned and he — not the bloke on the computer — decides when the show starts. The opener was *It's So Easy*, the second song I heard in the sand dunes 29 years earlier.

Now, if you are not a fan of this sort of music, you might wonder roughly why there were 40,000 more people here than the last time G N' R came to town. The answer lay in the bloke in the top hat and the skinny blond dude on bass. By adding Slash and Duff McKagan — who'd both left G N' R in the mid '90s — to his band, Rose was able to market this gigantour as a 'reunion' and move to stadia and megabucks. The lead guitarist reportedly has a divorce to pay off. Rose absolutely controlled the set list, including three songs from *Chinese Democracy*, on which he was the only original member to play.

The best of these, fittingly called *Better*, was completely murdered by Slash's new arrangement. Watching on *YouTube*, I had liked the way he played it at previous shows on this tour, but tonight it was an off-key disaster. And despite his stratospheric playing, I only saw Slash smile twice during the entire show. The goosebumps came from the usual songs — *Civil War* (which Myles Kennedy arguably performs better now), *Estranged*, bits of *You Could Be Mine*. Steven Adler, the original G N' R drummer who suffered a stroke following multiple years of drug abuse, came out for *My Michelle* and *Out Ta Get Me* but wasn't seen at subsequent shows.

But it was like I was back at Coachella. Not boredom exactly, but a long way short of exaltation. Seeing Axl, Slash and Duff on the same stage together again wasn't much more heart-warming live than it was on video and I have seen other, now derided, G N' R line-ups put on better shows.

Many others there were too young to remember these three icons together the first time around but, to me, the addition of Slash and Duff just gave Axl the opportunity to take an already-excellent show to a wider audience. Of course, concert experiences are subjective. If there was an easily accessible bar in the GA area, perhaps I'd now be consulting a thesaurus for superlatives. That said, here are the thoughts I had, as I recall them, as I made my way back over the pedestrian bridge around midnight …

Normally when I go to see an '80s band, such as Faster Pussycat or L.A. Guns or Skid Row, I suppress my temporal awareness. I willingly pretend it is 1989. While it is tempting to suggest this is because I did not see these bands regularly growing up, I can maintain the same level of excitement and wonder for those bands I did see, such as The Angels, The Screaming Jets and The Choirboys. But having witnessed every incarnation of Guns N' Roses since I hit play on my Walkman at the beach, the show I'd just seen seemed the least sincere, the least visceral, the most manipulative and rapacious performance of them all. At least in the days of Buckethead and Bumblefoot, you were witnessing someone's artistic vision.

Tonight, I thought, no one was doing exactly what they wanted. It was an attempt to present a nostalgic pop culture representation of Guns N' Roses to an audience at least as desperate for nostalgia as it was for *Sweet Child O' Mine*. It wasn't actually even an attempt to be, let alone a successful manifestation of, what Guns N' Roses actually was. There was no danger, no anger, little evidence of rebellion or camaraderie.

Over the years, I have been fond of telling people that if I lie on the ground, I can see 1987 clearly. I always pick 1987 because it was the year *Appetite* was released. I explain that my life did not changed in any appreciable way in the following 25 years. I had no kids, no mortgage, no house. It was a source of pride that while my friends had surrounded themselves with picket fences, I was still on the *Nightrain*.

That night in Nashville, trying to finish my sole IPA in a honky tonk bar, these anthems of Guns N' Roses seemed to have strangely lost some of their resonance. Instead of tattoos and jewellery, my mind's eye lingered on 2016 G N' R beer guts and lawsuits.

There was a steady incline as I walked back in the direction of my hotel, looking for a taxi or McDonald's, whichever came first. But I knew that even when I reached the summit of the hill, I wouldn't be able to see 1987 any more.

ANDREW JOHN LANGLEY SAYS: So after getting married you went to Nashville on your own to see Guns N' Roses? Awrighty then …

52 GAMES ... 52 GIGS

GIG 21 (JULY 15): Shihad at Factory Theatre, Sydney
It's a fact that I pretty much have no gig buddies in Sydney. I have about 2000 people who want to talk rugby league with me and only a dozen or so who will talk rock'n'roll. So what a fantastic experience to have a beer with departing Fairfax scribe Brad Walter and find that two others at the shindig, James Polson and Dominic Bossi, want to go see the Kiwi legends.

GAME 21 (JULY 16): Brisbane 30 South Sydney 10 at ANZ Stadium, Sydney Olympic Park
Doing the Saturday NRL blog from a ground is interesting. Everyone else is shooting the shit and you're embedding screen captures and instagrams. Back to reality and, aside from the ring on the finger, it's almost as if my wedding never happened.

GAME 22 (JULY 17): Melbourne 20 Newcastle 16 at Hunter Stadium, Newcastle
A long day, going to Newcastle on public transport. And it is too dark to film my new video magazine, *White Line Fever Kicks!* Brave performance from the Knights during a poor season.

GIG 22 (JULY 21): Carl Barron at Brolga Theatre, Maryborough
Comedians such as Carl Barron are popular in rural Queensland. I am tempted to say 'so are Trump and Brexit' but that's kinda mean. This is the first time I've seen live professional comedy. I last through about 20 minutes of humdrum observational gags and head for the bar. I like wordplay and humour based on ideas, not people commenting on car doors and the like. *Zzzz.*

52 GAMES ... 52 GIGS

GAME 23 (JULY 24): Cronulla 36 Newcastle 4 at Southern Cross Stadium, Woolooware
It occurs to me that with the contraction of the media, Sydney rugby league now feels small-time. There's no need to keep reporters out of the dressing rooms any more. There's hardly any wanting to go in.

GIG 23 (JULY 27): The Lazys at Frankie's, Sydney
Best described from the bar, on Facebook: 'Greetings from Frankie's. They're playing *Rag Doll* by Aerosmith. I've been married three weeks, in Sydney two. I'd like to take this opportunity to thank those of you who made the best day of our lives bester by being there and I'd also like to thank 30 or so people who have dropped everything to congratulate me since I've been back. Now playing *Take A Long Line* by The Angels. Not to put too fine a point on it, I feel loved and so does Sarah. Now a song called *Tooth and Nail* off a Lou Gramm solo album which is kicking my arse. Heard that solo? Where was I? ... I had some shit I wanted to say ... in 1988, I was a rock columnist and I was given all these free albums and I covered the birth of G N' R and Bon Jovi and Poison (hello Rob Goldstone), etc, and I just wanted to say there is as much enervating rock music now — stuff that makes you screw up your face and shed a tear of happiness — as there was then. In 1988, the mainstream hated us and they do in 2016. What's changed? Now they are playing *Mr Brownstone*.'

GAME 24 (JULY 28): Sydney Roosters 32 Brisbane 16, Allianz Stadium, Moore Park
A fun night on the sideline for Triple M. But still, I could live without it. In the time I spend doing this, I could write enough *Rugby League Week* stories to earn twice as much.

CHAPTER 15

ON JOURNALISM

The death of journalism through commercial and technological factors (that is, the internet) is one thing. To me, an equally compelling chin scratcher is whether we were ever doing it right to start with.

There was an interesting commentary on Brexit: that the BBC's chartered requirement to tell both sides of the story more or less equally misled people into making a bad decision at the polls. This strikes me as a post-journalism theory for a post-truth world, an argument that our personal objectivity must, at times, over-rule objectivity itself; that we must take it upon ourselves to say, 'I'm not going to give that person a platform because I believe they are bad/stupid/dangerous.'

Of course, journalists do practise this sort of censorship daily, to an extent. We don't report bomb threats. We don't give a forum to racism or homophobia or sexism to counter someone who is not proposing any of those things, to let people decide for themselves whether being hateful or anti-social might be a fun thing to do.

But should we extend the application of our own 'basic values' to covering an issue that is going to be the subject of a national referendum? If journalism is supposed to be an enabler of democracy, how can such interference in the flow of information be justified?

In my own little board-game corner of play-journalism, I had an interesting episode in August 2016 which caused me to ponder these issues once more. Bear in mind that alongside the intellectual and ethical dilemmas presented by *WikiLeaks* and Edward Snowden, this is a Malteser thrown at the sun. But it got me thinking, nonetheless …

A promising young colleague named Curtis Woodward had the sort of story on his website, *the81stminute.com*, that would make any mainstream reporter or editor salivate. Quoting un-named sources, Curtis said that the former Australia international Michael Cronin was opposed to, and was blocking, women's rugby league and Oztag in his home town of Gerringong. The story claimed The Crow did not want women playing on Mick Cronin Oval as long as it went by that moniker.

In my mind's eye, I could already see television networks camping at the oval, door-stopping local officials and throwing questions at them about outrageous sexism. I imagined Curtis acquired his story from aggrieved women in the town who wanted to play league against their friends in neighbouring towns. But I also immediately acknowledged this, with no sources named, was the sort of gossip piece that I would never have had the stomach to write myself and there was a vague awareness it might even be litigious.

Only one thing for it then: try to verify the story and give it a wider airing in the mainstream press. Make some calls. Get the story 'up', as it were.

My first call was to Cronin's pub. I left a message. The second call was to the Country Rugby League's PR, who on a Sunday was not immediately available. Next call was to the CRL chief executive, Terry Quinn, who doubted that there was any truth to Curtis' story but said he'd check it out. I was not sure what I would do with the item if he said there was no truth to it … I didn't even think about it, just moved onto another 'column par' in *The Sydney Morning Herald*'s *Set of Six* and waited for Quinn to call back.

When he did, I could scarcely believe my luck. He said he had been told by a Group Seven official that Curtis' story was on the money. The other teams all had women's sides but Gerringong refused to field one. This was enough for me.

(Before I go any further, I want to address another journalistic practice which you may find dubious but which in my experience is common. I put words in Quinn's mouth. He said he disapproved of the club's position, to which I replied, 'Well, it's illegal isn't it? It's discriminatory,' and he replied, 'It's discriminatory.' And I used that quote in my story.)

After deadline, with the item already online, Cronin called back. He said he wasn't responsible for any policy at the Gerringong Lions as he was only the coach. He was not opposed to women playing on his eponymous oval but explained the club was connected strongly with the local hockey team. It now seemed clear that it was for political and practical, rather than sexist, reasons that the Gerringong Lions were not big on women's Oztag.

I quickly rewrote the piece and, to me, it was the perfect news item in about six sentences. It started with an allegation, it had the voice of an identified authority (Terry Quinn) giving weight to the allegation and then it had another authoritative voice (Mick Cronin) denying said allegation.

(How do we deny an earlier version of a story that appeared online when it no longer appears anywhere? I got into that debate with someone on Twitter.)

My item still pissed off some people mightily — but airing both sides of the argument is the way I was trained.

Did I let down my constituents by not trusting my instincts, by not having the courage to dispense with accepted procedure and make an executive decision?

My mind and my emotions just don't work in such a way that I can discount what Terry Quinn said based on a hunch that the official he spoke to in Group Seven had an agenda, or on my belief that Mick Cronin is a good man. I've had too many years of what has become known as 'churnalism' to take that moral leap.

I've fallen in too many holes by abandoning the time-honoured methodology of newspaper journalism. I don't really trust my instincts. If I stray too far off the beaten hack track, I get myself in trouble.

Being able to stray successfully, I guess, is what separates the well-intentioned from the great.

Which begs another, orbiting, question: if I can grasp this distinction intellectually and understand a personal failing, could I have *been* great had I not embarked on a career in journalism?

In any case, I cannot say whether sexism is at the route of this little rural soap opera and I'm not sure who the aggrieved parties actually are. I do know that decent, honest journalism is about the quest for truth. You can't search for an objective truth without believing in its existence.

But most stories, in varying amounts of detail, just tell us about a search for truth that failed miserably.

ANDREW JOHN LANGLEY SAYS: You are overthinking something here that is of very little importance to very few people, aside from those directly involved. Let's have a drink.

Three Cheers for the Ref!

Saturday's was the first Challenge Cup final in five years I have not attended — which means I didn't get a vote for the Lance Todd Trophy.

But I've no doubt who I'd have voted for in the Hull FC-Warrington clash at Wembley: referee Gareth Hewer.

Working with Peter Sterling on *Monday Night Football*, I know the FC favourite son was a big fan of Danny Houghton getting the gong but for me the whistler had to be the man.

Rugby league officiating is beset with procedure, with technology relied upon in a way that is consistent and repeatable. Some people want it to be about feel, they want match officials to get their heads around how a moment can be ruined by unnecessarily consulting the video referee — or, in the NRL — the much-vaunted Bunker. But on Saturday, Hewer just pointed to the spot when tries were scored. The only time he consulted video referee Ben Thaler was when Hull's Steve Michaels claimed a touchdown. Although Hewer didn't have a clear view, it was sent upstairs as 'no try' and this was proven 100 per cent correct.

Hooker Houghton may have sealed Sterlo's vote as he stopped Warrington's Ben Currie from scoring in the final minute.

That's where Hewer won it for me.

There would not be a single referee in the NRL who would make a decision on the spot in the last minute of the final regarding a possible try. Certainly not with the side who claimed the try being down by two points. Hewer ruled knock-on immediately; he didn't even seem to consider consulting Thaler.

This got me thinking of a possible third approach to officiating in the technological age, an alternative to strict adherence to KPIs and an old-fashioned head-in-the-sand 'feel' approach. Why not use technology without fear of error? That's what Hewer did. He refereed the same way match officials do across the world on parks and fields. When he knew what he saw, he ruled on it without second guessing himself.

On the occasion when technology was available to help him make the right decision, he used it. He did not worry about being judged by his colleagues on Monday morning for not consulting Thaler in that last minute.

He was right. He understood that to be enough justification for his actions.

Technology is an aid to officiating. It doesn't have to be officiating itself. The video referee is there for when we aren't sure, yet box-ticking and mangled thinking has led us to a procedure where we have to tell him what we think before we use him.

If every Super League and NRL referee this weekend went out and controlled their games like Gareth Hewer controlled the Challenge Cup final, we'd have a lot of improved spectacles.

From **rugby-league.com,** *August 30, 2016.*

52 GAMES ... 52 GIGS

GAME 25 (AUGUST 4): Brisbane 12 St George Illawarra 8 at WIN Stadium, Wollongong
It's 4am. I am drinking with Michael Bolt, David Riolo, Keith Cole, Sean O'Connor, Josh White and Graeme Bradley. It's Rusty Steelers night — a reunion for the Illawarra Steelers; these guys were my heroes as a kid. My life ain't so bad.

GIG 25 (AUGUST 5): The Angels at Waves, Wollongong
Roughly 16 hours later I'm talking league backstage with Dave Gleeson. John Brewster points out a sign at the venue that says 'The Angles'. When I was a newshound, it would have been handy if there was a sign pointing me to angles. Boom-boom.

GAME 26 (AUGUST 8): Penrith 38 Sydney Roosters 18 at Pepper Stadium, Penrith
We give the man-of-the-match award to referee Gavin Badger for hardly consulting the Bunker. Gav refused to be interviewed on air, because — under NRL media guidelines — he is not allowed to be interviewed by us.

GIG 26 (AUGUST 11): Dio Driver at Agincourt Hotel, Sydney
Yes, $25 to see a Dio cover band. Before 2016 is out, I'm going to try to see close to the real thing (minus, understandably, the late Ronnie James Dio), and I doubt it'll cost me much more.

GAME 27 (AUGUST 14): Sydney Roosters 22 North Queensland 10 at Allianz Stadium, Moore Park
A regulation day on the sideline, although the interview with Roosters winger Latrell Mitchell is delightful. 'To see a kid looking up to me, I have to pinch myself,' he gushes.

52 GAMES ... 52 GIGS

GIG 27 (AUGUST 19): Palace of the King at Bald Faced Stag, Leichhardt

My friend Greg Truman from New York called to say he is in town, so I invite him along. There are half a dozen friends at the pub — and almost no-one else. So much for having no gig buddies in Sydney. It's just that before, I couldn't see them for all the other people at shows ... so the death of rock is actually quite convenient.

GAME 28 (AUGUST 21): Sydney Roosters 42 St George Illawarra 6 at Allianz Stadium, Moore Park

Sometimes, the Dragons feel like my side ... when they wear predominantly red. Their coach, Paul McGregor, always wears red in my mind as a Steelers great.

GIG 28 (AUGUST 24): Couple of Dead Bodgies at Merton Hotel, Rozelle

Couple of Dead Bodgies is a jam band organised by Greg Truman, who is related to rock royalty — his cousins, Anthony, John and Paul Field, formed The Cockroaches, which morphed into The Wiggles, Anthony is here tonight, and wants to talk about Wests Tigers. I meet a man who used to be on Wests Tigers' board and a surgeon who gives me a yarn that ends up on the front of *Rugby League Week* — complete with gory surgery photos.

GIG 29 (AUGUST 26): The Angels at Dee Why RSL

They say musicians can be stingy so I am pleasantly surprised when my Australian expat friend, a guitarist back home from Vegas, shells out on an Uber to and from Dee Why on Sydney's northern beaches. He is wearing a leopard print three-quarter length coat and a fedora. When my friend tries to get backstage afterwards, there's drama. Awkward.

CHAPTER 16

ON THE HOMEPAGE OF ROLLING STONE

In mid-September, my crappy podcast — *White Line Fever* — was on the cover of *Rolling Stone*. Well, the *home page* of *Rolling Stone*, but if that was ever a song I'd imagine it would be unlistenable, with lots of Auto-Tune.

The story was about Cherie Currie, whose thoughts on the meaning of life and being kidnapped by stalkers you can read elsewhere in this tome. The former Runaways singer had recorded an album five years previously with such luminaries as Slash, Duff McKagan, Matt Sorum, Billy Corgan, Brody Dalle, The Veronicas and Juliette Lewis ... which was never released.

During the podcast, Currie had revealed that her album was to finally be unleashed in September. She told me this in, maybe, May. I had sent her quotes out as a press release on September 13.

(OK, so maybe things changed ... I couldn't just ring her and ask.)

I've no idea how the *RollingStone.com* writer, one Jon Blistein, happened across my press release. I send them to ramshackle metal websites, not cultural behemoths with a dubious attitude to most of the music covered by ramshackle metal websites.

Because Mr Blistein had to put *RS*'s own stamp on the story, he did not rely solely on the quotes I had transcribed from my own interview. He went to the trouble of listening to it himself. And when he linked back to the podcast, he did not use the links provided in the press release but rather managed to find a page on my WordPress site, *stevemascord.com* (where do they come up with these names, right?), and linked to a playlist of the songs on the episode.

Your crappy WordPress site has been linked by *Rolling Stone*. The clicks form such a digital torrent that smoke emits from your server and you receive takeover offers from Time Warner.

Not quite.

Half a day after the story appeared, just 25 curious people had clicked on the link to see or hear the original interview. I have found the same thing every time a major news site has picked up one of my stories, even when they've done the decent thing and given attribution. If your audio is embedded in their story, you get a few plays.

Almost no one clicks.

When we talk about the decline of journalism, this is one paradigm that is not widely understood. It is reflected across both of my 'disciplines', music and sport.

Because readers are time-bereft, aggregation is where the money is. Aggregators are sites that trawl other sites, cutting things down to bite-sized chunks, without generating anything original. These are the sites that get advertising, sponsorship, takeover offers and those widgets at the bottom of each story

52 GAMES ... 52 GIGS

GAME 29 (AUGUST 28): South Sydney 34 Newcastle 12 at Hunter Stadium, Newcastle
The season is winding down now. The Knights have lost 16 consecutive games, the worst losing streak since Western Suburbs in 1984. Tomorrow night, I will be on the sideline for the final *Monday Night Football* game of this year and — given the proposed changes to the TV coverage for next season — perhaps of any year.

GAME 30 (SEPTEMBER 4): Penrith 36 Manly 6 at Pepper Stadium, Penrith
When I was living and breathing the rugby league round, the end of the regular season was something to celebrate. Not having to go to the football on Monday night is now what's worth celebrating.

GIG 30 (SEPTEMBER 5): Frankie's World Famous House Band at Frankie's, Sydney
The evening starts with Corolea Cameron, Jon English's ex-partner, and former Angels bassist James Morley at Frankie's, innocently enough ... if drinking nine per cent alcohol content beer like water can be innocent. It ends with James sitting in with the band and, it would appear, me deciding to break into a jog on the way home. I fall. I could have had an eye out. I wake up with my face glued to the pillow by blood. At 47, I'm running out of chances to get away with such misadventures.

which are sold by content brokers like Outbrain or Taboola. These are the sites that can afford to employ a journalist or two — in the world of hard rock such sites include *Ultimate Classic Rock, Loudwire, Blabbermouth* ...

And you know what? These lucky-to-have-a-paid-job journalists never interview anybody.

They are too busy scouring the internet, podcasts, radio and social media for interviews conducted by enthusiastic amateurs who just want to say they have spoken to a rock star on the phone.

The result is that hard questions aren't asked, fewer people are held to account. Musicians below the Metallica and Bon Jovi level these days must at first feel journalists really like them — before realising that the only people who will interview them are just fans who don't get paid. Sometimes these enthusiastic amateurs will ask a good question by accident, and the aggregator journalist in an office or working at home for a paltry fee will find the quote in the 47th paragraph of a 2000-word Q&A with Junkyard's new bass player ... and he'll feel like he's got a scoop. But he didn't get the scoop. Fifty-four-year old Chuck Mensch of Oklahoma City — owner of *spandexpants.com* — did. But he doesn't know what a scoop is.

Music websites such as, say, *Metal Scrotum*, actually transcribe and publish such exchanges as: '*Metal Scrotum*: "How are you today Wizzy?" Wizzy: "I'm great." *Metal Scrotum*: "That's great."' Pulitzer Prize stuff right there ...

In a shrinking media, professional journalists have become too valuable to dispatch to the coalface. Their training, and the money they must be paid, demands they be chained to a desk and bled dry as they sift through the work of clueless but keen hobbyists.

In mainstream sport, Fox Sports' website in Sydney have some of the best young rugby league reporters of the past ten years: Nathan Ryan, Dan Walsh, Ben Glover and John Dean. But you won't find them out on the road most days, going to media conferences and matches. Instead, they are based in the amazing St Leonards starship-like base of Fox Sports, monitoring the station's televisual output for angles and keeping an eye on social media, radio, newspapers and everything else you can access with the help of electricity, cables and transmitting devices.

When I was offered a job at Fox Sports a couple of years back, I was expected to be in the office five days a week, 9 to 5, throughout the off-season. If I was to criticise this trend, I would be quite some hypocrite.

Bar my work on Triple M, everything I do that pays my bills can be done remotely. I live-blog three games for Fairfax every Saturday from wherever I happen to be in the world and I have approached them to let me do the first and last match *and* write the match reports, saving them the expense of staffing those matches.

In 2016, there were many Saturdays when Fairfax Sydney had no one at any of the three matches. If the Raiders were in Sydney, they'd use the reporter from the affiliated *Canberra Times*. Even at Cronulla, the fellow from the *St George & Sutherland Shire Leader* would be there so there was no point doubling up.

News used to travel through a figurative pipe, through a big filter, to an opening at the other end where it was consumed by the public. The filter was the journalists themselves, whose main duty above all was to determine what was news, and then to check its veracity and dress it up in a manner that would justify a screaming headline.

What we have now resembles the funnel you use to put oil in an engine, but held upside down. Real, original content is poured through a narrow opening at one end — there's no one actually at the coalface gathering information any more because it's too expensive. The only people at the narrow end of the funnel are either those who must be there by virtue of their medium (television, primarily — even radio is now very often done from in front of a TV) or are there because of their saintly enthusiasm (websites, podcasts, community radio).

That material, gathered in a more careless way than ever before, is then poured through the narrow opening and propelled outwards through a vast ring of people sitting in offices, often with questionable knowledge of the subject or empathy for who is being quoted. Their job is to try to make the same stuff look different, before sprinkling it on the masses.

It's like petrol. Different brands. Looks, smells and works the same. We have a greater diversity of outlets in inverse proportion to the diminishing number of original sources, of reporters on the ground.

At this point you may be confused. I seem at once angry about the sinking ship, and yet shuffling to the stern and whistling in between panicked breaths into a dinghy I'm holding. That interpretation is completely accurate.

I'm an individualist. I generally interact with the world without the buffer of others. I don't think I can change things. Since I was a kid I have always had a core philosophy that I should behave as if anything bad happening to me was my fault. I should not complain about obstacles but find a way around them.

Journalism is in the sewer? Better get some nice tight goggles that cover the nose.

ANDREW JOHN LANGLEY SAYS: Actually, this stuff is interesting. You're not talking about boneheaded bum sniffers and long-haired deadbeats. Well, you're talking about talking about them — which is infinitely better than talking about them.

Cherie Currie on Personal Responsibility

The Runaways were, in many ways, a quintessential '70s band. 'When the group was formed in 1975 by music Svengali Kim Fowley, Sandy West was 18, Joan Jett 16, Micki Steel 20, Lita Ford 17 and Cherie Currie 15.

'Runaways' wasn't just a name for the girls who gave us *Cherry Bomb*. That's kinda what they were.

I ask singer Currie what she has learned from such a turbulent adolescence. Having done time as a drug and alcohol counsellor, she is eager to answer. 'Number one, don't ever ask anybody's opinion,' she says, down a phone line from Los Angeles, 'and if they give their opinion, don't listen to them. Because you've got a path in life, the same as they have a path. They can't see your path. Even asking is going to be a big mistake.

'Any time I've listened to other people or did what other people wanted me to do, I failed miserably. If I did what was in my heart, what that little voice in my head was telling me to do, I've never failed. Not once.

'So my strongest advice is you know in your heart and in your soul what you're doing on this planet. You know what your path is. Don't ask anyone else to understand or to believe in you. Believe in yourself and go for it and you can make it happen. You start listening to other people and it's going to be a disaster.'

Even being kidnapped and raped by a crazed fan can be viewed positively, she insists.

'For me, I was so blessed that I survived because I shouldn't have,' she says. 'So I walk away from that … I see people who are so much worse off, people who have lost their lives, for one, people that have been maimed forever from their kidnappings.

'I got away injured but I got away with all my limbs and everything else and I just am grateful. It happened when I was 17 years old and I've been speaking out about it ever since it happened. I really felt it was important for me to share my experience and I am a much stronger person. I'm a survivor, a complete survivor and I'm not a victim. People will argue with me on that. I did make mistakes. I got in that car. I didn't listen to that voice in my head, even though I was around my friends, there was even a guard there, something told me in my head, "You shouldn't do this."

'We always never listen. That was my mistake. Sometimes I even find saying that out loud on social media will get you in a lot of trouble. But I have to take responsibility for those mistakes. I think it's good that I'm still around to tell people, "It's OK, you survived and good for you. You're going to be a better person for it."'

*From the **White Line Fever** podcast, episode 88.*

52 GAMES ... 52 GIGS

GAME 31 (SEPTEMBER 11): Penrith 28 Canterbury 12 at Allianz Stadium, Moore Park

At no time in the past two decades would I have conceived of a year in which I only attended one finals series match live. But this is it. The Bulldogs' exit and coach Des Hasler graciously thanks the media for the year. He knows he will face pressure to keep his job over the off-season.

GIG 31 (SEPTEMBER 11): Devine Electric at Frankie's, Sydney

I don't feel like going but resolve to stand at the back of the room drinking lemonade and exit immediately Devine Electric's set is over. Arriving at the alluringly dark performance space, I buy a beer. One beer. Then I hear a voice shout, 'Mascord!' Andrew Johns. With him: Gorden Tallis. Elsewhere in the room are half a dozen friends — Brett Tyrrell and Ben Jacob of Release The Hounds are with Ross Young, the son of AC/DC's Malcolm. My friend Monique and her husband are sitting nearby. Half the band seem to know me. The Brad Fittler Medal is the next night and I have to cry off — even though it doesn't start until 7.30pm.

GAME 32 (SEPTEMBER 18): Illawarra 18 Newtown 10 at Leichhardt Oval

As much as I love anything in scarlet, I must admit Newtown are dudded this rainy afternoon. They are the better side and an out-on-the-full call by a touchie is clearly wrong. A pleasant debrief at the nearby Garry Owen Hotel, owned by my former *On the Street* magazine editor Margaret Cott, ensues.

CHAPTER 17

ROCKIN' WITH DOKKEN

'They're all Somalian anyway.'

I was sitting in a taxi in Sioux Falls, South Dakota, in the middle of a whirlwind six days in America on the way from the NRL finals to the Super League grand final. My day had started at 5am on three hours' sleep, so when I emerged from the small, airy airport terminal, I somehow missed a rank full of taxis.

My cab driver observed that I did the right thing in phoning for him. 'The guys on the rank are all sending their money back [to Somalia], it's funding terrorism,' he drawled as we sped past his mystified and miffed competitors. 'I don't know how the government allows it.'

This was my 'old' life. No, not talking to right wing, borderline racist cabbies. I mean, flying into Bumfukk, Iowa, for a show by some washed-up hair metal band. I did this sort of thing for a decade. Tonight, it was the first time the original line-up of Dokken had played a whole show together in more than 20 years. I was present the last time the four of them — Don Dokken, George Lynch, Jeff Pilson and Mick Brown — were on stage, at the House of Blues in Anaheim, California, for an encore in

52 GAMES ... 52 GIGS

GIG 32 (SEPTEMBER 28): Mr Big at Regency Ballroom, San Francisco

The most heart-warming thing I've seen since England warming up in *Keep Fighting Gaz* t-shirts during last year's series against New Zealand (at the time, league journalist Gary Carter was in a life-threatening condition in hospital following a brutal, unprovoked assault) is Pat Torpey, the drummer for Mr Big, sitting in for about half his band's set at this ornate Bay Area theatre. Torpey has Parkinson's and was not expected to play again. Tonight, Pat has a stand-in for the more demanding songs, but there's no one bigger in Mr Big now.

GIG 33 (SEPTEMBER 29): Stryper at Centerstage Theater, Atlanta

Security is tighter than the airport — we all received the full keys-out-of-the-pockets nine yards when we entered. Stryper have an app that allows you to decide what they play for their encore. The album sounds dated, to be fair. One girl is wearing a t-shirt she bought at the same venue on the original *THWTD* tour.

GIG 34 (SEPTEMBER 30): Dokken at Badlands, Sioux Falls

In putting the finishing touches to this book, it took a whole day to go back over the year and audit all 104 gigs and games. Between September 11 and September 28, and September 29 and October 14, I appear to have gone to no shows at all. My three shows in three American cities in three days during NRL grand final week would therefore have to cover three weeks. That's not in the rules. Does it sound like something I would do?

2009. Thanks to the singer's complaints, I got kicked off *YouTube* for posting that footage …

Less than two months before the presidential election, this was also a timely peek into the American heartland. Aside from my somewhat pink-necked cabbie, there was the venue for tonight's show: Badlands Gold, Guns and Ammo. That's right — a shooting range where one could avail oneself of the pleasures of an Uzi before attending a giant indoor pawn market in a room that was converted at night into a concert venue.

Not far from here, Native Americans were protesting a pipeline that was to cross their burial grounds. Twenty-seven days before my visit, construction workers had bulldozed sacred land despite the concerns — leading to attack dogs being unleashed on protesters, six of whom were bitten. By the end of December, there were still SWAT teams being called on the protesters. It was fair to say sympathies in Sioux Falls (pop. 153,000) lay with the pipeline, not the environmentalists who had succeeded in delaying work with the help of the Obama administration.

Even my Australian friend, whom I met for a drink before the show, said he will vote for Trump. His mid-west coffee shop wasn't doing too well, a previous business venture had ended in rancour, he believed America needed a shakeup and Hillary Clinton was, in his words, 'a criminal'. I was far from home, geographically and ideologically.

After two years of scrimping and saving to pay off credit cards, I had pushed the boat out on this 'transit' trip. First, three nights in San Francisco, culminating in an appearance on one of my favourite podcasts and a show by the band Mr Big at an ornate downtown theatre.

52 GAMES ... 52 GIGS

GAME 33 (OCTOBER 1): United States 20 Canada 14 at Eden Park, Wilmington
New Zealand would complain about conditions in Workington for their Four Nations game against Scotland. They should go to the US state of Delaware and drop into Eden Park, Wilmington. At this match, officials have to break into a switch box to turn the lights on and the players change in the car park. On the positive side, the food at halftime is great. And for the entire crowd — all dozen of us — it was also free.

GAME 34 (OCTOBER 8): Wigan 12 Warrington 6 at Old Trafford, Manchester
I'm pretty sure I covered the very first Super League grand final. It's matured into a great event — the RFL cops a lot of criticism but with a mixture of hymns and glitz I think they capture the spirit of their fans on the big occasions better than the NRL does. However, media mixed zones, where the broadcast and print media wait in a designated area for players and coaches, are increasingly frustrating. It's impossible to get anything for yourself.

San Francisco was sweltering. Jetlag only made the sweating more profuse and more pungent as I lugged my bag around the seedy Tenderloin, up a steep hill, looking for my lodgings. In truth, I had only chosen to stay at the Amsterdam Hostel in a nod to the lyric in Counting Crows' *Mr Jones* ...

'I was down at the New Amsterdam/Staring at this yellow-haired girl/Mr Jones strikes up a conversation/With a black-haired flamenco dancer ...'

It is so impossibly Bohemian, that song. When Counting Crows played Leeds during the 1994 Kangaroo Tour, I got singer Adam Duritz to sign a birthday card for my then-girlfriend (he misheard me because of my accent and spelt her name wrongly), who was back home in Brisbane. To me, she was a New Farm Bohemian — certainly more of a beatnik than anyone I knew in Wollongong.

(Legend has it that Kangaroos fullback Brett Mullins and the late Stone Temple Pilots singer Scott Weiland wrestled in the Roundhay Bar at the Crowne Plaza on the same tour.)

Somehow, when Duritz sang, *'When I look at the television, I wanna see me/Staring right back at me/We all wanna be big stars/But we don't know why, and we don't know how/But when everybody loves me/I'm gonna be just about as happy as I can be,'* he was being honest and ironic at the same time.

He wanted to be famous, he wanted to be beautiful, he wanted access to more women. But he was already beyond the naïve conviction that it would make him happy; he simply thought it was something worth doing anyway, just to make sure.

What Duritz discovered after the song went to No.2 in the US was that his darker suspicions were correct. On the 1998 live album *Across a Wire: Live in New York City*, he changed the lyrics to *'We all wanna be big, big stars/but then we get second thoughts about that'* and *'when everybody loves you, sometimes that's just about as fucked up as you can be.'*

To me, the imagery of the song was so powerful that I had even secretly cast a friend, the journalist Trevor Marshallsea, as the mythical Mr Jones (who was, in fact, Marty Jones of The Himalayans). I bought a brown jacket and threw my late-'80s black leather and bandanas into storage. I was alternative, man.

One afternoon in the '90s, before Google Maps, I spent a day traipsing up and down hills around North Beach, so desperate to stumble across the scene from the song that I resorted to asking strangers if they knew of the New Amsterdam.

Google 'New Amsterdam, Columbus, San Francisco' and you'll see I'm not the only obsessive when it comes to this subject. It was kind of like *Pokemon Go* for a select group of saddos 20 years ago.

The New Amsterdam is now, apparently, a sports club. The Amsterdam Hostel where I stayed is a perfect metaphor for Duritz rhapsodising about fame making him happy only to discover the opposite. Like fame, I suspect, the Amsterdam has its strong points but is nothing special. 'Good location but I wouldn't go back,' is one TripAdvisor review I'd agree with.

Michael Butler is a bass player with a wife, a daughter and a dog who paints houses and lives in the Outer Sunset area of San Francisco. His program, *The Rock and Roll Geek Show*, is one of the oldest music podcasts and one of the most popular. He's a bumbling, funny everyman with a repertoire of kooky affectations and an abiding and sometimes encyclopaedic knowledge of rock music, tending toward the punky end of the spectrum. Listeners call in for show reviews, always asking him at the start of their voicemails how he is and then pausing while he answers, 'I'm great thanks, couldn't be better.'

Butler, who was around 50, is at the vanguard of two financially tenuous oeuvres — hard rock music and indie new-media operators. If anyone can make a living out of podcasting about rock, it should be him. But the truck emblazoned with 'Michael Butler Painting' in his driveway told me no one can make a living out of podcasting about rock.

For the princely sum of US$100, I got to program the music on that night's episode, drink unlimited cans of Tecate beer and enjoy a meal of grilled fish and hush puppies. Michael's dog almost bit me before we retired to a cubby hole with two computers, a mixing board and two digital recorders to do the podcast. Above on shelves was all manner of rock bric-a-brac; Joan Jett gazed down at us from a record cover. It was great to be able to promote Australian bands such as Palace of the King and The Lazys to a rather large audience. If you listen to the show you'll detect that by the end I am starting to sound rather drunk.

Because I had an early flight the next day, I stayed the second night in San Francisco at an airport hotel, which allowed me to sample Uber for the first time, in the city where driverless cars were already being trialled. I left my camera in the back seat, didn't I? The driver found it and took it to my hotel, at no expense, which made my first experience with Uber rather positive, but Uber's first experience of me rather less so. But I was without my trusty Lumix for the Mr Big show, which was being held at the rather impressive Regency Ballroom. Built in 1909, it features a 10-metre ceiling and 22 chandeliers. You should know Mr Big from their 1991 hit, *To Be With You*. A much more recent song, *East/West*, was part of my wedding waltz.

Their 57-year-old drummer, Pat Torpey, had been unable to play due to Parkinson's disease so it was heart-warming to see him back behind the drums for between a third and half of the night's set. I'm not going to say it brought tears to my eyes because lots of things do that. But it did. So, I guess I said it.

The next morning I flew to Atlanta, Georgia, for the opening night of a 30th Anniversary tour for God-rocking Stryper's *To Hell With the Devil* album.

My hotel in Atlanta was so bad I actually feared for my safety. I changed rooms twice before finding one in which my odds of being garrotted felt like they'd dropped below 50 per cent. Even then, I refused to leave my luggage in my room when I went to the gig and secreted it behind reception.

Perhaps I should have prayed to Stryper.

That night in Atlanta, there were more security checks for the show at the Centerstage Theatre than at most airports. I had to go through the metal detector twice, removing my pretentious punk rock key-chain the second time. Were Christian rock shows now regarded as terrorist targets? Or was Atlanta itself as dangerous as my hotel?

Stryper did some interesting things. There was a countdown on a big screen before they came on stage. They also promoted a charity on the same screen. And as the show — which involved *To Hell With the Devil* being played in full, in order — neared its end, fans were invited to text their encore requests to a number displayed on the same screen. I suspect the charges applied regardless of whether they played the songs.

These middle-aged men wore ridiculous 1980s Spandex outfits and played ridiculously overblown 1980s hair metal. Separately, neither seemed ridiculous in the eyes of my dubious sensibilities. But fax machines, Filofaxes and liquid paper seemed cutting edge by comparison. 'I think our entire congregation was here tonight,' I heard someone say as I hailed a taxi back to Fort Apache.

Then it was on to Sioux Falls. Dokken had reunited for money, and said so openly. This was just a warm-up for a Japanese run which, Don Dokken said in one interview, would give drummer 'Wild' Mick Brown a nice nest egg. The two of them were in their own, separate version of Dokken already; George Lynch had Lynch Mob and his own side projects; Jeff Pilson was a full-time member of Foreigner. When I saw the words 'sold out' on the t-shirt stall, I reacted badly — until my expat friend pointed out that those words were actually *on* the t-shirt. A US medium is an Australian large; it fits fine. By the time they hit the stage after a support slot from LA chanteuse Gabby Rae, my expat friend and I were nicely buzzed.

The show itself? Well ... this was a tighter, more explosive Dokken than the one I saw before. Lynch and Pilson were masters of their instruments and the latter threw himself around the stage like it was 1985. Don Dokken, on the other hand, was no better or worse than the last time I saw him, at the end of the Rockingham Festival in Nottingham a year before, when he chided the audience for its apathy. Tony Harnell, the singer in such bands as TNT, once told me it's possible for middle-aged vocalists to get their range back with diet and physical and vocal exercises. If so, apathy would appear to be a two-way street.

The reality told me this had been a disappointing show. My childhood imagination argued that it was fantastic. I could still hear the two of them bickering as I dozed off in the motel abutting the venue/shooting range/pawn market.

The next morning, I was on my way to Wilmington, Delaware, to be at the United States-Canada rugby league international, returning to my hotel to live-blog the NRL grand final and, after a few hours' sleep, attend an open trial for the Toronto Wolfpack — the first trans-Atlantic professionals sports club entering English rugby league's third tier — in nearby Philadelphia. Soon after, I boarded an overnight trans-Atlantic flight, and then I pretty much headed straight to an Irish wedding. This, friends, is what I call doing it old school and what just about everybody else calls unremitting stupidity.

ANDREW JOHN LANGLEY SAYS: For once, your adult self is right. I see you growing out of many things relating to rugby league as this book goes on. It's only taken you roughly 37 years. I'm guessing 37 years after you first interviewed a rock star, you'll get over big chunks of that too. So, we're talking, what, 1990? Come back to me in 2027 and you'll see things differently.

THE CALL OF THE WILD

The things that make me happy are strange. One day not so long ago, I was sitting in Denny's near LAX, listening to Chickenfoot and Bret Michaels on my iPod, hoeing into an average t-bone and I was as euphoric as I've been for months.

Goosebumps-shit-eating-grin euphoric.

Euphoria, for me, is almost always achieved alone. Just me and my illusions, lying to each other. After two hours at the gym, I was finally ready for LA and Hollywood.

Another song I played was by a New York band I interviewed on my first visit there in 1990, called Company of Wolves. Their first single was *Call of the Wild*, which features a southern-rock-type chorus that bellows at one point, 'Ain't never going home no more … got a feeling in my bones.'

When I worked in AAP's London bureau for a month — when newspapers were still based in Fleet Street and the area bore no resemblance to its current upscale visage — I used to listen to *Call of the Wild* on the bus each day. I liked the sentiment. I had the same feeling in my bones. And although I eventually returned to Wollongong, that June, I still ain't gone home.

CHAPTER 18

DELAWARE VIA NEW YORK

'Issac Luke,' said the fellow next to me in a Manhattan bar, rather nonchalantly, sometime around midnight.

It would be disingenuous at this point not to reveal that the bar in question was called The Australian. And that it was owned by former Manly reserve-grader Matt Astill. And that Luke, at the time the South Sydney and New Zealand hooker, was playing on the TV in front of us.

But still …

It's a night that has stayed with me. It was early in 2013. There I was, 15,476 kilometres from 1300SMILES Stadium, watching a replay of the Test between Australia and New Zealand that was played in Townsville about three months earlier.

I'd been in the bar for a while. The 2012 grand final, Melbourne v Canterbury, was on before the Test, and during that game my future best man Jim Savage and I had been discussing the sameness of the Bulldogs' attack over Coopers Ale stubbies with labels printed in most colours of the rainbow. All the important colours, anyway.

I am not sure if Germans or Sri Lankans instinctively recognise each other when abroad ... but, with Australians, it is an inherent skill.

Or at least it's a skill that *I've* picked up. More than halfway through my 40s, I can identify my countrymen, almost like gaydar. Call it 'g'day-dar'. In the 1990s, we dressed differently. Australians abroad did not care what they looked like when they went out. They packed light. If someone walked into a Miami nightclub in a flannelette shirt, stone-washed jeans and Ugg boots, there was a high probability that he – or she – was Australian.

On this New York night, there were two groups of Antipodeans next to me in The Australian bar, restaurant and lounge on West 38th Street as the grand final and then the Test were shown on television.

The first group — two 20-something blokes from south-western Sydney — took an hour to spot me as a compatriot despite the way I was dressed and my gibber becoming progressively louder with each Coopers. And the fact that the bar was called The Australian ...

The second lot — two girls and two guys in their early 20s, maybe younger — took two hours. One of them, clearly not realising that the match had been decided some time before, asked who I thought was going to win the Test. 'I'll wager Australia by one to ten if anyone is keen,' I responded.

I'm not sure, at this point, if they'd worked out where I was from.

'I'll even have a go at first try-scorer,' I blithered.

But here's the thing: although I knew the final score, I couldn't remember who crossed for the first try in Townsville, aside from it being a Kiwi. I covered the game, filed while it was still in play, wrote about it the next day, even did a minute-by-minute account of the contest. But I couldn't remember who scored first. That's when one of the young Sydney fellas said, 'Issac Luke.'

I watched the slightly blurry picture, recorded from the Fox Soccer Channel, as Luke plucks the ball up out of dummy half, shrugs off one tackler, and dives over for the first try of the match.

Well, I'll be damned.

Matt Astill wasn't there that night. His wife Nicole had given birth to their first child the previous evening. Before being in charge of The Australian, which was frequented by News Corporation types and — I was impressed to hear — by heavy metal and hard rock DJ-cum-TV host Eddie Trunk, Matt tended bar at a place called Ship of Fools on the Upper East Side. He played lower grades for the Sea Eagles before moving to the US, where his greatest moment was being in the USA Tomahawks team that led Australia 24–6 at half-time at Philadelphia's Franklin Field on December 1, 2004. (The Kangaroos recovered to win 36–24.)

Of all the rugby league identities to visit The Australian, his favourite was Sea Eagles patriarch Ken Arthurson, who patted him in the shoulder and said, 'Matt, you mattered.'

'We get all the Aussie sports stars, all the big Aussie corporates, there's one fellow who is Rupert Murdoch's right-hand man,' Matt explained to me one night. 'The consul-general comes in a lot. Jac Nasser, chairman of BHP [Billiton]. A footballer walks in and I'll know everything about him; a big businessman and I may not ... [Australian basketballer] Paddy Mills, who plays for the San Antonio Spurs, brought a bunch of Spurs guys in.'

Moving to the Big Apple did not save Matt from the all-pervading scourge of rugby league politics. Until recently, the game in the US was divided. Matt is a loyal friend of David Niu, who ran the American National Rugby League. In the blue corner, the USA Rugby League, which — like Super League a decade-and-a-half before — is led by the country's dominant club, the Jacksonville Axemen.

But these are park comps, where games are sometimes forfeited because teams can't raise enough players and they have unlimited interchange, because occasionally too many players show up and they want to ensure everyone gets a run.

So how did Matt come to be in America? 'I'd been in contact with David Niu. He brought me over here,' said Matt. 'My wife, she made me stay. This is the start of '02. It's through David I got a sports visa. Luckily enough, I passed the test with my pretty average resume. I was meant to go to Philly, that's where Niu was, but — you'd like this — I had a friend who was in the music industry and he was a road manager whose mate was the tour manager for Guns N' Roses. I said, "Get me a job as a roadie," and he said, "I'll get you something better." I told Niu, "Can we start something in New York because I have a mate there and it's always a bit daunting moving over blind?" He said, "Sure." And that's when he hooked me up with [USA rugby league player and Manhattan bigwig] Bob Balachandran. 'He [Balachandran] got me a job at Chelsea Pier — this is when I was fitter — which was one of the big prestigious gyms in New York. I've been in the spa with Lou Reed there. It's one of those big, crazy-sort-of places. I showed Philip Seymour Hoffman how to do lat pull-downs. It's one of those things where you go, "Is this real?" But to make my visa legal and all that, I had to play rugby league.'

At the time, Balachandran was in charge of the redevelopment of Hudson River Park. Together, he and Matt started the New York Knights league team. That's how Matt met Glenn Treacher, owner of Ship of Fools. Treacher was one of the first players to sign up for the Knights.

'Ship of Fools was one of the first real sports bars in New York, where you had 40 TVs,' said Matt of the much-missed watering hole. 'We had the big flat screens before everyone else. It was voted Best Sports Bar in New York for a number of years in the late '90s, early 2000s. Glenn trained me up as a bartender and he could obviously see something in me. I ended up managing the place. I was living the dream — and then I met Nicole! At the same time, Glenn was talking about doing something with me. I didn't know how long I'd be in the States. I was just living this dream life for a while. But I met Nicole, our relationship became serious, and I started to look for something in terms of a career.'

The Australian was soon born.

'There was a little Aussie bar called Eight Mile Creek down in Little Italy. I used to go there all the time to watch the cricket when I was homesick, and put The Cruel Sea and Ackadacka on the jukebox. I thought, "If I could employ that sports bar knowledge to the Australian thing, have a bit of a crossover ..." Glenn said, "Let's do it." We put the wheels in motion in '06. We signed the lease in January '07.'

Matt did make it to Philly, of course, for that international against Australia at Franklin Field in 2004. 'One of the highlights of my life,' he said.

Michael Butler, host of The Rock and Roll Geek Show.

Tim Henwood, Palace of the King

Above: Ty Taylor,
Vintage Trouble

Left: Airbourne's
Joel O'Keeffe

Above: Black Stone Cherry

Below: The USA Hawks, Colonial Cup champions 2016

Images of Carcassonne:
Above: The sculpture of Puig
Aubert at the Albert Domec
Stadium. Right: The Hôtel
Terminus. Below: The road
to the medieval la Cité.

Above: Dave Sharp, Graham
Sykes and Stuart Sheard,
Stade du Moulin, Lezignan.

Right: A mural outside the
ground tells the story of
the Lezignan club.

Below: The Canal du Midi,
Carcassonne.

Toronto Wolfpack players after the club's first ever game, a 28-26 victory over Brighouse Rangers at Brighouse.

Glenn Hughes

live Nation Presents

Europe
Plus Special Guests

Saturday 12 November 2016
Main Space   Doors :7:00 pm

Level 1   Standing   Unres

£26.00

Adult   This is a smoke
free stadium

www.ticketweb.co.uk | London NW1 8EH | 0300 6789 222
Ticket no: 765   Ticketmaster
Ordered on: 4181695   4181695

ENGLAND V NEW ZEALAND
SATURDAY 7th NOVEMBER
THE STADIUM AT
QUEEN ELIZABETH OLYMPIC PARK
KICK-OFF 14:30, ENTRANCES OPEN 13:00

WEST STAND

BLOCK   ROW   SEAT
210   49   142

ENTER VIA MEDIA ENTRANCE
PRESS BOX

20M727
NO SMOKING IN THE STADIUM

BE THE WALL OF WHITE

70149952852150 1

Sunday 12 Jun, 2016   3:00 pm
Giants v Wakefield Trinity Wildcats

Press Box

Row: V   Seat: 6
Price : 0.00
Enter Via Main Entrance
Australian Press   186552
TO BE RETAINED   TICKET OFFICE NUMBER: 01484 484 123

First Utility
SUPER LEAGUE

Adult   Adult
6   6
Cash   Cash
0.00   0.00
186552
TO BE GIVEN UP   TO BE GIVEN UP

SEC: General Admission
General Admission

cketweb

Modern Media Presents

The Vapors

Plus The Circles
14+, Under 16 with an adult, valid ID required
Arts Club Loft

Arts Club
90 Seel Street,
Liverpool
L1 4BH

18 Nov 2016 07:30pm - PRICE: 25.00
Door Sales

GEN AD   Door Sales
-- 2500 x10

t

Badlands Entertainment Group Presents

Dokken

Badlands Pawn Gold and Jewelry
1600 W. Russell Street Sioux Falls, SD
Fri Sep 30, 2016 9:00 PM (Doors: 8:00 PM)
Price:$50.00

Order:095342490999   Purchased By:SN Mascord

0038RR085913077

THE HALLIWELL JONES STADIUM
HOME OF THE WARRINGTON WOLVES

Warrington Wolves vs Brisbane Broncos
Dacia World Club Series
Kick-Off: 18/02/2017 20:00

Block: WCS North L   Row: Q Seat: 325
Enter via Gate 14

Warrington Wolves   Internal   3728547   1176609

RED DEVILS
OF RUGBY
OFFICIAL MATCH TICKET

11 Feb, 2017
Salford Red Devils v
Press
AJ Bell West Stand   W04
Row L   Seat 113
Enter Via Main Reception
2297   Salford Red Devils

WIGAN. ALWAYS.

DACIA WORLD CLUB CHALLENGE
WARRIORS v CRONULLA SHARKS
SUNDAY 19 FEBRUARY 2017 3.00pm KO

PRESS BOX
BLOCK   ROW   SEAT
PB2   X   142

PRESS MATCH TICKET
ENTER VIA PRESS ENTRANCE

BETFRED
SUPER LEAGUE
47980
TO BE RETAINED   TICKETS 0871 66 33 552 WIGANWARRIORS.COM

errea   188BET
TO BE GIVEN UP   TO BE GIVEN UP

北京市延庆区
八达岭特区办事处

延庆
1211
参拾伍元

110290053398

1001683032
52116

6732686

WWRL

国万里长城 · 八达海
The Great Wall of China-Badaling

Above: With Cronulla captain
Paul Gallen before the 2017
World Club Challenge.

Right: Wigan's Sean
O'Loughlin lifts the
WCC trophy.

Possibly the first man to wear a Wolfpack jersey on the
Great Wall of China.

'John Cartwright being our coach, he took it serious enough to treat it more importantly than an exhibition game, but relaxed enough to recognise we weren't an NRL side. The day before the game, he got us to go through what the game meant to us individually. It was emotional, mate. We treated that game 110 per cent. In hindsight, the Aussies in the first half didn't take it as seriously as they should, as evidenced by the scoreboard, but I heard Wayne Bennett got stuck into them at half-time, saying, "Fucking pull your finger out." They came out hard in the second half and we still put on a decent showing. It was a great night for footy over here.'

Matt loves heavy metal but he was surprised to find that Aussie band Grinspoon was on his jukebox at The Australian, after I parted with a few greenbacks to play it. (The jukebox has since been removed because young people today don't really like rock — or any sort of proper music, do they?)

Afterwards, as I walked across the Williamsburg Bridge and looked back at Manhattan, it was hard to dispute that — for all its faults — the United States was easily the greatest nation on earth. They built all this in the last four centuries or so, taking people the rest of the world didn't want and institutionalising freedoms that encourage individuality and adventure.

Then, along came Donald Trump. There were times during the presidential election campaign when I considered banning myself from visiting the US, at least until he is gone.

But why let Trump ruin my fun?

JOHN PAUL BASILE, A pleasant, bald New Yorker, was sitting on the metal bleachers at Eden Park in Wilmington, Delaware.

'Is it always like this?' he asked. It was October 1, 2016, and a rugby league match was about to be played, between the USA Hawks (formerly the Tomahawks) and the Canada Wolverines. This was the second of two matches between the two teams for the Colonial Cup. The first, played a week earlier in Toronto, had been won 14–8 by the visitors.

Basile has been working with Australian promoter Jason Moore on a bid to host the 2021 Rugby League World Cup in the United States and Canada. (They would eventually be 'granted' — with some RLIF wriggle room — the 2025 tournament.) The former head of international development at the NBA, Basile hadn't watched a live game of rugby (either code) since going to see the Melbourne Storm when he was in charge of Disney on Ice in the Victorian capital in 1998.

Eden Park should not be confused with its Auckland namesake. This was more like a vacant lot, just off Interstate 495, which had been converted to a sports field by well-meaning locals trying to find something to occupy troubled local youth. The Test was set down for 6.55pm with an entrance charge of $10. There was no one on the gate to collect the money and the kick-off time seemed dictated by an earlier minor league American football game that — unlike the 'international' — had spectators and a couple of concession stands.

The absence of a gate steward seemed sensible, in the end; out of a total attendance of fewer than a hundred people, maybe 90 were there, not so much for the football but because they knew a player. Both teams, after arriving in a fleet of cars because the Wolverines had travelled some 10 hours, had to change in the car park because no one could get into the dressing sheds. The council worker with the key never showed.

The absence of that council employee became a bigger problem when the nominated kick-off time came and went and the Hawks players, their warm-ups finished, returned to the sideline. Why? You could barely see the ball now. The council worker also had the keys to the floodlights. Even the rotation of the earth has a set against rugby league.

After Basile became involved with Jason Moore, he reacquainted himself with rugby league and surprised himself with his depth of interest and even passion. He watched games on the internet, took part in forum discussions, formed well-rounded opinions on the sport's discussion points. Excited by the possibilities for rugby league in America, he had driven a couple of hours from New York City to the game so he could connect with the USA Rugby League, despite being warned that they were an amateur organisation unable to contribute much to the World Cup bid.

Basile had picked me up at Motel 6 in Essington, Pennsylvania, and quickly struck me as the sort of guy people instantly warm to — which probably helped him get NBA games played in such places as Brazil and Tokyo. He started our conversation by saying he felt the bid was doomed, that England would take the safe option.

I felt embarrassed. This was a high-flying sports executive and he was dealing with a world governing body that has one full-time employee. As a rugby league person, my disposition, as he spoke, plummeted to somewhere close to humiliation.

Basile told me that Gillette Stadium in Massachusetts, home of the New England Patriots NFL franchise, had called him, wanting 'in' for the RLWC. There was a meeting coming up with the Los Angeles Coliseum. The only parts of the United States that seemed dubious about hosting a World Cup game were the state of Utah and the city of Chicago where rugby union — surely not by coincidence — had strong connections and influence.

I wondered: *is rugby league about to throw away the opportunity to be 'rugby' in the eyes of the most powerful and wealthy nation on earth with barely a second thought? Is rugby league about to shun an open $10 million cheque because promoter Moore will take on all the risk.* (The 2017 tournament in Australia, New Zealand and Papua New Guinea is projected to make $7 million.) As we drove on, embarrassment gave away to anger. But as we sat there in the dark a couple of hours later, I had to admit to him: yes, it was pretty much always like this. I've seen games in many places, such as Malta, Hawaii and Bangkok, played in front of no one, on grounds that presented serious injury hazards for the players.

Basile knew the people who ran the local 22,000-seat soccer stadium in Philadelphia. They would have hosted today's game for next to nothing, he said. But had anyone from that stadium, or Boston, or LA, been here today they would not have wanted anything to do with the sport. With USARL president Peter Illfield back home in Australia, the indefatigable Daryl 'Spinner' Howland was trying to run this game over the telephone. He could not use the Starship Enterprise's transporter to get that key out of a locked room.

Rugby league is a terribly small-time sport everywhere but in places where, historically, a lot of people follow it. Then suddenly the marketing geniuses and cash flood in. But they are just trying to make a buck off the working-class people who like the code.

There is no one with enough gumption, courage, or influence trying to funnel that income into broadening the appeal of the platform, making the billboard bigger. Everywhere else, the working-class people who support rugby league are left to their own devices and you get train wrecks like this day in Wilmington — no dressing-shed key, no lights, team sheets you can't read, loving volunteers giving away pulled chicken rolls and hot dogs at half-time and being left with plenty to take home.

'There is not one sign here, *not one*,' says Basile, shaking his head. He had called a friend at Fox Sports in the preceding weeks to find out who was responsible for the NRL's relationship with the Soccer Plus channel, on which it is shown in the US. No one even knew who had negotiated the deal. The NRL has no head of international development. Outside the Pacific, it seems to have no ambition to even *do* international development.

The lights eventually came on. Someone had broken into the box. The referee suggested we skip the anthems and half-time only lasted five minutes. The match, on a muddy, unevenly mowed park played before few people — including one fellow in an Uncle Sam hat — was sometimes a little beautiful. Fearless running, courageous defence, brutal collisions.

With two minutes left, former South Sydney player Taioalo 'Junior' Vaivai — who had paid his own travel costs from Wollongong for the two Colonial Cup games — swooped on a loose ball and accelerated away to secure a 20–14 win for the Hawks. It was a great start to the young coaching careers of Boston-domiciled Dustin Cooper, brother of North Queensland Cowboy Gavin, and his assistant, New York-based Brent Richardson, son of South Sydney boss Shane.

Walking back to the just-opened dressing-room, Vaivai — a cousin of wrestling's The Rock — joked that he'd like to borrow Basile's fancy car to impress a girl on a date. He spoke about the satisfaction he derived from passing on knowledge, to kids hungry to learn, about the importance of getting rugby league into American schools and his hopes for the 2017 World Cup, in which the US will compete.

But these aspirations were undermined by our down-at-heel surroundings. Players stood around in their undies before gathering at the match's one sponsor — a local restaurant and bar. This international was played in worse conditions than a Sydney A-grade game on a Sunday morning. Basile copped an almighty spray from a Wolverines player who mistook him for a USARL official when Basile introduced himself at full-time.

Even the Wolverines' support contingent, the Toronto Wolfpack, including coach Paul Rowley and director (the former player and now actor) Adam Fogerty, left mid-match. They had lost interest. Rugby league began life as a social movement aimed at empowering the downtrodden worker — the player — who was making money for the toffs of Twickenham. There is now a new kind of tyranny: an administration in the sport's equivalent of ancient Rome rolling in money while the far-flung provinces starve. Winston Churchill did not say, as a rugby league trainspotter claimed to me he had, 'We must focus on the new world to save the old.' In fact, his statement was 'Do not let specious plans for a new world divert your energies from saving what is left of the old.'

As he dropped me back at Motel 6, so I could live blog the NRL grand final, Basile admitted he was simultaneously enlivened by rugby league's potential and afraid of its imminent death.

ANDREW JOHN LANGLEY SAYS: I understand you, you know. I guess that shouldn't be surprising because I am you. You see yourself as some sort of emissary from the rugby league Rome, out among the sport's savages on the edges of its empire, treating the wretched locals with respect other denizens of the footy Parthenon would not. But the empire of your mind will never exist. I'm trying to 'get' rugby league, but it remains merely a group of people who like running at each other and having their faces smeared in mud and those who like watching it. It's popular where it has history and unpopular where it has none. There is no more a rugby league 'family' than there is a universal brotherhood of spanner fanciers. You devote yourself to a cause that exists only in your imagination.

Ex-Referee Speaks Out on HIV

When professional punter Eddie Hayson sent a homophobic text message to *Sydney Morning Herald* reporter Andrew Webster in September, Michael Jones recalls thinking: 'What a goose.'

The 48-year-old retired NRL referee had never hidden his sexuality during a 100-game career, but rarely witnessed such risible bigotry. On the contrary, the rugby league world, he insists, is very accepting. But Jones — who is the second cousin of Dennis Bendall, the Balmain star who broke his neck and was forced to retire in 1979 — did have one secret: for his entire NRL refereeing career, Jones was HIV-positive.

Most of his fellow referees and sideline officials — men (in those days) with whom he trained so hard each day that during years of practice sessions he suffered broken ribs and a broken thumb — had no issue with him being gay.

But it would have been a different story if they found out about his HIV status. 'I reckon I would have been no chance. I was worried about them finding out because I would be ostracised. I believe if I'd divulged my HIV-positive status, my career would have ended then and there.'

Jones was diagnosed in 1998 as his partner Stephen was dying of an HIV/AIDS-related cancer. Those last days still haunt and Jones poignantly recalls coming out about his own status to the openly gay referee Matt Cecchin at a Potts Point hotel. 'I told him. He said, "Forget the coffee, let's have a double martini."'

The many misconceptions that still swirl around the issue of HIV/AIDS prompted Jones to request this story be held until the 2016 domestic rugby league season was over. He didn't want the performance of former colleagues to be affected in any way by the mistaken idea they may have been at risk.

To pass on the infection, Jones says, 'It has to be the exchange of certain bodily fluids. Even then, it's a very difficult virus to be infected by. Can you get it off a drink bottle? No, I haven't heard of one case in the world.'

During a 40-minute interview, Jones, who refereed his last match in 2008, gives a heartbreaking account of Stephen's death. It has been a difficult week for Jones: the 18th anniversary of Stephen's passing occurred last Tuesday. Jones does not want his partner's surname published out of deference to his family.

He recounts how his own test results were initially misplaced at a clinic, where he was told to 'come back tomorrow'.

Jones' HIV infection made him more determined to achieve his dream of reaching the NRL first-grade refereeing ranks, but the illness made it much harder than it was for others in the NRL squad.

'The training was sometimes very tough: anti-retro-virals can leave lactic acid in your muscles for up to 72 hours, whereas it's up to 36 hours clearance for HIV uninfected people,' he says. 'So that was painful. There was a lot of vomiting and pain and fatigue that went on.'

Jones was diagnosed at a time when the approach to HIV treatment 'hit hard, hit early'. He says of the four drugs (or 21 pills) he was prescribed to take concurrently in 1998, some are now no longer prescribed in Australia.

His motivation for going public, he says, is to provide education for others, remove the shame some may feel about their condition and show people who may be frightened that others have made it through, and that HIV does not mean the end.

'By the law of averages, in the NRL arena — every state, every grade, every referee, every administrator — I can't possibly be the only one.

'This has been a few years of mulling — what can I do to help make this better for someone else? I'm not a martyr, I'm not an Australian sporting superstar, I'm not an Olympic athlete.

'I was an NRL sideline official who lived the dream — there were only about 28 of us — and I did 100 games plus a City-Country and two reserve-grade grand finals. I'm no Bill Harrigan, I'm not a household name. My motivation is ... I remember having moments after I found out when I thought, "What would happen if someone didn't have a support network?" I was fortunate to have that support, but I worry about those who may feel abandoned and [like] they're the only person in the world with HIV.

'Depression and anxiety are realities these days, seven suicides a day in Australia. For someone to be diagnosed HIV, they can be ostracised by their families and lose friendships.

'I thought if I could actually tell my story, link it into an elite sporting level, and show how resilient and disciplined I needed to be to push myself. It was even more of a win, because I was living with a condition at a time when people were dying. It was about not allowing HIV to take away my dreams.

'I've turned 48 and decided to get rid of the stigma by telling my story.'

Jones' primary carer, Andrew Lloyd, head of infectious disease and inflammation at Prince of Wales Hospital, says much has changed since 1998.

He says there are wonderful treatments for HIV that reduce risks and allow people to continue to take their places in society and realise their potential.

'While a case can be made for stringent controls where people work in areas that could involve a high risk of infection — such as blood-to-blood specialist work — it does not hold for most of us, and that certainly goes for refereeing NRL,' Lloyd says.

Looking back, Jones says drugs have changed life expectancy for many.

'Stephen was not so lucky. My journey in many ways has been the continuation of his spirit,' he says.

From **The Sydney Morning Herald,** *October 23, 2016.*

ON THE ROAD

Take this day from the 2013 Rugby League World Cup as an example ...

It could have been any time of the day or night when I stirred, given that my room at a dilapidated Manchester hotel featured not a single window. But it was 10.14am ... and checkout was at 11.

Dragging my home — sorry, my 25kg wheeled suitcase — across the cobblestone paths of the Northern Quarter, I visited the yard of the Sixt car rental company. Your correspondent, it may come as no surprise to you, had left his iPod in one of their vehicles, travelling between Wrexham and Wigan for the Challenge Cup quarter-finals the previous weekend.

I knew the answer before I even asked if it had been found. No. Should I buy the little black box which would be dubbed 'Steavis' ninth iPod' immediately? No time. No money.

Soon, Thunderbird 5 and I would be at Manchester Piccadilly train station. On the way, after taking a seat at Yo! Sushi, I was interrupted by someone saying, 'Sorry, mate!' as he brushed past me, brandishing a bottle of lager. This fellow Antipodean was informed by staff of the rules surrounding open bottles of beer imported from outside the arbitrary block of floor leased by Yo! Sushi, took the instruction warmly, and then we got talking. 'My brother's over here playing in the World Cup,' said Dane Cordner, brother of Boyd and 'a pretty handy footballer himself', according to someone on Twitter.

Taking my leave, I assure the waitress that not all Australians know each other and it was off to today's destination: Buckley in north Wales. The reason? The Darkness — they of sequins, high voices and roughly one-and-a-half entendres — were playing there and it fit nicely into my schedule.

Things were going relatively smoothly until I glanced at my electronic itinerary at the same moment my Arriva train stopped at a station. The hotel I'd booked and paid for, the Coach House, was not in Buckley at all but in a place called Hawarden, apparently. *Hmm.* Hey, look at that weird Welsh name of the station we're at. And there it is in English underneath.

Hawarden.

Ding, ding, ding. The doors were locked tight despite me feverishly hitting the one with the green arrows. I guessed the mothership and I were going to Buckley, then.

There, where it had been snowing that morning, leaving me thinking that the hole in my jeans was rather eighties, I got the local cab company's phone number from a friendly bus driver. 'We've got nothing till five,' the operator informed me. So did another. Their drivers had to take kids home from school.

So I guessed it was wait on the station in sub-zero temperature for the train back to Hawarden (it was 50 minutes' walk, according to Google Maps), check into the hotel there and figure out how to

52 GAMES ... 52 GIGS

GIG 35 (OCTOBER 14): Goo Goo Dolls at Hammersmith Apollo, London

The less said about this, the better. I enjoy some Goo Goo Dolls music but this is mostly insipid. I do like Johnny Rzeznik's self-deprecation, though. He reasons that most men in the audience just want them to play *Iris* so they can leave. 'No chance!' he says. 'I know how you feel, though. Sometimes my wife makes me sit through a Matchbox Twenty show.'

GAME 35 (OCTOBER 15): Wales 50 Serbia 0 at Stebonheath Park, Llanelli

These are the journeys to cherish — four hours in each direction to the valleys, navigating strange streets and overgrown parks with Google maps. So far from the NRL you can barely utter the letters without feeling alien — and yet there's a kid who is starstruck by Serbia prop David Andjelic because he saw him on *NRL Rookie*. I've never seen *NRL Rookie*.

get back here again for the show, and then how to get back to the Hawarden hotel at the end of the evening.

At this point came a helpful text from online retailer See Tickets: The Darkness had cancelled. I called the venue. Justin Hawkins had an infected throat.

You are no doubt sensing my gut-wrenching frustration, but I looked upon the whole fiasco as a blessing, really. Now I could just go straight to London for the World Cup semis the following Saturday, even if I'd lost the night at the Hawarden Coach House and tomorrow's train ticket, which, combined, amounted to more than 100 quid.

A ticket that night to London's Euston Station cost £78.

Dinner in a pub near Shotton Station was served by a lad who read *The Sydney Morning Herald* rugby league page every day.

But the direct train from Chester to Euston was delayed, then cancelled. Irate fellow passengers rushed to catch an alternative train to Crewe, connecting to London, but I stayed in my seat and asked when the next direct service is. 'Not for two hours,' the conductor said.

'That's fine, I'll wait.' I am very fortunate in that the only place I had to be was at about 100 rugby league games a year. The rest of my work could be done almost anywhere. After what I had already endured, what was the big rush? When I emerged from the delightful coffee shop at Chester Station to catch that direct train, a female conductor told me she was so impressed with my stoicism that I had been upgraded to first class.

It occurred to me that my luck had finally changed as I shuffled over to a sweets machine, inserted 85p and pushed number 143 for an Aero bar. The metal coil turned, and turned, and the Aero bar got stuck.

Even extreme stoicism has limits.

After handing the machine a half-hearted slap, I decided to buy another Aero bar and walk away with two (but resolved not to insult my waistline by eating both immediately).

I threw in 10p, then 20, then 50 … and ran out of coin.

Alas, there was a treasure trove of shrapnel in another pocket. Both chocolate bars tumbled into the tray.

The conductor who upgraded me pointed me out to her colleague but as I shivered on platform three, this lady conspiratorially informed me that this train — too — would be late.

Self-discipline, like stoicism, also has its limits. I reached into my black leather bag — which had been slowly eroding the stressed discs in my lower back throughout this odyssey around Britain, Ireland and France — and searched for the second Aero bar.

Instead, I felt something else. It was a similar shape, but cold and unwrapped.

My iPod.

CHAPTER 19

ON RUGBY LEAGUE PLAYERS

Professional rugby league players can be quite a curious breed.

There was a day not too long ago when I was in a suburban Sydney café with a couple of officials, who were in full, almost blindingly colourful, club garb of the local NRL team. In loped a hefty prop and lithe centre from the same club, wearing the same clothes. They sat at the next table. They did not acknowledge their co-workers. Not a word.

There are two exceedingly peculiar things about this. One: co-workers at any other business in this suburb would at least nod to one another — unless they hated the other group. Which brings us to two: that being the case, why sit at the next table?

It is my experience that the majority of professional rugby league players in Australia — not a 'vast' majority, just the majority — enter most rooms with blinkers on. They do not meet the eyes of others. They certainly don't engage strangers spontaneously in conversation.

When I was a cub reporter, I figured this was how all important adults behaved. But as I grew older, no one else took up ambivalence as enthusiastically as Australian rugby league

52 GAMES ... 52 GIGS

GIG 36 (OCTOBER 18): Steel Panther at Manchester Arena

My ticket is sent to a friend's place in Wigan. When it arrives to be signed for, he is at work. That means that after arriving in Manchester by train from London, I have to go on to Wigan in driving rain, find the dispatch office before it closes, return with my ticket to Manchester, get into the arena in time to see opening act Buckcherry and buy a drink. Hard work — all achieved, only for my Zimbabwean friend Jono to say his favourite band on the bill is friggin' Bowling for Soup. Is he serious?

GAME 36 (OCTOBER 22): England 40 France 6 at Parc des Sports, Avignon

If language really is a reflection of culture, then I am assuming there is no French word for 'taxi'. Badly hung over, I wait until it is almost too late to walk from the centre of Avignon to Parc des Sports before, unable to attract a cab, I set off on foot. I do not see a single taxi on the way. Wayne Bennett opens his tenure as England coach with an unconvincing performance. The highlight of the weekend is my first visit, since the 1994 Kangaroo tour, to the Palais des Papes and the stunning adjoining gardens.

players. If their club has a 'media session', they sit in the corner like shy girls waiting for someone to ask them to dance.

Why?

There is a fear of the media, often justified, though I feel that the worst of the enmity between the second row and the fourth estate, as it were, has cooled. We no longer see stories as page leads about players parking in handicapped spots, and when someone is in trouble for urinating near a police car, social media or the constabulary's own public-relations department beat the mainstream hacks to the punch.

Nonetheless, there is still this 'bubble' around our stars. I can identify a number of reasons for this.

There is the sense of camaraderie formed on sand hills, at military training camps and a hundred brutal training sessions, of which a natural by-product is the shunning of others. You don't talk much during a beep test — communication is done with nods and grunts and many players take this restricted vocabulary into their daily lives.

Bear in mind, most of these fellows are not being paid to 'play sport' in the sense that you may imagine that concept. 'Playing sport' implies fitness, skill and competitiveness, yes, but it also implies a sense of guile, risk taking and adventure. Very little risk taking is encouraged in the modern NRL.

If you were walking around in anticipation of simply running repeatedly into a wall (albeit with a little footwork) at the end of the week, would you be cracking jokes and shaking every hand in the room? You would have the visage of someone about to be turned into mincemeat.

I can only put that down to comparative intensity — not of the competitions but of the media coverage and the coaches. Only three of the ten national dailies in the UK have a rugby league writer (not full-time or staff — not even a regular stringer!)

And then there is the pampering by clubs of individuals plucked straight out of school. The learning of basic social skills such as saying 'hello' and 'goodbye' to people in your presence does not seem to take a high precedence.

52 GAMES ... 52 GIGS

GIG 37 (OCTOBER 25): Ryan Koriya at The Half Moon, Putney

Ryan Koriya is a young Zimbabwean singer-songwriter who seems to spend most of his time in Scandinavia. Jono is the one who invites me to The Half Moon, a truly charming venue that specialises in jazz and blues. The gig, according to my tastes, is only OK but what's fascinating is seeing an artist almost beg to be filmed and tell the audience between songs where they can find his social-media channels — repeatedly. Most of the bands I see still regard *YouTube* as something that's stealing their soul (along with exposing their inability to hit high notes for the last decade). Koriya's merch girl is from Whakatane in New Zealand, which gets a mention from the stage because of the way it's pronounced. When I mention Benji Marshall to her, she responds, 'My auntie used to cut his hair when he was a boy.'

GAME 37 (OCTOBER 28): Australia 54 Scotland 12 at Craven Park, Hull

If Kingston Communications is so daft it will buy naming rights to two neighbouring stadia and call them both very similar names, they'll not get a plug from me. Oh, they just did ... The Four Nations is underway. The next day leaving England-New Zealand at Huddersfield, I am feeling particularly content and pleased with myself. This is never a good sign. Reaching into my pocket to buy a sandwich before returning to London, I realise I have lost my wallet — for only the second time in my life. I lose a lot of things; my strategy is to make all efforts to recover said item but not to change plans unless I've no choice. I return to London, and Uber home from Kings Cross. I'll never see the wallet again.

I also blame coaches. Coaches use the public utterances of rivals to motivate their own charges. While journalists are supposed to be governed by a code of ethics in what they report and how they report it, there are no such pleasantries among the clipboard carriers.

In 1993, Wayne Bennett distributed to his team an entire tactical tip sheet purportedly compiled by his grand final rival, St George's Brian Smith, which Bennett said had come into his possession. Covering the game for AAP, I could not understand why Broncos players were openly willing to take swipes at Smith after their 14–6 victory at the Sydney Football Stadium. As far as they were concerned, he had derided them. Kevin Walters believed Smith had described him as a defensive weakness. Smith had done no such thing. Bennett had motivated his men with a lie. He wrote the tip sheet himself. This is the real story behind Allan Langer encouraging a crowd to sing 'St George Can't Play' later that night.

But the real sting is this: most of the 1993 Broncos would be *grateful* they were lied to. Lies are sometimes the currency of rugby league, the catalyst for getting things done when reality indicates you are just a bunch of men dressed in bright colours with socks pulled up like schoolboys, running into each other to sell alcohol and punting to the western suburbs of Sydney. Rugby league is sometimes a form of voluntary self-hypnosis — we know what we are being fed is horseshit but we *need* a bit of horseshit in our diet.

And if that involves hating the opposition, or the media, or anyone, even though we have no logical reason to do so, then so be it. Winning is as far above logic in rugby league's list of priorities as Mt Fuji is above a leaking nuclear reactor.

Having said all that, there are gregarious people in rugby league as well as introverts. Former winger Anthony Quinn, now of the Rugby League Players Association, calls them 'social butterflies'. Wests Tigers' Aaron Woods and veteran Willie Mason are butterflies that were never slugs. Others, such as superstar Johnathan Thurston, have become approachable and amiable with the end of their careers in sight. That is not to suggest Thurston is disingenuous — he has clearly matured with increased responsibility on and off the field, including fatherhood.

It takes courage to play rugby league — but it also takes intestinal fortitude of a different kind to break from the playing group in a social situation and go shake hands with a sponsor or a media person. Football teams are intensely conformist units and individuality is tested and tacitly discouraged during a pro's career. It's one of the few areas in sport where a comparison with the army is not gauche.

I covered a number of Brad Fittler's misadventures as a player — from missing a flight back from a New Zealand tour after a big night out to being late for an Anzac wreath-laying ceremony in the week before a trans-Tasman Test when he was captaining his country — and only really developed a relationship with him after he retired. I can remember Freddie as a 19-year-old, on the shuttle bus to the plane which took the 1991 Australia side to PNG, engrossed in a copy of *Hustler*. Today, I find him inspirational — he's been through the wringer of coaching since all that and approaches television commentary as something that everyone else can take seriously if they like.

Football provides opportunities for working-class men — and only a small percentage of those opportunities are directly connected to playing the game. Players are dealing with people on an almost daily basis who they would not have met had they gone to work at the local paper-clip factory. These people can teach the players things they would not otherwise learn and create job opportunities that would not otherwise be available.

But who am I to lecture about lost opportunities? I've frittered away what would otherwise be called 'my life savings' on plane tickets, beer, CDs and taxi fares.

In some ways, during my 30 years covering their exploits and quizzing them dozens of times a month, rugby league players have made the complete transition in society from hunters to hunted. In the '80s and early '90s, I witnessed some appalling behaviour. The Queensland-appointed manager on Kangaroo tours always seemed to be fair game to be belittled and even roughed up by players. Property was damaged wantonly at times on these tours. I recall a drunken player smashing the heads of two English broadcasters together and spitting in the face of an opposition player's wife — within minutes. I witnessed a player call a female fan 'a buzzard' at a post-match function in Parkes. I received a letter from a traumatised production assistant who was horrified and disgusted by the behaviour of players during the shooting of the 1997 Super League TV commercial.

By comparison, today's stars are seraphic.

But it is as if the public and media are intent on punishing the current batch of footballers for the boundless sins of the previous generation, none of which they can prove due to the absence of Vine, Facebook, Instagram or even a Polaroid or two.

So today's NRL footballers, by and large, keep to themselves.

I find Australian players in Super League to be completely different. For some of them, perhaps it is because I'm a familiar Australian face a long way from home.

But in this age of NRL players joining Super League clubs and then returning to the NRL, we have the stunning phenomenon of aloof fellows suddenly becoming personable and approachable — and then returning to aloofness again! Tonie Carroll is one I can think of — a man whose warmth came out in frigid climes and whose coldness returned in the sun.

Many of today's young players have been kept so far from the media that they can have had no 'bad experiences'. Yet, I can remember as recently as 2006 being told by a sports editor to ring every Parramatta player photographed standing under the goalposts for a quote and having no trouble doing so — without going through the club. I lost one of my early mobile phones and when I got it back, the finder asked, 'Why have you got the entire Canberra Raiders team in there?'

Today, some reporters have various players' phone numbers but if they were to quote that player without the club PR being aware of the conversation, the Hounds of Hell would be released.

'It's a lot different to when I started,' Robbie Farah told me when he was the Wests Tigers captain. Farah made his NRL debut in 2003. 'Back then, you used to have relationships with some of the [media] guys. There were ones you liked and ones you didn't like, ones you would talk to. Nowadays it's very structured. You get told where to go, what to do, who to talk to. It's part of the obligation of being a footy player.'

Fair dinkum club PR staff will not insult you with claims that this sterile process is about 'being professional'. They'll admit it's about 'controlling the message'. They don't want their players becoming mates with media men, who not only pass information onto the public for a living but also deal with other clubs. But 'controlling the message' often leads to no message at all ... just sanitised and innocuous club-sanctioned reports. Rugby league from Monday to Friday becomes a monochrome product and the mainstream media is left with only bad news to report.

The game is at (yet another) crossroads. If it continues to hide its practitioners away from the public, more and more they will become just like other entertainers — out of touch, eccentric, anti-social. With no reference points to the outside world, problems are magnified and, resultantly, so is the danger of self-harm.

Yet rugby league does not reward players sufficiently for them to be able to retire on their earnings. What happens when the music dies and the circus leaves town? What happens when those curious rugby league players have to rejoin the rest of us?

ANDREW JOHN LANGLEY SAYS: Stephen, your profession is dying. The footballers' is not. Retired players will replace you, asking soft questions and getting paid more in a week than you ever did in a month to do it. You seek to put your finger in the dyke of professional sport becoming nothing more than stage-managed content. But, in essence, it isn't anything more than stage-managed content, there for the diversion of the masses each weekend. What you write from Monday to Friday is, at best, a sideshow, something to put between the adverts. I suggest you move on. Start writing books or something ...

An Audience with Mal Meninga

They even named the hotel after him.

Your correspondent meets Mal Meninga in the compact breakfast room at Birmingham's *Malmaison*. There's a set of scales adjacent to the buffet area and I wonder aloud if the small travelling press corps have to be weighed after bacon and eggs, too. The team PR, former *Sydney Morning Herald* colleague Glenn Jackson, finds us a corner in the coffee shop downstairs, orders us coffee (me) and tea (Mal) and leaves us to it.

Meninga's career traversed my own transition from a fan: sitting up watching the 1982 Kangaroos and taping news bulletins on VHS, to reporter: covering his final match in Béziers, his ill-fated club coaching career and involvement in the Super League War. Mal is now 56; I am 47. He unwittingly finds himself the target of a third incarnation of my own rugby league odyssey, that of a beard-scratching columnist who can go weeks without having any contact with those about whom he writes.

Meninga says he follows me on LinkedIn — so he knows I regarded the selection of Semi Radradra in the Anzac Test as 'an embarrassment'. He knows I don't think the Australian team should receive preferential treatment from the NRL. He knows I don't think fans in Australia will flock back to international rugby league just because his side is winning.

Perhaps because he knows these things, he told Jackson he was especially keen to do this interview. We start off with five minutes for my *White Line Fever* podcast, in which he reminisces about partying with AC/DC on the '82 tour in France and discusses the Vanuatu heritage he shares with centre Justin O'Neill.

But this is the first time I've done an interview like this — throwing three or four opinion columns up to a major rugby league identity and getting them to argue their case. My first question is one I've been dying to ask since Meninga came to power on a platform of simultaneously making international football popular in Australia once more and leading the Kangaroos to the top of the world rankings …

Rugby League World: Isn't this a conflict given that rugby league often benefits when Australia loses?

Mal Meninga: No, I reckon the international game benefits if Australia's winning. It's like the All Blacks. In my opinion … everyone wants to be part of it, everyone wants to come and watch them play. Hopefully they hold them in awe. They've got that aura around the footy team. Regardless of who they play, they want to come and watch the best players in the world play. I think Wayne [Bennett] being involved in England is going to help them immensely with the team itself. They've always had some really great players but just actually bringing them together as a group, playing for each other, is one of the things that hasn't occurred with English sides. Whereas the Kiwis, under Stephen Kearney, built a really strong culture around belief and respect for the jersey. You could see that in the way they play. So the top three teams, I think, will get better with the people involved but I still think a strong Australian side, going to different places, playing in Papua New Guinea as an example … whilst the score line isn't flattering, it still brings people to the game. It still brings people who want to watch it, they want to be involved with the players. That's a positive.

RLW: But in Australia people have drifted away to the Wallabies and the Socceroos. They see it as a strong competition. I understand what you're saying, about being the Harlem Globetrotters or whatever, but how do you get people to come back and respect not just you but the teams you're beating?

MM: I think it's around the quality of the people in the footy team, around the quality of the team when they play, how they carry themselves, the humility and the respect that they have — not only for the game but for the people who want to be involved in the game. If we start setting up an environment where it's built on great character, it's built on strong leadership, it's built on quality people and great players. That's what the game should want. That's what New Zealand's trying to achieve, that's what the English game is trying to achieve. Having a personality like Sam Burgess involved, having Wayne Bennett involved, can only aid the game and lift the profile of the game.

RLW: But do you accept that scorelines like 64–10 in 2002 was bad for rugby league? Or do you

think if Australia had continued to win by those scores it would have been good?

MM: What I'm thinking, what I'm saying is that it's about the external messages that come out of international rugby league. It's not about the internal stuff. You're going to have those scorelines. It's about how you win, it's about how you carry yourself, it's about how the players are perceived outside of playing. It's what they do every day that I think is more important than what they do on the footy field. They're all talented individuals but it's more about the quality of the person and how they talk about the game and how they carry themselves as individuals.

RLW: As you would have read on LinkedIn, I personally don't think Australia should use the residency rule. I don't think you should have picked Semi Radradra because I don't think it's good for the game …

MM: Well, those are the rules at the moment.

RLW: … Which have changed.

MM: Yes, and that's fine. We just played by the rules. Semi Radradra was the best winger in the game. He was eligible for Australia at that particular time so we picked him. We're not going to discriminate. You give us the parameters and we'll abide by those regulations.

RLW: The other thing I've been saying is that the NSW and Queensland teams are both drawn from the NRL and it doesn't openly favour either of them. But the chairman of the NRL reads out the Australian team and the entire New Zealand team is also drawn exclusively from the NRL.

52 GAMES ... 52 GIGS

GIG 38 (NOVEMBER 1): UFO at The Assembly, Leamington Spa

Phil Mogg can't remember the name of this British rock institution's latest album. He's their singer. But no matter, you've got to love days like these. I go to the Australian team hotel to interview Mal Meninga, rush to finish my copy in a dowdy B&B, hop on the delightful Chiltern Railways to Leamington Spa, have someone at the local Wetherspoons give my chicken korma to someone else, get a refund, down five beers and see an iconic band.

GAME 38 (NOVEMBER 5): Italy 76 Russia 0 at Leigh Sports Village

Walking from the bus station, I meet John. He's spent the whole day travelling from Cumbria, taking a day off work. I know about one-tenth of the crowd. Italy have a couple of NRL stars, Russia don't even have 17 players.

MM: That's not the NRL. It's the Australian Rugby League Commission's decision, with the Australian side. It's a New Zealand Rugby League decision with the Kiwis side. We've got to start playing more games in New Zealand to help propagate the game there but also to help them financially over there so the New Zealand Rugby League is not drawing from the Australian Rugby League Commission. We've got to leave some money in countries so they can fund their domestic programs and also their development programs.

RLW: NSW and Queensland, they would target kids at a very young age who could have played for other countries. Is that something you are now doing with Australia?

MM: No, I don't target kids. I believe you've got to follow your heart when you make those decisions. Jason (Taumalolo), he made that decision based on his heart and his family. He made that decision to stay with the Kiwis even though he played junior, all the way through, with Queensland. I think that's fair. Kalyn Ponga's doing the same at the moment. It's where the heartstrings lie. I'll be honest with you, there were things that were said through Origin — I never chased one player. Not one player — because it's their decision.

If they don't gauge it from the heart, they're not going to play well. There's going to be some doubt in their mind if they're doing the right thing or not.

RLW: Your *Courier-Mail* and *Sunday Mail* columns in Brisbane are often very controversial. Stuff like rats and filth trying to undermine you, Wayne Bennett trying to undermine you. What is your strategy there? Are you trying to stir the pot? Why do you write these things?

MM: It comes from impatience and frustration and people having digs at me — not internally but externally. People saying things about me that are not true. Eventually it gets to you. I'm a very patient person but at the end of the day, you've got to stick up for what you believe in and the way you do things at times. It's a very successful program, the Queensland program, and the way they kept chipping away at me, trying to break down that leadership … That's an intentional thing. It's planned. It gets to you eventually. You get frustrated.

RLW: Who were the rats and filth?

MM: Everyone below the border at that time.

RLW: And out of the second column I mentioned, the great unanswered question is: how is Wayne Bennett trying to undermine you?

MM: Every article, comments, statements during the year, ever since I got the position. Again, there's only so much you can take. Again, I was put in this position to not only improve the footy team. I don't think anyone really understood what the position was. I don't think that was publicised too well. It's more than just coaching the Kangaroos. It's more about the game itself internationally. It's more about looking after the Jillaroos and all our elite programs. The Junior Kangaroos … it's a bit more than just turning up for six weeks out of the year to coach a footy team. It's a dedicated position. Put 120 days in a year, constantly travelling, constantly doing things behind the scenes, trying to commercialise the brand, trying to add value. It's a lot more than just coaching and I don't think people understand what it entails.

RLW: Everyone loves this soap opera and this drama. Do you think Wayne's primary objective is to prove a point?

MM: Yes, to prove a point. But I've got to prove a point too. That's what makes it so competitive. That's why at times I get a bit frustrated with things. People just don't understand what's going on.

RLW: What were the mechanics of the decision to leave Andrew Fifita out?

MM: It was about his behaviour. It's as simple as that. I've put some rules around the team, some core values, we call it the DNA and we're going to abide by that … But that doesn't mean we're going to discriminate against him. If he gets his off-field stuff right and everything's cosy and he's playing good footy next year, he will certainly come back into calculations.

RLW: One last question: is an Australian loss ever good for rugby league?

MM: No.

This interview took place on 4 November 2016 and first appeared in the December issue of **Rugby League World**.

CHAPTER 20

CHIPPY, IZZY AND ALL THAT

It was finally over.

I was sitting in a south London café full of yummy mummies during the final week of November, contemplating the cost of having covered the rugby league Four Nations tournament for the last six weeks.

The cost to my waistline had been considerable. Bitter, kebabs, buffets. While I didn't exactly look very different, I felt appalling.

I don't particularly like news gathering any more … but I do. In the same way the previous sentence conveyed the idea that I don't really like beer and kebabs any more … but I do. In all likelihood, I considered, I'll drink beer, eat kebabs and gather news in the next 24 hours, even though I was acutely aware of how bad they each were for me.

As seems to be always the case when I 'dip my toe' back into day-to-day reporting these days, the Four Nations merely reinforced my strengths and weaknesses as a journalist. They hadn't changed. The weaknesses hadn't evaporated because I didn't want them to.

The best stories I wrote during the Four Nations were administrative yarns. That's my specialty because, frankly, it's what interests me most. I've no interest in what interests you, sorry. So, I reported, there will be no punching ban in the Four Nations as we had in the NRL … The pitch for the final at Anfield will be nine metres short … Kangaroo tours will be back in 2019 or 2020.

They were my yarns.

Because *The Sydney Morning Herald* does not hold for the next day's print edition stories that happened earlier in the day, Australian time, I was also able to get a competitive advantage filing stories about England's Australian coach Wayne Bennett straight away. When the Australian coach, Mal Meninga, claimed Bennett wanted his job, I filed the news immediately, even though it was in the early hours of the morning in Oz. The same when Bennett attacked the press at an extraordinary media conference.

My direct opponent at the Four Nations was Michael Carayannis of Sydney's *The Daily Telegraph*, filing for the entire News Limited group in Australia. The yarns he got, that I missed, were injured Australian winger Josh Mansour talking publicly for the first time about the knee injury he suffered on tour, Australian reserve Shannon Boyd discussing his selection (having never travelled outside Australasia, he found the different currency in the UK 'pretty annoying') and some interesting comments from Valentine Holmes about Ben Barba testing positive for cocaine.

Now Michael was on expenses and often stayed in the team hotel. Being on no expenses, I commuted backwards and forwards

52 GAMES ... 52 GIGS

GIG 39 (NOVEMBER 9): The Last Vegas at Camden Underworld

These guys don't go close to filling the Underworld but they're on their fourth visit to the UK and seem to know every rock chick in London. Which means, as I said .... they don't go close to filling the Underworld. They're like Aerosmith. I'd go see them again.

GAME 39 (NOVEMBER 11): New Zealand 18 Scotland 18 at Zebra Claims Stadium, Workington

Whenever international rugby league history is made, I tend to have a personal marker. Tonight, the first time the invited fourth team, Scotland, gets a competition point in Four Nations history by drawing with the Kiwis, I almost break my neck falling down wet stairs at my hotel. This, without doubt, will be the highlight of the tournament. No, not my fall. The game! St George Illawarra centre Euan Aitken, after scoring the late try that forces the draw, dedicates the moment to his Scottish grandfather who died when Euan's father was two.

GIG 40 (NOVEMBER 18): The Vapors at Arts Club, Liverpool

This is like stepping into an alternative universe, the new wave universe. I know how these devoted fans view me when I video *Turning Japanese* and then leave because I've sneered at people who do the same for *I Remember You* at a Skid Row show or *Rock Me* at a Great White gig. A fascinating night. Listening to the rest of The Vapors' set helps you understand where, creatively, an all-time classic pop song came from.

from London to the north, so in the circumstance I thought I fared OK. The point is that my journalism is always about asking the right person the right question at the right time. It is rarely about anything deeper. There is most often a convenient quote in the third paragraph. This is about as far from Woodward and Bernstein as you can get.

I am not good at cultivating people so they come to me with information. I am not good, as explained in an earlier chapter, at sticking my neck out and taking all the heat from a story, because I am a woefully bad judge of character. As a result, I was always the guy that could get you the best story of the day, six days out of 10, the best story of the week two weeks out of four, the best story of the month one month in six, and never the best story of the year. If you asked me the biggest story I ever broke, I'd have nothing for you.

The biggest story of the year usually comes from a tip-off, a relationship, a deep throat or thorough investigation. The last of these is no longer possible in most newsrooms through sheer lack of resources.

(I read a wonderful *LA Times* piece about Guns N' Roses reclusive guitarist Izzy Stradlin, the end result of extremely high journalistic standards, hours of travel and the checking of public records across the US. I'm willing to bet this accomplished writer is also an Izzy nut in his spare time and simply applied his professional skills to a personal obsession, with what he was paid for the piece falling a long way short of covering his expenses, let alone the time invested.)

In any event, Michael and I both missed the story of the tournament — Australian winger Valentine Holmes and New

52 GAMES ... 52 GIGS

GAME 40 (NOVEMBER 20): Australia 34 New Zealand 8 at Anfield, Liverpool

Could Mal Meninga be right? Could Australia flogging everyone be moulded into something that's good for the international game? The 40,042 crowd proves that the Kangaroos brand is a bankable commodity in the north of England. If we can build up countries No. 2 to No. 8 to be competitive and have the Kangaroos as something akin to Australia's Harlem Globetrotters, maybe it could work.

GIG 41 (NOVEMBER 23): Dead Daisies and The Answer at Electric Ballroom, Camden

'Jaw-dropping' was just another over-used superlative they sprinkle in reviews until I see Cormac Neeson perform the second song of tonight's The Answer set, *Beautiful World*. 'Jaw-dropping' is apt tonight. Amid swirling lights and with just a little oomph in the vocal effects pedal, his is the most powerful, larynx-driven delivery of a simple song I can remember hearing. The Poles next to me call the Dead Daisies 'a cartoon band' by comparison. Perhaps. But who doesn't like cartoons?

Zealand back-rower Jason Taumalolo travelling to LA on the way home to trial for the NFL.

This is the reality of journalism in the 21st century: you can go to the other side of the world, churn through $10,000 in expenses, stand on muddy sidelines early in the morning watching boring training sessions and still get scooped by someone lazing on their couch at home who is mates with a player agent.

The most startling example of this from my recollection was the story of the 2003 Kangaroo tour thief. So much stuff went missing from players' rooms on that, the most recent such tour (which I incorrectly reported recently as being in 2001 — even though I was there. *Doh!*), that members of the touring party actually set up a 'sting' operation in which property was left sitting around in the hope of nabbing the culprit, who was suspected to be a player.

The story was broken by the Nine Network and *The Sydney Morning Herald*'s Danny Weidler, who was at home in Sydney. Those of us on tour — principally me and the *Telegraph*'s Dean Ritchie — knew precisely nothing about it. Sure, it was our job to know. As explained above, this is the part of my job I am incapable of doing … or unwilling to do.

Dipping back into being a roundsman for a couple of months here and there allowed me to reassure myself that my probably-antiquated approach still works, and perhaps show some of my younger colleagues the way we used to do things. Initially, I tried to park my Four Nations work in a corner marked 'money' and proceed with writing this book and doing everything else I would normally do in a day. By the end of the tournament, however, I had abandoned all pretence of normality. I wasn't going to the gym, I was reading my stories repeatedly on the *SMH* website, I was waiting with breath baited for what the opposition wrote, I became indignant at the smallest slight.

An email debate with a member of the RFL media team about the way I reported something that England coach Wayne Bennett had said became a black cloud following me around Teddington, where the Australians were based. This was no way to live. In 2004, when veteran Sydney rugby league writer Peter 'Chippy' Frilingos suffered a fatal heart attack while sitting at his desk and trying to get a story from then NRL chief executive David Gallop that would keep Chippy on the back page, many in my profession were spooked. Columnist Jeff Wells promptly quit, fearing he would go the same way. He now writes books.

Even the most dogged reporter with journalism in his sinews, such as my close friend Brad Walter, can't resist the siren's call of redundancy. Society needs journalism but, increasingly, even those who seem born to do it aren't willing to pay the price.

ANDREW JOHN LANGLEY SAYS: I can kind of understand how journalism could be addictive. You start every day on zero, regardless of what you did the day before, and you compete. No wonder reporters hang out together. Aside from the unsociable hours, there's the fact that they've been labouring in isolation for hours and probably feel the need to talk about it with someone who understands those reference points. From this perspective, it seems quite sad that it is dying.

CHAPTER 21

STAND UP FOR ROCK'N'ROLL

'G'day mate.' Ryan O'Keeffe brushed past me and headed towards the stage of the still-empty Electric Ballroom in Camden, London. 'They're learning some new songs. They'll be a while,' said Matthew Harrison, from Airbourne's support band Palace of the King.

Ryan and older brother Joel formed Airbourne in 2003. In four hours, the brothers and bandmates David Roads and Justin Street will confront a seething, sold-out 2000 crowd. It was their second no-tickets-left night in a venue that dates back to the 1930s. The touts outside Camden Town tube started early tonight.

It's tempting to think of the O'Keeffes as walking in the footprints of giants such as their heroes, AC/DC, and of Palace of the King — in turn — walking in theirs. Seeing a band with which you're very familiar tread foreign boards is one of the highlights of gig-going and if you've followed the Games & Gigs timeline in this book, you'll know how familiar I am with Palace of the King.

April 2016 was the 40th anniversary of AC/DC's first UK tour. On April 1, 1976, they arrived in London after a 36-

hour flight (with stops in Singapore, Hong Kong, Mumbai and Bahrain). But the tour on which they were booked, with Street Crawler featuring former Free guitarist Paul Kossoff, had been cancelled while they were in transit. Kossoff had died, one of the better reasons for cancelling a tour.

Holing up at 49 Inverness Terrace, Bayswater, the lads waited to be rebooked and finally made their Old Blighty debut three weeks after landing in London, at the Red Cow pub. Allegedly, the 10 people present for their first set, which featured Angus Young on Bon Scott's shoulders along with the guitarist's signature duck walk and back-spin, all left before the night was over ... to tell their friends. By the time Ackadacka came back on, the place was full.

Tonight, four decades on, at the Electric Ballroom, it was as though those same 10 people had been on social media for the last 40 years whipping up support for Airbourne. The testosterone level directly in front of the stage was almost flammable, annoying and reassuring, all at the same time.

'I know you're only watching us so you get a good spot for Airbourne,' said Tim Henwood, the singer for Palace of The King and a former member of Adelaide post-grungesters The Superjesus. 'That's OK.'

A collective with a predisposition to long jams, Palace of the King were not well suited to a half-hour support slot. But Henwood still managed to introduce every member of the band — and we got a drum solo from Travis Dragani, who resembles *The Muppets'* Animal more than any skinsman touring.

Second-on-the-bill, American band Crobot, were a revelation. Or, more precisely, singer Brandon Yeagley was a revelation.

'Acid rock', to me, implies someone stumbling onto stage mid-hallucination and spitting out a few nonsensical lyrics while staring at the rafters. Brandon Yeagley was like David Lee Roth. He spun, he twirled, he jumped and swooped, he used the microphone stand like it was one of his limbs, snapping it back to his face just in time for his next high-octave vocal. He was a heavy metal James Brown, frankly astonishing.

Airbourne were greeted uproariously (after The Poor's *Trouble* announced their arrival). 'I'm in a band that plays rock'n'roll,' Joel O'Keeffe once sang on a bonus track, *Kickin' It Old School*. 'We sing songs about ... rock'n'roll.' Well, that and sex ... unless *Chewing the Fat* really is about having a good chat. Joel smashed a can of beer on his head. He climbed the PA. He was carried through the crowd (since he is Angus and Bon rolled into one, he needs a roadie for this). It was a scene that tempted the writer to use a variation of a cliché used earlier: 'Standing on the shoulders of giants.'

But the truth is that there was even less similarity between AC/DC in 1976 and Airbourne in 2016 than there was between the London of 1976 (*Carry On* comedian Sid James died on stage within days of Angus and Co's debut) and 2016.

In 1976, when *New Musical Express'* Phil McNeill wrote of AC/DC, 'they could well clean up', there was a sense that popular music really was a pot of gold, there to be stolen. *Blue for You* by Status Quo was the No. 1 album in the UK. Brotherhood of Man's *Save Your Kisses for Me* was in the middle of a six-week run at the top of the singles chart. Music papers such as the aforementioned *NME* and now-defunct *Melody Maker* helped shape opinion, as did TV shows like *Top Of The Pops*.

Nowadays, rather than a pot of gold, popular music is more like copper coins scattered in long grass. 'The last 10 years, the crux of our career, have been the worst 10 years since music was invented, basically,' Ryan O'Keeffe told me, perhaps a little hyperbolically. (In fact, the first 10 years were pretty poor, what with the market in cave paintings going through the roof and people becoming obsessed with these new things called 'words'.) But a band like Airbourne makes its money from ticket sales and merchandise; maybe every third person at the Electric Ballroom had either worn an Airbourne t-shirt here or purchased one on the way out.

Yet in a deeper sense, Airbourne were further from the centre of popular culture than Angus and Malcolm Young could even have imagined being in 1976. Airbourne's success has been of the word-of-mouth-generated kind that Brandon Yeagley was clearly relying upon at the Electric Ballroom. Airbourne's airplay has come almost exclusively on satellite and internet radio. The vast majority of interviews they had done prior to the show were for websites, not physical publications. They have survived by constant touring ... and then more touring.

There won't be another massive rock band simply because there is no rock mainstream any more. Our entire perception of mainstream culture is already fragmented and the fragments are getting smaller. Your Facebook stream is full of people who agree with you, you hear only about bands and films that social media algorithms know you will like. Phil McNeill's concept of 'cleaning up' is therefore obsolete.

For Airbourne, the modern paradigm is both a positive and a negative.

On one hand, they could make a living with a low level of mainstream awareness that would have killed AC/DC in the womb. If I had asked anyone around Camden who was this band that have sold out the biggest venue in the area on two consecutive nights, unless the person was wearing one of their t-shirts, I'd have drawn a complete blank. 'We're seeing a change — money is coming back in (to the industry) through streaming services and such,' said Ryan O'Keeffe. 'It's easier to listen to a song on *Spotify*. People want what's easy.'

But on the other hand, there is a glass ceiling for Airbourne that they can never really hope to break. It is difficult to imagine the O'Keeffes headlining arenas in the UK, Australia and the US, even if they continue playing until they're 90. The seats beyond the floor in such venues will remain unoccupied because those who ideally would be occupying them will never get to see or hear Airbourne. Word of mouth only spreads so far. In the end, the social media algorithms leave their fans preaching to the already converted.

(Perhaps their only chance is to send up themselves and their genre, ala Steel Panther. Stillbourne, perhaps?)

For Ryan O'Keeffe, there is no way of dealing with this. He said it was dangerous to even spend too much time pondering it. To borrow from Bon, they're just going to 'ride on …' And for them, as for me and perhaps you, it is the touchstones of their youth that keep them riding. Mythologies inspire reality, even if they don't accurately reflect it.

'Ever since my brother and I started that band, there was never a plan B,' said Ryan. 'And that's honest. We moved the whole band to Melbourne to basically go on welfare, for the purpose of only trying to find gigs. We didn't get jobs. As far as we were concerned back then, we were going to keep going, we were going to move up and that's the way it was going to be. The mentality still remains today: there's no plan B and there's not even a thought of things dropping off.

'And they haven't.'

ANDREW JOHN LANGLEY SAYS: Stephen, have you thought of a Plan B?

RYAN O'KEEFFE ON HUMAN NATURE

Airbourne started life in Warrnambool, Victoria, and now play pubs, clubs, theatres and festivals around the world. I've seen the AC/DC acolytes stun crowds from Grafton to Sweden, singer/ guitarist Joel O'Keeffe scaling towering PAs without a net, being carried out to the mixing desk on a roadie's shoulders, smashing beer cans on his forehead until the aluminium splits and the stuff sprays everywhere.

Joel's brother, drummer Ryan O'Keeffe, says he's learned a thing or two about human nature.

'Common sense is not that common, that's one,' said the 30-year-old. 'People are very influenced, unfortunately, by media. Once you tour the globe a few times and start seeing things from a different perspective, you see people can be manipulated quite easily. '[But] people are generally friendly everywhere you go. Being in a rock'n'roll band, your job is to give people a good time. That's kind of what we're about. Come to an Airbourne show and lose your mind and forget about your troubles.'

CHAPTER 22

MEETING THE SORCERER'S APPRENTICE

'Gig 26'

That entry in the Gigs & Games ledger for this book remained blank for an eternity. I just couldn't remember what I'd done that week. Weighed down by the responsibility of earning enough money to eat, it was not always possible to diarise punctually. But some four months later, when I saw two former members of the original Dio in the band Last in Line in concert 16,951 kilometres away from where I was for the mysterious Gig 26, I remembered: I'd witnessed a Dio cover band in a bar off Broadway in Sydney.

When singer Ronnie James Dio died of stomach cancer on May 16, 2010, aged 67, I was involved in a Triple M rugby league commentary at Parramatta Stadium. I remarked, off air, to colleague Dan Ginnane that it was indeed a sad day.

'I don't know who he is,' Ginnane responded with a shrug.

More than any other performer, Dio separates those who know and love heavy metal from those who have a vague idea who Iron Maiden might be. The impish American replaced Ozzy Osbourne in Black Sabbath in 1979. Despite Gene Simmons' competing claim to the distinction, Dio invented (or at least popularised) the 'devil horns' sign that thousands of people around the world are making at any given time, even if they are Dan Ginnane.

The Australian cover band, Dio Driver, charged $25 entry. That caused a couple of friends to turn around and go home in disgust. Last in Line, featuring two original members of Dio, charged £17 ... which on the day of the show equated to A$28.97.

(This reminds me of the apocryphal tale of an Australian Crawl 'tribute' band out-drawing a solo performance by the well-known Australian Crawl singer, James Reyne, when the tribute band and Reyne both played the same country town on the same night.)

What I got out of the rather loud Dio Driver was the quality of Dio's songs. They played tunes from throughout Ronnie James' career, including his time in Sabbath and proto-metallers Rainbow. Dio's songs were as sensitive as a fragile flower and as forceful as an axe, all at once. Aggression and love all wrapped up in silver jewellery and black leather. As canvassed in the earlier Iron Maiden chapter, these are largely allegories and folk-tales. Humans have always had an appetite for wizards and dragons, the little fella was just giving it an update for the BMX-and-blowdry '80s.

But my journey to the Last in Line show in Sheffield was about more than downing three-quid cylinders of Red Stripe and inhaling a midnight curry. (Although I did both.)

I hoped to find the answer to a question at the core of this book. Millionaire Def Leppard guitarist Vivian Campbell, who is behind Last in Line, was in the original Dio but was not on

52 GAMES ... 52 GIGS

 GIG 42 (NOVEMBER 28): Airbourne, Crobot and Palace of the King at Electric Ballroom, Camden, London

At one point, I fall over. Clumsy, yes. Drunk, also. Unfortunately, it is right in front of the merch stand at a heaving Electric Ballroom. I am convinced afterwards that members of Palace of the King, who got me in on their guest list, saw me topple. Why do I care so little about what footballers think of me but so much about what musicians think? I'm 47 years old.

GIG 24 (DECEMBER 2): Last in Line at Corporation, Sheffield

If you've been looking for gig 24, here it is. Back in week 24, I'm sure I saw a band or two, but I never diarised it. I wanted my 'catch-up' gig to be a good one. I stay the night in clean and basic £50-a-night accommodation provided by the Church Army, which is like a more evangelical Salvation Army, as best I can tell.

GAME 41 (DECEMBER 3): Queens 46 Sharlston Rovers 10 at Meanwood Road, Leeds

There are no touch judges, Sharlston appears to have no reserves, players banter with a shivering crowd, no-one knows the score, the crossbar is bent like a banana and at least one of the uprights is rusted through. A fellow is sent to the sin bin and when leaving the field gestures menacingly at an opponent, but later exchanges jokes with the same fella as he runs past him to score a try. Queens were sold to me as the most notorious club in England. Notoriously good humoured, perhaps.

especially good terms with the singer. In interviews, he has claimed that Dio's wife, Wendy, was at least partially responsible for turning him, Jimmy Bain and drummer Vinnie Appice into side men. In the end, he says, he was sacked.

'I've always been a very positive person but when I got my cancer diagnosis (Hodgkin's lymphoma, now in remission) back in 2013, it really did heighten that emotion in me,' the 54-year-old told me, standing next to a rickety table backstage. 'I do realise, more than ever, how fortunate I've been in my life. I was fired from Dio. It was actually misrepresented for years that I turned my back on the band, which is completely untrue. It left a very, very bad taste in my mouth and I wanted nothing to do with [Ronnie] Dio, the band, the music or even the genre of music. A lot of things happened, one of which was the passage of time, obviously. Another was the fact Ronnie passed away six years ago and … it gave me the chance to reflect on a lot of things. I look at that time in my life and that music very, very differently now. For years and years and years I denied it was part of my legacy, but it's as much my legacy and Vinnie Appice's legacy and Jimmy Bain's as it was Ronnie's because we wrote those songs with Ronnie. But we weren't allowed to have ownership of them for years. I still haven't been paid for them and I never will be. That's beside the point. They're still part of our creation.'

At no time during this excellent show is Ronnie James Dio — who presumably sacked Campbell — mentioned by name even though most of the songs, save a handful from this line-up's new album, were made famous by the band named in his honour. Yet Jimmy Bain is the subject of a heartfelt tribute mid-show. The

Scot died of lung cancer, age 68, in his cabin on the *Hysteria On The High Seas* cruise in January 2016.

'The thing about Jimmy, Jimmy couldn't really cope with life very well,' the distinctly N'orn Irish Campbell told me. 'If he would get a parking ticket, he'd tear it up and throw it in the bin. If he got a bill from the tax man, he'd do the same thing. He could have been eligible for ... Medicaid. Jimmy didn't have much money. He didn't have a pot to piss in, to be honest. He wasn't very good at managing his money and to be fair he was short-changed by a lot of people he worked with in his career. He would have just put his head in the sand (regarding his illness). Jimmy died with his boots on. We knew he was ill about a month before he died. We were rehearsing and did some shows ... we offered the week before [the cruise], "Jimmy, you don't have to do this. Your health is more important." But Jimmy wanted to do it. To Jimmy, this was important. He must have known that he was that ill. We knew he had pneumonia but it turns out that was a by-product of the lung cancer that actually took his life.'

I had stumbled across the best example of the delineation between art and artist I could possibly encounter. The former collaborators of an artist, in this case Ronnie Dio, honouring and building on *their own* contribution to his work without specifically canonising him.

I must admit that, initially, I saw something dishonest about Last in Line. It looked like they were profiting from Dio's legacy without actually liking him. Dio's widow Wendy endorses another cover band, Dio Disciples. But I misread the situation entirely — these guys were honouring their *own* legacy. Ronnie James just happened to be the singer in that band.

In Last in Line, Vivian doesn't say anything negative about Ronnie James Dio. He doesn't say anything positive. He doesn't say anything at all. He is able to go up on stage in front of people who worshipped Dio every night and deliberately put his emotion and skill into the art, not the artist. He feels no awkwardness; his relationship with the man everyone in the audience loves is irrelevant. 'I've always subscribed to the theory you should never meet your heroes because you'll always be disappointed,' he replied when I asked him the general question. 'And most of the time, when I've met people whose music I've admired, I've been disappointed. Not because of anything they've done but more likely because of what I built up in my imagination what I thought they should be or could be.'

Campbell's message was that music makes you feel good, and everything else about it should be ignored. What people created and who they were, he insisted that night in Sheffield, 'are two very different things. You should never try to look beyond what it is that is the immediate, and gives you pleasure. If you enjoy somebody's music, just take it at face value.'

ANDREW JOHN LANGLEY SAYS: Now you're finally getting somewhere. The nature of fame, the futility of hero worship, the intrinsic value of art. I'd have written this myself — if it wasn't about godawful headbangers.

CHAPTER 23

THE RAMBLER

Around the time I received a letter from the social services in New South Wales identifying my 'putative' old man (if you're reading: Hi Dad), I drove to Canberra for the NRL game between the Raiders and the Bulldogs. That was my game for week 15.

These days many rental cars don't even have CD players but just in case, I threw in a couple of CDs I'd recently purchased from Utopia Records on the way to work. One was the 2016 Cheap Trick release, *Bang, Zoom, Crazy ... Hello,* which I thoroughly recommend even though it could just as easily have been called *Brush, Washing Machine, Nuts ... Frying Pan* and made no less sense. The other was *Kentucky,* by nu-southern rock (I just invented that genre before your eyes) foursome Black Stone Cherry. I liked Black Stone Cherry but sensed that they had been drifting further away from their Lynyrd Skynyrd-inspired roots with every passing year, stripping the blues from their music and morphing into a passable modern rock quartet.

Listening to *Kentucky* confirmed my fears. After five songs, I had chastised myself for wasting money, consigned them to my mental list of bands to stop following, and worked out a place in my off-site storage room for said compact disc.

Then the LED display clicked over to track 13 (that number again): *The Rambler.*

There is nothing modern rock about *The Rambler.* It's a gentle, countrified lament with a story to rival Kenny Rogers' *Coward of the County.* And that story — a father writing to a child he never met — instantly installed a lump in my throat.

'You were born in a southern fall/It might've been Sunday but I can't recall/All the birthdays I must have missed/Your first steps and your first kiss/I don't even know if you know my name/But you should hear the truth before it's too late/So I hope this finds you, on some highway …'

As I sped past the Goulburn Roundhouse, I felt tears welling. I'd had 47 years of telling myself I didn't care about my biological background, that I was a self-made man blissfully free of inherited baggage. But having parents you never knew carries a complex psychological and emotional weight. For 5:08, it was as if the rope that had suspended that weight had been suddenly snapped.

However, before long I was running up and down the sideline at GIO Stadium and I forgot about *The Rambler.* All I could remember was that *Kentucky* was worse than those breadless burgers KFC tried to market. I wouldn't be going near either of them again.

Our story now moves forward six months, to London's Shepherds Bush. I was tapping my foot impatiently at a kebab shop, about to see *An Evening with Black Stone Cherry* at the grand old local venue, the Empire. It was built in 1903 by Frank Matcham who can't have imagined the unkempt rockers who would one

52 GAMES ... 52 GIGS

GIG 43 (DECEMBER 5): Black Stone Cherry at Shepherd's Bush Empire

'Seen 'em before?' asked a balding man of 60 next to me at the bar. My answer — that I once saw Black Stone Cherry on a ship in the middle of the Caribbean — seemed to befuddle him. It is true. Black Stone Cherry were on board for the fourth annual *ShipRocked* cruise that left Fort Lauderdale, Miami, in December 2012, and so was I.

GAME 42 (DECEMBER 10): Carcassonne 42 Avignon 16 at Stade Albert Domec, Carcassonne

Is it possible for a ground to be redeveloped, with a new grandstand, and yet pale by comparison with your memories of it? The answer? When the redevelopment was done to suck up to rugby union. And the food isn't a patch on what it used to be.

day play there and at his other ornate creations, the Coliseum and the Palladium.

But I was not *really* impatient because I didn't care if I missed the start of the show. In fact, if not for the one-gig-a-week premise of this book, I may not have bothered going. Modern rock, remember ...

Inside the Empire, it was a diverse and friendly crowd. When Black Stone Cherry came on for their acoustic set, just after 8pm, my expectations remained low. Singer Chris Robertson was a big lad, like an '80s rugby union prop, perhaps. Guitarist Ben Wells was the blond rock star. Bassist Jon Lawhon seemed like someone you might find in a bar in Louisville and drummer John Fred

Young … well, he was pretty much like every other drummer I've described in this tome.

Things started rather casually with *In Our Dreams* and *Hell & High Water* and by the time these 'kids' (all aged about 30) came to the agreeable *Like I Roll*, I'm glad I didn't eat in at the kebab shop. Acoustic rock, done well, can be soothing.

'This next song,' said Robertson in what I am bound by journalist union rules to describe as a 'southern drawl', 'if you know it then please feel free to sing along. But if you don't, I'd ask you to stop and listen to the words and you might understand why it means so much to us.'

He strummed his guitar. Oh shit. It was that song.

The Rambler was co-written by Jasin Todd, from the … *ahem* … modern rock band Shinedown. The official video, which tries really hard but pales by comparison with the actual song, even stars Billy Ray Cyrus as the prime protagonist.

I can recall tentative tears that took the entire song to reach my chin. Telling his child about the encounter with his or her mother, the main character croons, *'She said the songs you sang made the whole room cry/And that night I told a young man's lie/When I said I would call her/And I said I'd write'* …

At the end of the acoustic set, Robertson said, 'I know someone here in the crowd is struggling. I know someone is having trouble coping. I just want to say that you're not alone. If there's one thing I learned from the period where I suffered depression, where I didn't want to sing, when I thought about suicide, is that you think you're alone but you're not. Why do people with depression have to prove they have it, unlike other illnesses? People just think, *He's crazy, he'll get better.'*

Robertson came across as an astonishingly wise, self-assured and soulful man. He's a decade and a half younger than me but I found myself aspiring to be more like him and being ashamed of my dismissive musical snobbery at 110kph on the way to Canberra all those months ago. And suddenly, this wasn't just a rock concert. By stripping back the instruments, and then his own soul, Robertson and his friends turned the Empire into a non-religious congregation. I photographed the emo group to my right, chatted to the young Italian couple in front of me.

The wonderful bluster and machismo of an electric rock'n'roll set followed a short break. *In My Blood*, with its tale of compulsive travel and the strain it puts on relationships, is one of my very favourite songs of this century. Perhaps there is no excuse for the behaviour depicted therein, or for that of the fictitious *Rambler*. As gender roles evolve, both sets of lyrics may be condemned ... if, as is unlikely, they are remembered by anyone of note.

But while the morality of each narrative can be questioned, the tangible impact on me of each cannot. I felt goosebumps, I tasted tears. The argument that my emotions have been shaped by a lifetime of clichéd stimuli did not hold water — because my eyes did. That's what tangible means — measurable, real — regardless of the electronic impulses in the limbic system of my brain which cause them.

'I met a devil in an old motel/It seems I ain't got much of a soul to sell/My glass is empty/My hands are blue/And the doctor gave me about a month or two/Well I thought I would make it to you this year/So forgive me one last time my dear/And tell your mother/I won't be coming home' ...

I couldn't tell my wife about how *The Rambler* had made me feel when I got home, lest I sounded hopelessly drunk and sentimental. Or that the second reason I was listening to the song repeatedly while she lay next to me later that night was that this was an end I'd always seen for myself, from which she appeared to have saved me.

But mostly, since I am not allowed to contact my 'putative' father, *The Rambler* does and — and unless he calls me — probably always will represent his voice. It helps me feel I know something unknowable. Is that real? Is that tangible? Does it give music intrinsic value beyond the expensive videos and subconscious association between words, colours, memories and involuntary emotion?

To make sure, I listened to the song again while I wrote this chapter ... sober, far from Shepherds Bush, Goulburn and my wife.

I still cried. It's still real.

ANDREW JOHN LANGLEY SAYS: I thought we went to these shows to get drunk and forget about the world ...

'The Game'

What I want to discuss in this column is the use of the phrase 'the game'. Your correspondent always objected to the ARL and the NRL referring to themselves as 'the game'.

'The game' taking back the Immortals concept, for instance, argued on behalf of a group of suited men at Phillip Street or Moore Park. It always seemed the absolute height of presumptive self-importance. Likewise, the idea that just 16 clubs — out of the million-plus people who play versions of the game worldwide — are 'the game' seems completely outrageous.

I went to a suburban ground in Leeds on Saturday to see Queens play Sharlston Rovers in a Pennine League match. I didn't see any sign of the NRL. I didn't see any sign of any NRL clubs. Now, there were also no touch judges. One team had no reserves. The crossbar was shaped like a banana and one of the uprights at my end was rusted-through at the top. The observance of the shoulder charge ban also seemed somewhat lackadaisical.

But I could have sworn it was 'the game'. I could have sworn they were playing 13-a-side. I assumed it was four points a try, although the ref was just about the only one there keeping track of the score. If this wasn't 'the game', then what was that woman at the canteen talking about when she told a little kid — and this did happen — 'it doesn't matter how fat or skinny you are if you want to play,

it's in there', as she put her hand over her heart?

And what was that bloke on the gate — I think it was Ryan Bailey's father — giving up his time for, collecting a pound from every spectator in return for a ticket in a raffle for a bottle of plonk? The ref, the canteen lady, what were they there for if not 'the game'? You might say that's another country but this scene is repeated in Australia hundreds of times each weekend over the winter months ...

NRL clubs sit at the top of a pyramid that rests on volunteers, juniors, live spectators, television fans, magazine and newspaper readers, people doing websites and podcasts for nada. For any of them to suggest they are the entire sport is unspeakable arrogance. The NRL is not just there to sell the games in which they are involved for 30 weekends every southern hemisphere winter.

The NRL is charged with maximising the number of people who watch and play an entire sport. And no other organisation in the world has the resources to provide that service for rugby league aside from the NRL.

By all means take a side in the current imbroglio. But don't let either side tell you they are 'the game'. They are just people, companies, employees, logos and intellectual property holders.

You are the game.

This story first appeared in **The Sydney Morning Herald** *on* **December 5, 2016.**

CHAPTER 24

FRANCE

In 1994, we almost convinced Bill Harrigan — who was refereeing Mal Meninga's final match the following week in Bezier — that French for 'get back 10' was '*je t'aime*'.

We — the travelling Kangaroo tour press, that is — were in a Perpignan hotel room with Harrigan. But when he waved an arm aggressively and shouted '*je t'aime!*', there was no way we could keep straight faces. (Just like the time on the same tour we *almost* convinced Bob Fulton that Warrington, where he was born, was dedicating a statue in his honour right next to Brian Bevan's one.)

Roughly every third year since 1991, your correspondent has wandered the back streets of French towns with Kronenbourg and baguettes sloshing around in his guts. In 1997, I followed the South African rugby league team on tour here. In 1991, I toured with Papua New Guinea. That was the trek which ended in one of the game's great apocryphal stories: the one about a couple of intoxicated Kumuls liking the local shows (perhaps those after 10pm, if you know what I mean) so much, they unplugged a television set from their hotel room and attempted to take it back to Rabaul.

52 GAMES ... 52 GIGS

GAME 43 (DECEMBER 11): Villefranche 33 Ferrals 18 at Stade de la Fontaine, Ferrals-Lès-Corbières
Can there be two prettier grounds than those I visit today, at Ferrals and Lezignan? Stade de la Fontaine sits on a river, next to a gorgeous old bridge. It's seven euro to get in. The view is arguably better from outside.

GIG 44 (DECEMBER 15): Reef at Pyramids Centre, Portsmouth
Why have the bands of the '90s aged so much worse than most '80s bands? Reef used to be brash, cheekbone-blessed men about town. Now they look like they've been in suspended animation for 100 years on a mission to Mars. 'They had better drugs in the '90s,' is someone's answer.

GAME 44 (DECEMBER 17): Toronto Wolfpack 28 Brighouse 26 at Brighouse Rangers Sports Club
Unique occasions don't come around too often; a trans-Atlantic sports club making its first appearance against a team that dates back to the schism qualifies as one such occasion. The Wolfpack's low-key millionaire owner David Argyle even speaks in the clubhouse, thanking RFL CEO Nigel Wood who at this time is somewhat beleaguered over events at Bradford, where the Bulls, it seems, are facing imminent extinction.

In a quarter century, my French has not improved but my understanding of *frisson* has. The south of France is one of the few places in the world where one can attend rugby league in December, and — with its fine light and finer wine — must also be one of the leading venues for what is known as a 'writers' retreat'.

Now it was mid-December and I was in the historic Hôtel Terminus, Carcassonne. Three lads by the name of Stuart Sheard, Dave Sharp and Graham Sykes read about this book in *Forty20* magazine and invited me to join them on their planned *treiziste* sojourn. We met a Chelsea fan called Dermott when he chuckled at my answers to a consumer survey to which I was subjected in the departure lounge. He had a holiday home in Carcassonne and was talking, moving, breathing and thinking more slowly. Following his example was not terribly difficult.

The Hôtel Terminus isn't just another lodging. It is famous for its staircase, a double spiral if you can picture that, and the lobby is old world in a way that makes the airy acoustics almost hypnotic. In World War II, the Hôtel Terminus was Nazi headquarters; there're still bullet holes in a nearby bridge where locals were shot on the final day of the German occupation.

By comparison, the banning of rugby league, and the handing of its assets to rugby union by the Nazi puppet government based in Vichy seems rather trivial. But there was a synergy there, a connection, that made the Terminus seem like a rugby league landmark in a way that ran much deeper than the dinners, lunches and piss-ups it has hosted for the sport over the years. Stepping out of the antique lift upon my arrival, the first thing I saw was a pre-war tourism poster for Vichy.

I first tried *cassoulet*, the local specialty made of white beans, pork and sausage, at this hotel one evening in the '90s. And across the road, at the La Rotonde restaurant, is where I consumed it again with my three new friends on the opening night of this mini-odyssey. Stuart, Dave and Graham are retired Huddersfield fans (retired from work, not from being Huddersfield fans), with

Stuart also a prominent official in amateur rugby league. Dave ate a snail because, let's face it, someone had to. As we became acquainted, proceedings moved to the town square, Place Carnot, and to a venue the name of which translates roughly to 'Cave of Beers'. The Leffe Ruby beer was a particularly tasty stalagmite as we discussed pressing (*pression?*) matters such as the age of Jake Mamo and why a prominent player of recent times came to be known by a name other than his original surname.

In a high-ceilinged second floor room overlooking a largely ignored Christmas fair, I sequestered and wrote on my second night while the boys attended — cough, splutter — a rugby union match. My second excuse for not going to a rugby union match; there was paper to be kept dry, and energy to be preserved as the weekend schedule consisted of three French league games, one from the Elite One competition and two from Elite Two. (If you're asking what my first excuse was, you obviously don't know how I feel about rugby union.)

I had only ever seen one French club game live — in Toulouse in the '90s. I'd watched a few on television over the years. When I worked for AAP in London in 1990, an early version of satellite television featured a French game a week with commentary overdubbed by the likes of Ray French. Ray once admitted that he once got to half-time and realised he had completely mixed up one team with the other — calling each player's opposite number for the entire 40 minutes. He got it right in the second half and hoped no one would notice.

Game one pitted Villegailhenc — a village 15 minutes' drive the other side of Carcassonne Gare — against Lescure. Our taxi driver offered 'good!' and a thumbs-up when we told him we were off to see *rugby a XIII*. This was in sharp contrast to a taxi driver in Toulouse who once insisted *rugby a XIII* was not rugby at all but *jeu* à *treize*, or 'game of 13'. This was the law in France from 1949 to 1991 — rugby league was banned from calling itself rugby anything; I am constantly overcome with regret that I did not order that cabbie to stop immediately and exit his vehicle in the middle of the street. Our driver today professed a love of *'l'equipe d'Wigan'*, which he had once seen play at Wembley. He liked Andy Farrell and singer Phil Collins. Would he have known where Villegailhenc's home ground was had Phil Collins performed there? Because it didn't seem to help his sense of direction that the sport Andy Farrell once graced is played at the venue.

Turning right off the unprepossessing main street, the driver thought we'd gone too far while my companions — who had been there before — insisted we'd not gone far enough. Turned out our driver had been to Wembley but, in the words of Charlene, he'd 'never been to me'. (I didn't ask him about being undressed by kings, but who knows?). The men from the birthplace of rugby league are right. Stade Jérôme Rieux could have figured in any Bruce Springsteen song that references 'the edge of town' — this was as far as Villegailhenc went. It was like any suburban ground in Sydney, although with an impossibly lush grass surface. There was another striking difference too — 2.4-metre high vertical bars around the field. It's a curious aspect of sport in France, these stark fences ringing the playing arena. Considering that the players were in danger of out-numbering the crowd today, the bars seemed excessive.

But on the side of the ground nearest what seemed to be a vineyard, there was a small grandstand unobstructed by the stalag-worthy fence. And there was a bar of another kind — the plastic table where people were flogging espressos also offered cans of Kronenbourg at two euro a pop.

It wasn't long before my companions spotted familiar faces. Vinnie Anderson, formerly of the New Zealand Warriors, St Helens, Warrington, Salford and AS Carcassonne, was warming up with the backs of the home team. Elsewhere, given his age is 37, Vinnie would be with the forwards or — far more likely — standing alongside us. Dave observed that one of the touch judges was 'from the English school of skinny linesmen', and Graham rather wittily responded, 'Never mind skinny linesmen, he's [just] from a school. He must be 14.' Indeed, the young fellow officiated like a startled gazelle and when the sun got in his eyes later in the afternoon and he raised his flag for a goal that missed, he was immediately forgiven by all and sundry.

The football itself was wonderfully entertaining, in many of the idiosyncratic ways you expect French rugby league to be. At one stage, the home side made a break, enjoyed a three-on-two overlap, and the halfback chip kicked to the corner. The ball dribbled touch-in-goal, a certain scoring opportunity gone, and no one in the crowd seemed too bothered. Not only did the players banter with the crowd but so, too, did the referee! I had no idea what was said but I'd like to think the fellow next to me yelled, 'Get a pair of glasses,' to which the official responded, 'Your wife says it's time you got a prescription for Viagra!'

At Stade Jérôme Rieux, I encountered something that had always frightened me the way some of you may be scared of heights or spiders or fingernails on a chalkboard — a squat toilet. Everything about going to the toilet, particularly *numero deux*, is pock-marked with phobias and hang-ups for me. It's enough to make me avoid the entire continents of Africa and Asia whenever possible. What's worse, being nervous about having nowhere civilised to have a shit just makes me need to shit more. I made an unsuccessful visit to the facilities at Villegailhenc and silently prayed for a comfortable throne later that day at Stade Albert Domec, where Carcassonne were to take on Avignon at 6.30pm.

After Lescure beat Villegailhenc, my companions informally interviewed the side's utility back Jordan Tansey, who had arrived only four days previously to take up a contract and set up a nice try with a chip kick much better conceived than the one described a couple of paragraphs back. Tansey, previously of (now pay attention here) Leeds, Sydney Roosters, Hull, Dewsbury, Crusaders, York, Castleford, Wakefield and Huddersfield, said he was staying until May and would fly his family over after Christmas.

Our cabbie, the chairman of the Phil Collins Fan Club (Carcassonne chapter) showed up at 15 seconds past the assigned time of 5pm to take us to Stade Albert Domec, named after Albert Domec, who played rugby union for France in the late 1920s. Domec is not to be confused with Sid Domic, who played for (sorry about this) Brisbane, Penrith, Warrington, London, Wakefield and Hull.

Sid Domic, sorry Albert Domec, Stadium was, in some respects, unrecognisable from the place I'd last visited in 1991. It has a new stand, named after the medieval la Cité which sits imposingly in the distance, funded by the council following the arrival of — cough, splutter — rugby union. I also remembered bewildering gastronomic options inside and outside Domec;

tonight the pickings were rather thin — *merguez* on a roll from a caravan outside the stadium, or *frites* inside the arena (*steack Americain* on a baguette was offered later). All purchases within the stadium were made with tokens. When the man in the token tent asked in halting Anglaise, 'One glass or two?', I assumed he was referring to how many beers I wanted. In truth, he meant the plastic glasses themselves, which are loaned to spectators. Once you hand you glass back in, you get a yellow token back and this you redeem for cash. In the end, I gormlessly took my ASC XIII glass and token back to London with me.

Once more, the rugby league was enterprising and entertaining with much more ball movement and daring than you would see in a whole weekend of NRL or Super League. The other abiding French stereotype — indiscipline and short fuses — was mostly unsupported, save for a sin-binned forward kicking over a water bottle in the second half with Carcassonne well on the way to a handsome victory.

Doing a lap of the ground (outside the fence, not inside holding my cup aloft), there were signs of decay. The old grandstand I remembered from 1991 was mostly deserted, the gate on the old-town side of the stadium was closed. The outdoor *pissoirs* that had fascinated me so much in 1991 had been torn out and the statue of Puig *'Le Pipette'* Aubert, French rugby league's greatest player, was forlornly 25 or 30 metres from the nearest spectator. But the most alarming observation was one I thought impolite to make in the company of three older men — until Graham said it himself. 'Look at the age demographic of the crowd,' he said. 'Who's going to come when they go?'

Mike Rylance, who wrote the acclaimed *The Forbidden Game* about the dark days of World War II when Germany occupied France and the defeated country's collaborationist Vichy government supported rugby union and discriminated against rugby league, has thought about Graham's question. '[The] observation about the game being followed by old men is certainly true of regular fixtures although for finals and so on you'll see a better demographic mix,' he told me. 'Young kids do play the game in numbers, usually in the écoles *de rugby*, the junior sections of open-age clubs. As they get older, as elsewhere, it's a matter of keeping them, either as players or spectators. The French haven't been too successful at that.'

Certainly, the academy game that preceded our only Elite One match of the weekend was entertaining, skilful and well supported by the few hundred who were there. By the way, rugby union money has at least produced one overwhelming positive — western toilets. *Ahhhh* …

A few pints at The Celt pub, populated by local ne'er-do-wells zonked out on cheap Christmas-market wine, followed. The young bar manager, who despite his red beard was not Celtic at all but rather from Quebec, Canada, had his hands full kicking them out.

The next day, planned mainly by Dave in intricate detail, comprised a visit to the town of Lézignan, followed by a speculative journey to the Ferrals-les-Corbières and the home ground of the Ferrals team (in Australia, 'Ferrals' would be a subversive nickname for a team) to watch their match against Villefranche.

In the morning, we met for the short train journey to Lézignan, which had two major attractions — a 'vine and wine museum' (why not add a few exhibits dedicated to 'drunkenness' and 'urination' to complete the depiction of the process?) and a rugby league team. A DJ was spinning *YMCA* at the Lézignan clubhouse ahead of what appeared to be a Christmas lunch when we *four treize-a-teers* showed up wanting a look inside their ground. Lézignan were playing away at St Gaudens but their ground, Stade du Moulin, even when empty, lived up to the promises my companions made that it was one of the most picturesque, atmospheric and devilishly charming sporting venues in the world.

The former orchard boasted an impossibly quaint wooden grandstand on one side and a mural depicting the history of the club on the other (with one panel vacant — presumably for a hologram). Think Leichhardt Oval, but without whatever it is you don't like about Leichhardt Oval, in radiant French sunshine. There was time to kill at a café before our taxi driver was due to arrive to take us to Ferrals. We had more time to kill than we thought; the cabbie was waiting for us at Carcassonne station.

For jaw-dropping beauty, Ferrals's ground out-does even the Stade du Moulin. The clubhouse's top level is on the main thoroughfare, the second floor comprises dressing-rooms and the bottom floor is adjacent to the lush playing surface. The river Orbieu meanders past the ground, under a grand bridge that leads into a small town of about 12,000 people. Looking back at the ground from the bridge is almost dream-like. In the match, a field goal was kicked before half-time, rival players chatted to each other at full-time as they corkscrewed up the clubhouse building to their dressing-rooms, and I finally made my peace with a squat toilet. (I won't go into detail except to say any illusion of not having gained weight over the past few weeks explodes quicker than your bowels when your guts are pressed up hard against your thighs.)

It is apparently an unspoken tradition in France that if you are beaten at home, you do not help the victors find the post-match banquet. And so we left the Villefranche players wandering aimlessly around Ferrals-lès-Corbières as our taxi took us back to Lézignan, and from there we caught a packed train to a pizza restaurant on Place Carnot … all of which was well and good, but what did it tell us about the role of rugby league in these communities in the south of France? What did the sport do that is intrinsically worthwhile? Perhaps sadly, rugby league seems inextricably linked with the past in these parts. The young boys playing in the Domec curtain-raiser were engaging in a long-standing tradition that is deeply connected to geography. Rugby league is kind of like *cassoulet*.

'Since professionalism came into [rugby union] 20-odd years ago, union's profile has expanded enormously, even into previously *treiziste* towns like Carcassonne and Albi,' Mike Rylance explained. 'As we know all too well, it's not that what they have to offer is more entertaining, but simply that [rugby union] has a national significance which league lacks. It's because of that that local councils will dole out far bigger grants to their union club than to league and why bigger crowds are attracted to [union, bolstered by] a sizeable percentage of fans who used to watch league.'

Carcassonne's old town, where, in 1990, Kevin Costner was working on *Robin Hood: Prince Of Thieves* when he hung out with the Kangaroos, attracts a staggering four million people a year.

They eat *cassoulet*. Why should they not sample rugby league, and why should rugby league not be as big a source of pride? Said Rylance, 'Fortunately, we have the Catalan Dragons, who have done a lot to boost league's image — not so much nationwide, but certainly in the heartlands, where they've given hope and encouragement to those who want to see league be successful. [The Dragons] have also had the effect of draining away fans from other rugby league towns, because they see the domestic championship as second rate. And if [the Elite One] champion team, Toulouse, heads off for the third tier of the UK competition, what does that say?'

Then, Rylance delved into the politics of league in France. 'It's true that [former Fédération Française de Rugby à XIII chairman] Nicolas Larrat saw the future of French league through the prism of the UK competition, believing that the domestic clubs would be incapable on their own of bringing themselves into the modern professional era. But what does that leave you with in France? Towns like Carcassonne, which feel they've been marginalised in spite of a glorious past, rose up against [Toulouse president] Carlos Zalduendo in the last elections, even though they have no concrete plans to construct a new future.'

After the three Englishman left, I hiked up to la Cité. It was mostly deserted on a cold afternoon, but no less spectacular. I was the only person in a military museum on the restaurant-lined road back into town, where a curator told me about the Nazi atrocities that left their mark on the bridge near my hotel. 'They were children, woman, people working at the clothing factories who were passing by,' said the moon-faced man with bow-tie and cauliflowered ears. The local headquarters of the Fédération Française de Rugby à XIII was just a few metres across the canal from the memorial for those murdered.

Carcassonne has recovered from World War II with the help of tourism but has not forgotten. French rugby league has, in almost every quantifiable way, failed to recover from the war. But it is doggedly determined not to be forgotten, either.

It's not easy to get a cab in the south of France. After waiting half an hour, mine finally arrived and when in the back seat on the way to the airport, I noticed *Radio Nostalgie* on the radio LED display. 'Monsieur, wasn't it you who took us to Villegailhenc?' I asked the driver. 'Oui! *Rugby a XIII*! Wembley! Wigan! Andy Farrell.' For the sake of this chapter, I wanted to ask him which Challenge Cup final he saw but he just rattled off the names of every team in Super League.

'Hey!' said the fellow who checked my boarding pass at the airport, 'Were you at The Celt the other night?' It was the bar manager, the guy from Quebec. This was his other job.

Three days earlier, on the sideline at Villegailhenc, while a winger joked with a spectator standing next to us, my English friend Graham boasted, 'I've been to every racecourse in Britain, you know. But I don't like the big ones. Ascot, you can't move. I'd rather go to the smaller courses. It's like being here. If the winner at my race is going three seconds slower than the one at Ascot, what do I care?'

I spent some time trying to work out what the last few days had been worth. Sport itself can link us to the past, through handed down lore and monuments like the statue of *Le Pipette*. But this adventure might have proved nothing more than it's nice in France and I had a good time with three men from Yorkshire who are *literally* trainspotters.

The point is: if I wasn't doing this, I'd be doing that. Or I'd be doing something else. Whatever I was doing, it was worth it if I enjoyed it, and I certainly enjoyed my time in the south of France. It had worth, whether or not French rugby league is being gobbled up by rugby union and the third tier of Super League.

Sure enough, as the sun began to dip and I crossed the tarmac to board my Ryanair flight back to London, there was a familiar fellow in a Chelsea shirt walking towards me. 'Have a good time?' said Dermott.

'Yes, a great time,' I responded. 'The three Englishmen were wonderful fellas.'

'Ah good,' he nodded with a warm, relaxed smile. 'Well, that's all that matters.'

ANDREW JOHN LANGLEY SAYS: I like France. I like travel writing. You go on this trip and who do you meet? Three league tragics from the north of England, a Chelsea fan and a barman from Quebec ... except for one cab driver, it sounds as if you never talked to anyone from France! And yet, these new mates of yours seem like genuine people ... you know, I don't like saying this, but the amount of friends you have makes me a little jealous.

CHAPTER 25

HOWL LIKE A WOLF, BOY

I've been overweight most of my life. Not actually 'fat'; I've only been 'fat' for a sixth or a fifth of my 48 years. Most of the time I've been what Dan Ginnane once kindly described on Triple M as 'puffy'. What that means, in a practical sense, is that going to the gym is pretty damn important to me now.

I get cranky with myself if I don't go, or if I don't stay there long enough. I assign very precise times to my gym visits. For instance, in Sydney in winter I will leave to go to the gym at 5.30pm, which gets me there at 5.41, which gives me 49 minutes of stretches and weights before watching *NRL 360* from the treadmill until it is over, or until one geriatric knee or the other seizes up.

On this occasion, I was 22 minutes and nine seconds into a half-hour treadmill stint when the *Noize In The Attic* podcast was interrupted by a call from someone I will describe here as a 'creative' with close professional and personal ties to rugby league. It would be unfair to him to be any more specific as I'm sure he hopes to continue working in the sport. He offered to call back in seven minutes and, as I flailed away, I allowed myself to imagine what he might want.

52 GAMES ... 52 GIGS

GAME 45 (DECEMBER 18): London Broncos Academy Trials at Trailfinders Sports Ground, West Ealing
OK, this barely qualifies. But they do run, pass and kick — if not tackle. And Martin Offiah is there by complete co-incidence. 'Do you want to trial?' a Broncos lady asks him. 'I wish ...' responds 'Chariots', who is only at the ground to watch an earlier kids' rugby union tournament.

GIG 45 (DECEMBER 22): Geoff Tate at Voodoo Lounge, Dublin
Reading interviews with his former Queensryche bandmates, you could be forgiven for thinking Geoff Tate is a tyrant. Yet the Gaelic band he has picked up to support him on this solo jaunt through Europe never stop smiling. A wonderfully compelling evening.

GAME 46 (DECEMBER 27): Warrington 28 Widnes 18 at Select Security Stadium, Widnes
My first 'Festive Derby', reached after setting off from Fethard, Tipperary, at 4am. Best remembered by me for doing live updates on my own radio station.

GIG 46 (DECEMBER 30): John Coghlan's Quo at The Half Moon, Putney
It seems a fitting end to a year of celebrity deaths: seeing Status Quo's drummer six days after guitarist Rick Parfitt died. But John Coghlan prefers to tell a story about Parfitt's cooking to shedding a tear. Boogie just doesn't lend itself to grief, I guess.

Was there some exciting project on which he wished to work with me? The small window I had allowed myself for today's workout was ruined by his incursion but if there were some dollars involved, that would be OK.

At first, when he rang back, my man wanted to know if there had ever been a definitive history of rugby league published. Yes, several, Tony Collins' *Rugby's Great Split* among the most forensic. Then he wondered if anyone had drawn a family tree of the game, how it had spread, in which direction, showing the dead ends (of which there are no doubt many). An intriguing idea. Did he want me to work on this with him? Would I have to fly to some exotic locale for meetings?

As it turned out, no. It was the dead ends that my man was interested in discussing with me. He was calling to have a moan.

'Denny Solomona, Chris Sandow, James Segeyaro — I've never felt more disheartened as a rugby league fan,' he opined. Those three players reneged on their contracts with Super League clubs for 2017. One went to rugby union and was being sued, the other two refused to return to England after taking a break back home in Australia. I looked longingly back at the treadmill. Not that I wasn't up for a group moan but, you know, I had a beer gut that needed irradiating.

'The most exciting transfer for next year is Kevin Brown to Widnes,' he continued, 'a fellow just going down the street. The whole sport seems to be flat-lining.'

There is a strange dichotomy when you are a newspaper columnist about having conversations with people about the things you've written. While I may have mustered considerable outrage in order to write said piece, by so writing I experience catharsis. When I've written about a contentious issue and your words have been read, I am most often sated and the subject itself becomes 'work'.

Of course, if I've done my job properly, I have simply passed on my outrage to many others. And then they want to talk to me about what to me is now 'work stuff'. Rugby league fans like to whinge but, near the end of 2016, in purely objective terms, most aspects of the sport as we looked ahead to 2017 were depressing.

The NRL and its clubs were at each other's throats over the same issue that begat the sport itself — money. Alex McKinnon was about to sue the League and a rival, Jordan McLean, over the tackle that left him in a wheelchair. Scotland, on the basis of its 2016 Four Nations appearance, is fourth in the world but has just a handful of domestic teams and pretty much no RFL funding. Wales had its own cash from Red Hall dramatically slashed and had to lay off two full-time employees. The RFL was retrenching people. England was planning a training camp in Dubai, where the sport is illegal.

Grim, grim stuff.

'Eventually,' I counselled my friend, 'you have to accept what rugby league is, its place on the food chain.' In almost every respect bar aesthetically, it is a sow's ear dressed up as a silk purse. One of the worst mistakes an "insider" can make is to see a silk purse. We're supposed to know that such illusions are intended strictly for outsiders only. In many ways, we're expected to assist in the deception of outsiders, not fall for it ourselves.'

But, of course, as the poster says, 'I Want to Believe.'

The Toronto Wolfpack, the 2025 World Cup in America … these things tease us like a girl half our age in search of a free drink. Objectively, the only expansion franchise in rugby league to have experienced sustained success is the Melbourne Storm, but that did not prevent me travelling from London to Brighouse in west Yorkshire and back in a day to see the Wolfpack strip make its competitive debut.

Most of the time, they will really be the Brighouse Wolfpack. Their home games, at Lamport Stadium in Toronto, will actually be away matches for all intents and purposes with the coach and players spending pretty much all their time in Yorkshire. Still, when I spied someone in a Wolfpack cap on Atlas Mill Road, I fantasised that he would sound like a member of Men Without Hats when I asked him for directions to the ground.

He sounded like one of those Men With a Cloth Cap.

Without exception, my previous visits to Brighouse (a derivative of 'Bridge House'; the bridge across the Calder dates to the 1200s) have been because the headquarters of League Publications are located there. I've had a few meals at the Wetherspoon pub over the years, lodged at the Black Bull and visited the bank and some cafés. With those experiences, my expectations of the match venue were not particularly high.

Twenty minutes' walk along Bradford Way, fittingly named because the late, great Bradford Bulls marketer Peter Deakin used to live there, Brighouse Sports Club was a revelation. The site was bought with the proceeds from Tesco's purchase of their previous field in the town centre. There was an ample but muddied cricket oval, a sturdy and well-populated clubhouse, and a nice roped off rugby pitch ahead on the right, as you looked from the road.

'I first came here about six weeks ago,' said David Argyle, the deliberately low-key owner of the club, after he surprised the MC by asking to address about 350 fans inside the bar area. 'And as soon as I saw this club and this clubhouse my eyes watered up because I knew we had found the Toronto Wolfpack's home base in the UK.'

Argyle is a banking executive who made millions in the mining industry. He speaks with a weird mid-Pacific accent that reflects his Australian and North American roots. His claim that he cried at the sight of a rugby pitch in Brighouse strikes me as somewhat odd. Me, I'm a schmuck. Life itself is enough to make me sob uncontrollably.

But really, do rich dudes get involved in owning professional sports teams for any reason *other* than emotion? Chances are, the bigger emotional wreck you are, the more money you will blow on some spoilt brats chasing a synthetic bladder around. So, given that the Wolfpack players are on modest pay packets and entering National League One, Argyle is probably quite in control of his senses compared to other gazillionaires who own sporting teams.

Today's game was not an official Toronto Wolfpack fixture, not even an official Toronto Wolfpack friendly. Instead, it was a run-out for 18 trialists discovered at 'try-outs' in Canada, the United States and Jamaica. Somewhat bizarrely, the already-contracted players were having their Christmas party at the same time, with our MC inviting fans to 'get autographs and photos before they get too much drink in them'. Perhaps this concept would catch on in the NRL — combining fan days with Mad Monday would allow the smallest kids and the biggest players to wear the same fancy dress and everyone could get their own photo with Joel Monaghan and his friend Rover.

The contracted players moved to the sidelines, beer in hand, to cheer their would-be team-mates against Brighouse Rangers. With each try the Wolfpack aspirants scored, they howled like wolves. At the try-outs, they made *sober* players do this for the cameras. The Rangers were an amateur team in the midst of their off-season; one of their reserves warmed up in a knitted Christmas hat and the entire reserves bench encroached on the field at regular intervals to get a better view of the action.

The Brighouse field is one of those venues where you can't kick for touch on one side lest the ball be lost; instead, the referee takes the ball off the player who would have these duties and walks the pill 10 metres downfield himself. I wonder if a referee has ever failed to find touch this way and been dropped for it.

By early in the second half, in front of an appreciative crowd that numbered around 1000 (and paid £2 each admission to a venue you could have reached for free by just walking across the cricket pitch in contravention of a sign expressly forbidding it) the home side led the Yanks, Canucks and Rastas by 26–12.

The Wolfpack were fearsome-looking chaps and floored anyone they got hold of like androids out of *Westworld*. But they were a little naïve about some of the more cunning attacking ploys, such as anything initiated by a dart out of dummy half. Considering a handful of them had never played before, and that American football is so specialised you almost have someone whose only job is to sneeze, a blown-out scoreline seemed assured. Instead, the Wolfpack fought back and with four minutes to go, one of their outside backs (they wore numbers at the try-outs in Delaware but, strangely, none in this actual match) passed deftly in the tackle to a teammate and they drew level. The conversion was a cinch and rugby league's most exotic professional club kicked off with a win. The players, most of whom would go back from whence they came, embraced Argyle at full-time. 'That took real character,' he said, with his mangled Australian vowels and American consonants.

Oh, I almost forgot. I'm supposed to find meaning in these events, right?

Er, look no further than Nathan Campbell. The Jamaican winger was named three days later as one of a trio of trialists to win a Toronto Wolfpack contract. Previously, his Facebook page showed him graduating from the Jamaican Institute of Technology and playing in a local 'Parish Of Residence' game, and revealed that he received an offer to play rugby league in the British midlands.

Now, thanks to an Australian mining magnate, Campbell was going to be commuting between Yorkshire and Toronto for a living instead of eating ackee and saltfish under a palm tree each morning.

That's got to mean something. I'm not sure what … but something.

ANDREW JOHN LANGLEY SAYS: Let me get this straight. Every expansion team bar the Storm has been failure. Ever. But there is a team from Toronto playing in England and you are wildly optimistic about it. You know the definition of insanity, right? Doing the same thing and expecting a different result.

CHAPTER 26

TEAM ROCK

Is hanging out with people of similar interests, in itself, unhealthy?

At the start of 2017 I spent an enjoyable mid-week night at The Black Heart bar in London's Camden Town. The event was a benefit show for the retrenched employees of Team Rock, publisher of *Classic Rock* and *Metal Hammer* magazines. Some 70 staff were made redundant the week before Christmas with no severance pay and Ben Ward, hulking singer for doom-metal band Orange Goblin, had organised this fund-raiser for them. This included a *JustGiving* page (which raised £85,000) and the show. Three days after the gig, the *Guardian* reported that Future Publishing, which had sold the various magazine titles, licences and brands to Team Rock for £10.2 million in 2013, had bought them back for £800,000.

No sooner had I arrived at The Black Heart than I made a friend, David. He lived at St Albans, seemed to attend every rock festival in the UK, and wanted to help the journalists, photographers and designers whose work he had been consuming for a large chunk of his life. He introduced me to his equally enthusiastic wife Maria, who had been outside chatting to Ben Ward, and we had a splendid night.

52 GAMES ... 52 GIGS

GIG 47 (JANUARY 5): Team Rock Benefit at The Black Heart, Camden

The entire staff of *Classic Rock* and *Metal Hammer* were laid off when their parent company, TeamRock, went into receivership a few days before Christmas. Tonight, Orange Goblin singer Ben Ward has organised a benefit for them. I like The Black Heart, hidden around the corner from the famous Underworld (famous for its rude staff, in my experience). I don't particularly like Orange Goblin but I'm not here for the music. Having paid my 10-quid donation, I watch three songs from the headliners and go home.

GAME 47 (JANUARY 7): London Broncos 54 British Army 8 at Trailfinders Sports Ground, West Ealing

And a good afternoon is had by all. About 150 people on hand, carrying drinks in and out of the clubhouse at civilised intervals. Great to see Andrew Henderson and Adrian Purtell afterwards.

A couple of days later, I was at a London Broncos friendly against the British Army. Howard Scott, to whom you were introduced earlier in this book, came to meet us and he introduced me to two friends. One, who used to coach army teams, told me he once had three players arrested between the warm-up and kick-off. 'One minute I'm watching the warm-up and thinking, "We've got a strong side here." Then we're crossing a road and the police come along and arrest three of the 17 for brawling the previous night. I'm thinking, *The side doesn't look as strong now*!'

David and Maria in Camden Town were dressed in black, pretty much head to toe, with piercings. These chaps (Howard has gone off the Broncos in recent years but was warmly welcomed back to the fold) have caps and polos of that peculiar shade of blue that the London side wears. David and Maria would have nothing in common with those I was with today, but my experiences interacting with them were surprisingly similar — in-jokes, knowing smiles, jargon, camaraderie. We might have been talking about Jamie Soward or Mike Portnoy, but the cadence of the conversations is almost identical. Mention a name or a place and there were knowing laughs, gentle put-downs. Having such interests represented a wormhole in the friendship universe that can take you from point A to point Z-to-the-power-of-608 in a nano second.

This is called tribalism or neotribalism. The theory, championed by the likes of Billy Shurtz from Arizona State University and French sociologist Michel Maffesoli, postulates that we spent most of our time as a species in tribes and still seek such gatherings wherever possible now, even in a profoundly depersonalised world. Shurtz seems to think we'll eventually go back to the forest and reject all the conventions of modern society. If that happens, I am really concerned about what common ground I'm going to find for the London Broncos fans and the doom rockers when we move into our well-appointed new cave.

THIS BOOK IS ABOUT the passage of time, as much as anything, and the passage of time seems to have treated Jizzy Pearl well. I first met Jizzy in 1990, when he said — after he and his band Love/Hate had brought down the house at the Marquee in London and we ran into each other at the St Moritz Club — that I reminded him of Donny Osmond. Unlike every other journalist he'd encountered, I had short hair and wore a shirt that wasn't black. Hence Donny.

Twenty-three years later, as I crossed the border from California into Nevada at around 1.30am, I was wearing a black tee. They're the only type I now have. Eventually, I reached the bright lights of Vague Arse, found a hotel — sorry, casino — on the outskirts of town, slept a little, and then texted Jizzy, born James Wilkinson and now 54, at a reasonable hour in the late morning.

In the rock interviews of yore, you would read how the temperamental singer 'sauntered' into a bar, where he and the hack became 'sequestered' in a booth. But despite what I repeatedly tell myself, it is not 1986.

Pearl walked into a casino. He sat on a stool in the cafeteria.

He was thin, sported jet-black hair, a discreet facial piercing and carried intangible rock cache, although more punk than glam rock. When I'd last seen Jizzy, he was completely consumed by the trappings and illusions of rock stardom. 'It's hard to describe what goes through someone's head when they're in that microcosm of having a record coming out, working your whole life, starving and having no recognition and no money and all of a sudden praise is being heaped on you by the truckload,' he said, sipping a coffee. 'You've made this brilliant record, every chick wants to bang you, everyone wants to buy you a beer — especially in the UK where we were initially very popular and to this day still have a loyal following. Having a big record deal, it goes to your head. It's called "rock-staritis". It went to *my* head. It went to everyone's head. You just think you can turn water into wine … And when that doesn't happen, you board up the house and you just have them slide the pizza under the door for a year or two.'

It is just a little disquieting to think that many of the rock gods you sang along to in the shower are now of more modest means than you. Had Pearl wanted to fly to New York, rent a car, drive to Boston, find a hotel and then text me that morning, would he have been able to afford it?

Of course, he would have. He was just not as stupid as me. He had domesticity; we would have met at his house except for 'the new puppy'.

While I saw mainly flat terrain since 1990, he had scaled considerable heights and plunged horrible depths. Being forced by the loss of a record deal to return to the same squalid flat from which he once emerged to screw supermodels while snorting Colombia must make for an especially repugnant slice of *le pie du humble*.

Pearl was now back on his feet financially and had played with L.A. Guns, Ratt and Quiet Riot. He was estranged from the other members of Love/Hate and after guitarist Jon E. Love threatened to sue, announced he would bury the band name altogether. Then he kept touring under 'Jizzy Pearl's Love/Hate' anyway.

Driving through the Nevada night, I listened to Hair Nation, which still plays Love/Hate's *Blackout in the Red Room*. Buckcherry's Josh Todd said, 'For me, that record is right up there with *Back in Black* and *Appetite for Destruction*.'

Pearl, and Love/Hate, didn't sell many records but they certainly had the appetite of which G N' R spoke. Being put up in a New York loft at the record company's expense to record the follow-up to *Blackout* hastened their demise. *Wasted in America* was wasted *on* America and as his career fell apart, Pearl actually climbed the Hollywood sign and tied himself to it. 'By crucifying yourself on the Hollywood sign you were making a statement that this is what it took to make it in Hollywood,' Pearl wrote in a memoir. 'Any actor or musician can immediately identify with this feeling — years and years of unrequited labour only to have your hopes dashed again and again …'

He was hauled down by law enforcement officers, and, when interviewed by a police psychologist, said he was making a plea to the rock gods. 'And the cop gets all serious,' the singer recalled, 'looks me in the eye and says, "Jizzy, there *are* no rock gods."'

By connecting yourself to things rather than to people, as I would now say I did for some 40 years, you spare yourself the lows but kill any shot at the dizziest highs. Yet you can't be completely aloof in a band, or a football team for that matter.

'I do Love/Hate these days for fun,' Jizzy told me. 'I enjoy it but I wouldn't want to tour in a van eight months out of the year and play dives every night and age in dog years.'

Ah, maybe what some of us do is *mature* in dog years.

Pearl would rather drive a cab to raise money for a new CD than hit up a crowd-funding site like *Kickstarter*. He said some of his contemporaries struggle to sing, not because of their age, but because they're just plain lazy. 'You just have to have your shit together. By that I mean, you gotta do your cardio and you gotta get your chops together. If your chops are together and you've been running every day and you've got your wind, then it's basically … you can just do it. But if you don't … which is why a lot of these guys from our generation just can't hit the notes any more — because they're not doing what needs to be done. You know what I mean? Like sit-ups, for one thing. Or stop eating so much. Or quit getting so fucked up on stage. Now that the era of *YouTube* is here, it really behoves everybody to have your shit together. That's how I feel. It would embarrass me if *YouTube* came out and I was at 60 per cent. It would make me want to work harder.'

I don't eat as much as I did in 1990 and I don't get drunk as often. I had just assumed this was because I was old. But Jizzy said society's expectations have changed; if we were that age again, we'd still be healthier. Today's role models don't walk around swigging from a bottle of Jack Daniels', like mine did.

'I gotta own up to the fact that we all drank liberally,' my interview subject conceded. 'But everybody did. I mean, I could tell you stories of famous rock stars who pissed their pants every night, regularly. That wore diapers regularly because they were so fucking drunk. The '80s and the '90s, people got fucked up all the time. When we used to play in LA, there was this band called Motorcycle Boy. Back then they were semi-popular. The singer would be so drunk that the audience would have to hold him up because he was gonna fall. That's how drunk people got all the time and it was accepted and it was cool. Times have changed. It's not cool to be that fucked up any more. It's not cool to be on drugs any more.

'A lot of people thought heroin was cool and, you know … they're dead.'

ANDREW JOHN LANGLEY SAYS: On one hand, you have reached the quite sensible conclusion these subjects are just socialising mechanisms. You like football. I like freeform jazz. They don't really matter themselves; what matters is that they give us something to talk about. I like that conclusion. But doesn't that negate this whole book? I mean, the whole friggin' thing?

New World Order

On Sunday, the contracted players for the first-ever professional trans-Atlantic sports club made their debut in Hull, east Yorkshire. The Toronto Wolfpack colours had already previously been seen when their trialists, competing for spots as part of a reality TV show, played an amateur team and won.

The Wolfpack, featuring mainly Brits with a smattering of players from North America and the Caribbean, held the Challenge Cup holders (who'll be competing two divisions above them this year) to a 26–20 defeat. They should have, at least, got a draw.

The Hull coach, Lee Radford, predicted Toronto would 'walk through' the English third tier, National League One, this year. His two-try winger, Mahe Fonua — who knows a thing about expansion, hailing from Melbourne — said they'd be in Super League in two years.

One club, however, is not going to restructure an entire sport and we know rugby league's record of expanding into areas where it has no history. It's terrible; aside from the aforementioned Victorian capital, none of these areas are represented in the Super League or the NRL and there is a long list of failures like Adelaide, Cardiff, Paris, etc.

What can change the order of things, however, is a confluence of events.

It was reported over the weekend that a Florida consortium is preparing a bid to enter the British system, starting at the bottom like Toronto. Eric Perez, the man behind the Wolfpack, wants a second Canadian team and finally, Australian Jason Moore is planning a semi-professional league in North America in the lead-up to the 2025 World Cup.

Suddenly, the goalposts have moved. There are more fulltime jobs for rugby league players worldwide. While in Australia and the UK we need rugby league teams to have a significant market share in order to be viable, in the giant North American market they can be barely visible in a national sense and still be able to pay the bills. Suddenly, North America is opened up to Super League as a television, merchandise and membership market.

It can be tiny in an American sense, a pin-prick, and still drag players away from the NRL. Imagine a Super League in 10 years with three North American franchises. At the very least, Australasia would no longer have the player market cornered; it would be impossible to hang onto every decent player.

It's the theme of a hundred science fiction movies. Only when the aliens invade do the earthlings learn to work together for the common good.

And the NRL desperately needs an alien invasion right now.

From **The Sydney Morning Herald,** *January 24, 2017.*

52 GAMES ... 52 GIGS

GAME 48 (JANUARY 8): Hull KR 40 Hull 16 at KCOM Stadium, Hull

Forty-seven-year old reporter, me, is talking to 66-year-old coach, Tim Sheens. A Hull KR PR in his 20s thinks it's OK to stand 60 centimetres from the two of us and listen in without saying a word. Is he going to tell the former coach of Australia he shouldn't have said something? Is he going to ask me not to quote someone I've known for 35 years? Hull FC aren't any better; they wheel in just one player for me to interview and say no-one else is available. After a January friendly! This job just isn't much fun anymore.

GIG 48 (JANUARY 14): Accept at Brixton Academy

My wife likes traditional metal. She didn't know she did.

But of all the bands I've taken her to see, she likes Judas Priest and Accept as much as any. Funny. She hated it when her sister put an Iron Maiden poster on their shared wall because the band members were, in her words, 'Ugly.'

GIG 49 (JANUARY 19): The Quireboys at The Iron Road, Evesham

I have now interviewed the Choirboys and the Quireboys for my podcast. Today's pre-gig interview upstairs at a pub across the road from Evesham railway station has been a year in the making after a series of misfires from both sides. Nice lads. Great show.

GAME 49 (JANUARY 20): London Skolars 26 Wigan 22 at the grounds of the Honourable Artillery Company, London

There was apparently an all-in brawl at the start of the second half. I don't know for sure; I was otherwise occupied at the time. Wigan coach Shaun Wane says there was nothing in it; referee Matt Rossleigh says there was. The game finishes in a scuffle, too.

52 GAMES ... 52 GIGS

GAME 50 (JANUARY 22): Hull 26 Toronto 20 at KCOM Stadium, Hull
There are actual Canadians in the crowd, I am told. Apparently, the Wolfpack jerseys are only available at the club shop outside the ground, and it is closed at halftime. I know that, because I walk outside and check. They're unlucky to lose, too, the 'Pack ...

GIG 50 (JANUARY 26): Tyketto and Romeo's Daughter at Islington Academy
There's a couple at the next table in the noodle shop beforehand who I've seen all over the world at rock festivals. I even picked up the girl's passport when she dropped it at immigration after getting off a cruise in Miami. Yet they look straight through my wife and me. We gossip about whether they've put on weight and what they're wearing. They don't know we exist.

GAME 51 (FEBRUARY 1): Huddersfield 12 Warrington 0 at Halliwell Jones Stadium, Huddersfield
Last year, in my weekly *Home & Away* column for the official Rugby Football League website, I 'credited' Mike Cooper with a mistake he didn't make. His father complained. Tonight, I apologise to Cooper (junior) in person.

GIG 51 (FEBRUARY 2): Glenn Hughes at The Fleece, Bristol
First impressions: this room sucks and this gig is going to be only fair to middling. But after skirting up the right flank, I find myself directly in front of the former Deep Purple star. And we soon discover that Glenn's mother died the day before. His ruminations on life and death are right up this book's alley.

UNFORCED ENTRY IX

GIBBER

I had an idea when this project started. I would write whatever came into my head when I was drunk and I would be banned (by myself) from changing it. Compared to some of the rules I've come up with, it was genius. Republish one column a month? Go to a game and a gig a week? Lame by comparison.

The bottom line is that my motor neurons are spitting most out of the neuron muffler in the middle of a gig after three beers. I've no idea if the emissions are a honey apple vape smoke or pure carbon dioxide but I do know I feel unsatisfied they are never recorded for you to decide.

Sometimes I have what seems like an insight standing in front of a prancing guitarist in a packed club and then it's gone, like an 8am dream. I can almost see it driving away with the fake smoke from the flashpot.

Tonight, I saw former Deep Purple bassist Glenn Hughes perform in Bristol. After four songs, I was pretty much resigned to being semi-bored for the rest of the night. It wasn't hitting the mark; I loved his *California Breed* project in theory — it sounded like something I would like — but I've not listened to it in a couple of years. The gig was a bit like that.

Then he mentioned 'stuff that's been going on in my personal life' and my Clark Kent ears pricked up. I didn't know what had been going on in Hughes' private life but as it turned out his mother Sheila had passed away the day before.

'Thirty years ago, I probably wouldn't have shown up tonight,' the 65-year-old said. 'I would have been hammered. But what I've learned about reality in life is you have to love. I do know, without spooking you guys out, that there is another place after this. I've seen some incredible things happen in hospitals this last couple of months. If you remember this gig for anything … celebrate life. Celebrate your own life, your family's life, your friends' lives. Life is so friggin' precious in this fucking world that we live in now … what's going on in the country I live … we gotta come together.'

Hughes then sang *Long Time Gone* — which features lyrics that refer to 'my one and only' and a 'black light so lonely' — as he had never sung it before, and may never again. At one point, I looked to the right and saw his drummer fighting back tears.

Hughes apologised for 'sounding like a hippie', but then shrugged, 'That's because I am one.'

What beer-addled insights descended from such a touching night? That perhaps — despite my forays into website administration, video production and podcasting — I may not be able to escape the fact that my primary role in life is to tell you about such a touching night. It was such a strong compulsion that I came straight home and started typing this.

Secondly, that it costs money to be a sensitive artist like Glenn Hughes. He refuses to call people 'fans', preferring 'friends I know from the internet' (that means something else for a swathe of other people, right?). If he wasn't a former member of Deep Purple living in Los Angeles, would he have had time to write a record while recovering from a double knee reconstruction (after giving up alcohol and drugs, Hughes took up obsessive running in late middle age)?

So, following that thought to its conclusion: is the death of the music industry stopping people being creative; people who would otherwise have brought us life-enriching, maybe even life-saving, truths? It's a rather sobering thought, even after four Red Stripes.

'Eighty per cent of people in this room, if we have an indifferent day at work, come home, put on headphones and listen to music,' said Hughes that night in Bristol. To make that music, however, it helps to not have to go to work …

If you can put food on the table, an artistic life seems like a good life. If you have to blog 18 hours of rugby league — as I've been known to do — to buy that food, it's a small price to pay.

CHAPTER 27

SWIMMING WITH SHARKS

Event merchandising is not one of British rugby league's strong points. While rock bands have mastered the art of the one-night-only t-shirt, the closest thing you get in the north of England most of the time is the half-and-half scarf. You know the ones. One half has the colour and name of one team, the other has … I'll let you figure it out.

A week after the 52nd and final match I was duty-bound to attend to complete the quest that was the motivation for this book, I bought, outside DW Stadium before the 2017 World Club Challenge, a half-and-half scarf for my friend in China. He's based in Beijing and would dislike me telling you any more about him. He's private, his job requires it — not on social media, etc, etc. That's not to say he's bad. He is, in fact, good China. But anyway, he's a Cronulla fan and he considered returning home for last year's grand final, the one I covered from Essington, Pennsylvania, the one in which the Sharks beat Melbourne 14–12, securing Cronulla's first premiership.

As *The Sydney Morning Herald*'s WCC man, I followed the Sharks, NRL premiers, around for a week in Britain in February.

52 GAMES ... 52 GIGS

GIG 52 (FEBRUARY 10): Anthrax at Kentish Town Forum

At a meeting with sports-desk staff, a Fairfax Media executive once declared that sport served only a perfunctory role in *The Sydney Morning Herald*. 'I'd be really offended,' said a racing writer, 'if I knew what that meant.' Tonight's gig is perfunctory for me. I go so I can write that I went; in for about five songs then off to the kebab shop.

GAME 52 (FEBRUARY 11): Wigan 26 Salford 16 at AJ Bell Stadium, Manchester

A train, the Manchester Metro and a bus from London before a short walk in the company of a mother and daughter who've travelled from 'the other side of Manchester'. Salford seem to have few supporters at any given home game, yet those who are here today come across as uniquely passionate and loquacious, the sort of people I'd invite to my last game of 52.

I met them at the airport, where coach Shane Flanagan answered a question about whether the game would be fiery by daring WCC opponents Wigan to put on a stink. Captain Paul Gallen told me he fancied a playing stint in England; it was a worthwhile ride on the Piccadilly line for a reporter, then.

At Teddington, where the Australian Four Nations side had boarded three months previously, the Sharks' likeable media manager, former golf professional Rob Willis, turned back the clock a couple of decades by letting AAP's Ian McCullough and me approach whichever player we liked as they left the training field, as long as we didn't like Andrew Fifita. That was the way things used to work, before sponsors' back-boards and 'controlling the message' became the done thing. And the Sharks made all the right noises about wanting to add a world title to their still-rather-echoey trophy cabinet.

But they did go to Paris for a day. Now, would they go to — say — Broken Hill for a day of sightseeing in grand final week? I mean, there's no Eiffel Tower in Broken Hill and the local answer to the Champs Elysees is someone's landscaped front garden, but you get my drift. It wasn't a great preparation for a game you're desperate to win. Then reports emerged of a big night in Manchester on the Thursday before the match. I had a big night in Manchester that Thursday and I didn't win the World Club Challenge so that must be it.

Cronulla did not beat Wigan. Not even close. The 22–6 defeat, coming on the back of Warrington upsetting Brisbane 27–18 the previous evening in the first game of the World Club Series, shut up even the worst Chicken Littles in the British game for a few hours (although one Wigan fan apparently told league writer Phil Wilkinson at full-time, 'I'm worried what it will take out of them for Friday's game against Widnes').

But the fact remains, Cronulla won the NRL premiership in 2016. That's pretty remarkable. 'One of the boys said to me, "Can you actually believe we won the comp last year?"' Chad Townsend told me in London.

Before we finish looking at the tangible value of sport, we probably should examine the tangible value of *winning* at sport — of winning big, winning in such a way that even four months after you've won, you are prone to express incredulity to a team-mate.

'I had more people say, "Thank you" than "Congratulations",' said Sharks back rower Wade Graham. 'You think when you win something, people say, "Congratulations" but there's more people in Cronulla, life-long fans, life-long members, saying "Thank you for bringing a premiership to Cronulla finally". Mate, it blew me away….'

When I'd put the same question to Michael Morgan during our conversation in Townsville 11 months ago, he responded in a similar way. Born and raised in Townsville, the 2015 premiership victory has special significance for him. I slipped in the question for the book: 'What does it all, like, mean?

'In a way, I don't know if I'm answering it the way you want me to, but for that week or even months after the actual game, when the trophy went around, we were able to give people a lot of happiness — just from winning that game,' Morgan answered. 'One game brought so many people so much happiness. I think for that period of time, people forgot about their problems — whether it is not having work, struggling financially … To know we could actually make a difference in people's lives like that … to know you've, by playing well and working as hard as we all did last year, made people we've never met extremely happy for a long period of time … Even now, people still talk to you about the game and where they were for it, what they were doing, how they reacted, who they were with and everyone's got their own story now of where they were when the Cowboys won their first premiership. It feels pretty special to have done that.'

In 2016, James Maloney was in his first year at Cronulla. Having left Sydney Roosters, the popular narrative was that the bubbly — some would say pesky — pivot's career was beginning its descent. 'I probably didn't understand leading into it, until it all happened, the scope of it, being the first side,' Maloney told me. 'I never thought about it too heavily. You get people you see who have been staunch supporters for 40 odd years, 50 years, who never got to see one [grand final win] and didn't know if they would. Just what it meant to them, that was pretty awesome.'

Chad Townsend is a Cronulla local who was forced across the Tasman to the Warriors for a couple of years. Turns out, he's a pretty thoughtful guy and gave a detailed response to a question about underlying meaning which may sound, to some footballers at least, rather wanky. 'Throughout the year, when we won those 15 games in a row ... we didn't lose a game for four months straight and everyone was loving going to training. And people were saying in our team, "If we don't win the comp, it's been a failed season for us." That's just how we looked at it, you know? We were focused on winning the comp. We were talking about it. Everyone was talking about it; how good we were going. It was, like, "We *have* to win." That was our mindset. Then, when we actually did it ... Luke Lewis said, "Can you actually believe we won?" You just have to kick yourself every time and wake up to the fact that we actually did it and how hard it is, I guess. Guys like Chris Heighington and Luke Lewis who won comps, you know, 11 and 16 [sic] years ago, they talk about, "You don't get the chance very often to do that stuff so you need to make the most of it."'

These guys who lived it are trying to help explain it to us but if you're not a sports fan, their attempts may still sound a little clichéd. However, it should be evident by now that it is intellectually dishonest to just say, 'Sport doesn't matter, it's a bunch of guys chasing a pigskin around a paddock.'

Why? Because even if it *shouldn't* matter to the people doing it, there is no denying it *does* matter to lots of people watching. These are cultural tropes with deep historical roots in pretty much every society. I don't particularly like the expression 'in and of itself' but, anyway, in and of itself playing sports is a very unimportant job — and writing and talking about it are exponentially more trivial. People plotting and planning on going on the Mars Mission, for instance ... we don't deserve to deploy a toilet brush on their excrement.

However, the jobs of athletes — and even those of us who inform the general public about what they're doing — are not like making a sandwich and then selling it, or building a website for someone. It's not goods, exactly, and it's not services, exactly. Like musicians, athletes keep alive customs that give humans comfort and have done for centuries. Despite the hyper-commercialisation of sport over the last 30 years, their earnings are still not related in any direct way to the extent of their impact. You can be paid a lot of money as a football player and not make that many people happy that often — and vice versa. And that gap between the quantifiable aspects of your job and the impact of your work on others is where the magic lives, in both sport and music.

That's why I say that trying to assess the importance of sport by simply assessing what these athletes do is intellectually dishonest. Hydrochloric acid, sitting in a beaker, is also unimportant and ineffectual until it comes into contact with something. You can argue the surface it eats through in seconds shouldn't be so weak — but the effect is undeniable.

'As the semi-final series went on, you could feel how important it was for everyone,' Chad Townsend recalled. 'You're getting clapped out of cafes during the week, people are running across the road to say hello. We'll go for lunch down the [Cronulla] mall and old guys will just come up to us, look you dead in the eye and say, "Thank you," and just walk off. You're, like … "No worries!" To be able to touch someone's life in that way is, I guess, an amazing thing to be a part of and something that this team and this squad will never forget."'

The lesson? If you can go to Mars to widen the footprint of mankind, by all means do. Otherwise, play for Cronulla.

ANDREW JOHN LANGLEY SAYS: People follow sporting teams. They are often the sporting teams of their parents and even their grandparents. They want to see these teams win. Even a non-sports person like me can understand this. You and I can critique the significance of sport until we fall asleep or are given our own TV show, and it won't matter to these people. The result of a game made them happy. Full stop.

Oh, and one more thing … next time you go to a Wolfpack game, and you go to the merchandise counter (and I know you will), pick me up an away jersey. Extra large. It will remind me of your trainspotter friends and your own trainspotting.

CHAPTER 28

THE END

So, this is it.

February 19, 2017, and I was sitting in the press room at DW Stadium, 90 minutes before the 2017 World Club Challenge between Wigan and Cronulla.

For all the questioning I'd done over the last 12 months, all the efforts to reject that to which I have tied my entire identity for decades, I was surrounded by stimuli that still pulled at my subconscious. Why had I felt this morning like I was heading to the Sydney Cricket Ground for a semi-final in the 1980s, starting with under-23s at midday? Why was there a shapeless sense of elation, which for years I associated with the end of the season?

Because in England it was spring. The birds chirped, there was pollen in the air, and for years, for me, spring was when the league season in Australia and work was about to end, when overseas adventures beckoned, when the slug could have another shot at being a butterfly. These environmental factors remind us we are animals, I guess. They affect my behaviour … the speed at which I walked down here from Wigan North Western station, the smile on my face, the warmth of a handshake.

They're things that defy the intellect — even after 12 months of trying to apply my intellect (such as it is) to everything I do.

A few feet away, Toronto Wolfpack coaches Paul Rowley and Brian Noble were gossiping about players with Batley's John Kear. The cadence of Kear's voice had a soothing quality, evoking 50 or so muddy Yorkshire winters.

I heard John's voice rise and fall, I thought of Sheffield beating Wigan at Wembley without even listening to what he was saying. I needed to think hard to get these images out of my head, to not smile to myself, to not feel reassured in some vague but tangible way that the future will be OK because something from the past was in close proximity.

For your correspondent, there were things that had changed profoundly over the past year and others that stubbornly refused to. When I returned to Sydney in March, it struck me, I will not even be accredited by the NRL. Three organisations I worked for each assumed one of the others had applied on my behalf, and none of them had, and as a result I was not on the accredited list.

A year ago, sitting in the café at Headingley with Amanda Murray and Barrie McDermott, this would have appalled and scared me. Now I felt liberated, enlivened.

So, today, as I finish this book, here's what I've learned:

Going to rugby league games was an addiction; rugby league matches were boxes in my mind that needed ticking, always open while other boxes remained closed. These closed boxes were labeled 'relationships', 'family', 'financial responsibility'. My wife — through faith, persistence and some accidents of history — managed to prise open these boxes for me. Now the rugby league boxes are less demanding of my attention.

At the start of the book, I spoke about 'tangible value'. Four games in four cities in four days had very little tangible value aside from allowing me to write about it here. It's rather unusual that I learned to give up something by force-feeding it to myself for the previous 52 weeks — but there you go.

However, I have not — as I thought entirely possible — weaned myself off rugby league itself. I've a new love of standing on the terraces with a beer, of watching games on a plasma screen, of talking crap and not having to remember scores or scorers. My time on trains to Campbelltown may have been wasted but my time among the people of rugby league has not. Eleven hours drinking at a civilised pace before and after a London Broncos game, a half-hug from former St Helens and hero of Brisbane club football Phil Veivers ... small things that reassure me that any questions I had about the value of the friendships the game has given me have been soundly and convincingly answered.

What have these last 52 weeks told me about rock'n'roll?

That answer is a little more nuanced.

I no longer feel like a spectator at the rock circus. The rock circus has fallen on even harder times than any actual circus; I feel like I need to be a participant, a contributor, sharing new music with as many people as possible, helping the un-appreciated gain appreciation.

The star system described in my chapter about Iron Maiden is but a minor annoyance. At a Camden Underworld show by the bassist Marco Mendoza early in 2017 I noticed in the crowd the singer Nathan James, of Inglorious. He was there with an older woman, who I assumed to be his mother, to see his brother guest on lead guitar. I had interviewed Nathan James and got on quite well with him but when I motioned an informal 'hello' he looked straight through me. So what? If I had spent the last 20 years interviewing bands instead of rugby league players, he might remember me. A young reporter from Featherstone interviewed me in a Wigan pub the day after the World Club Series; he had met me before but I didn't remember him. You can only remember so many people; that's not arrogance.

As long as you don't fall for what Axl Rose called the 'prejudiced illusions' that pump the blood to the heart of the business, you don't have to worry about this.

The tangible value of sport is that it is a socialising mechanism. It really doesn't matter if you are standing between your two best friends that some NRL games are frightfully boring. Once upon a time, bonding with your fellow tribesman could save you from a rampaging wildebeest. Today, it might still get you home in one piece, albeit asleep in the back of a cab.

But watching every single Super League and NRL game on your own, to the exclusion of family, friends and fellow North Wales Crusaders supporters, is probably bad for you. In my humble opinion you, like me, are using that habit to substitute for something else you need, something that is almost certainly much better for you.

Following a band, or a musical genre, can be a more solitary pursuit. I remember putting Def Leppard's *Hysteria* on a turntable in 1987 and arranging the speakers on either side of my head before letting rip with *Women* (and I wonder why I have tinnitus). I can't help but think that's the way Mutt Lange intended it to be consumed, given the US$4.5 million spent on the album.

The only unhealthy aspect of being a music fan that I can see is slavish devotion to those who create it. Bowie should have sung 'we *should* be heroes just for one day' because any longer seems to be unwise for all parties concerned, as Vivian Campbell indicated in chapter 22. The inability to separate the art from the artist at least has the potential to ruin appreciation for the art.

And sometimes obsession with the artist, and the way that affects the artist, wrecks the art itself. Axl Rose found a million dollars that someone forgot and wanted to get in the ring with critics, duly writing songs about these things, which prevented him writing about *Nightrain* wine, sweet children of his and rocket queens. That was not a good thing.

In the cases of both sports and music, it's important to scoop the cream off the top — the stuff that makes you happy, that you consciously *want*, and discard that which you think you *need*. Because, really, you don't. These things are there to enhance life, not to take it over.

I am finishing this book at Poole, in Dorset. The south coast of England is where I found that my fiancée knew about my whole biological family and this led me on a journey to find out about them, and about myself.

Walking along the beach yesterday, I allowed my mind to wander and for the things that excite me to flood in. Strange, exotic women aren't there any more but Poole Bay to my left and the quaint, boarded-up cabins to my right — the real world — are but a diaphanous curtain in my mind's eye.

Behind the flimsy drapery of reality still loom rugby league heroes of the 1980s colliding heavily and rock gods breathing fire, shooting rockets from their guitars. Knowing them, witnessing their banal normality at close quarters over 12 months and 25 years, did not erase them after all.

They are what keeps me walking.

ANDREW JOHN LANGLEY SAYS: Stephen, I believe one of your friends once told you he envied you and pitied you simultaneously. I wouldn't be surprised if many of your readers feel the same. They envy the travelling, the proximity to notorious people and the ability to indulge childhood passions all day, every day. But they pity the endless searching, the absence of a real home, children or an ever-present circle of supportive friends. The constant overthinking and questioning seems exhausting, as does the dedication to pursuits that bring so little financial reward.

But as someone standing at the end of a path that diverged from yours at Crown Street Women's Hospital in early 1969, I think it's time for you to stop worrying about what I think. You were parachuted into a loving home and your genes drove you in a singular — yes, obsessive, idiosyncratic and even kooky — direction which has nonetheless served you well. Look at all the people you know! You weren't a 'victim' of your circumstances because whatever Elizabeth passed on to us allowed you to navigate those circumstances and to thrive. I have those same qualities, those same flaws, the same emotions and ways of thinking. By revealing and explaining in this book the reasons behind your obsessions, you have eliminated them as being central to your character. You've conclusively proven they are merely expressions of who you and others are, the language you speak. That's all.

You know what that means, don't you? There is no difference between us in any sense that is significant. In any alternative universe, or even in any sensible theory, I simply don't exist.

ENCORE

It was round one of the NRL, 2017. Week 53, if you like.

The first draft of *Touchstones* has been with the publisher for eight days and I was up at 5am in London, ready to blog three NRL games for Fairfax Media in Australia. Even though I have supposedly spent a year researching what we should hold onto from our childhoods and what we need to let go, I was still suffering from inner turmoil.

How much did I care about the start of this new season — by my count the 38th to which I have been betrothed as a fan or journalist — and how much did I only care because I still thought I should, or because I liked social media and websites, or because I needed to cover the season to earn a living?

The iPad was perched stupidly on a bundled-up duvet as the wife I didn't have when I started this book slept beside me. Perched on my nose as I glared into my MacBook Air in this darkened pre-dawn room were glasses I didn't need when I started this book. The iPad was slow but the Premier Sports picture soon flickered to life — St George Illawarra v Penrith from Kogarah Oval, a ground to which I dragged my mother on Mother's Day in 1981, where I lined up for autographs from Brad Buchanan and Michel Sorridimi.

The Dragons were going to be crap in 2017 — wooden spoon contenders — and Penrith were a chance of winning the whole darn crapshoot, apparently. I described the tries, lifted the code from Twitter to embed the videos … it was quite enjoyable work. And after 80 minutes of play — by roughly 7.15am BST — the Dragons, the team that was supposed to represent the dreams of my primary school years and the geographical reality of my childhood, had won 42–10.

This is okay, I thought as Sarah made me coffee. *Not a bad way to make money.* But if I didn't have to be up now, I'd have been snoring.

Then came the second game.

North Queensland v Canberra from the ridiculously named 1300SMILES Stadium. Late in the contest, Johnathan Thurston attempted a conversion to put the Cowboys eight points ahead. Raiders centre Joey Leilua had been such a pantomime villain, you want to scream, 'He's behind you!' at the TV; he punched Gavin Cooper and no one but the few hundred thousand watching on TV saw it. Thurston was kicking from the left side of the field, where he apparently only missed one shot the previous season. He was on 1999 career points in the NRL. He missed.

The Raiders levelled the scores and Thurston shot for field goal in the final moments to win the game and claim his 2000 points. But the shot was deflected. We were into overtime with JT still on 1999. Five minutes into golden point, Thurston was in front of the Canberra posts. A field goal attempt. If successful, it would give his team two competition points and himself 1000 times that many. But the ball deflected off the cross bar and landed in the in-goal area in such a way that it stopped almost dead.

The ball just sat there. And when the camera switched to the one located in the corner of the in-goal area, you can see who was winning the race to it. Thurston. Although it was Gavin Cooper who overtook him to ground the ball. The Cowboys won the match.

The greatest player in the game today, Johnathan Thurston, walked off what was once Thuringowa paceway a winner — but he was still on 1999 career points. As I watched him, goosebumps rose on my arm, the way they usually only respond to a handful of songs; my inner-cynic was utterly demoralised as I breathlessly repeated the narrative throughout the rest of the day.

There was another game and some faffing around before I dashed across London to see the Toronto Wolfpack make their National League One debut against London Skolars, at New River Stadium near Tottenham. This was my last full day in London for a couple of months and Sarah had gone ahead to the ground while I finished the blog.

Turns out, the girl who accidentally knew my biological family also accidentally knows the sister of the Wolfpack's owner, David Argyle. Not just 'knows' — they were old buddies.

Adam Fogerty, he of the Philadelphia 'try-outs' all those pages ago — pointed me in the direction of the pre-match function, saying, 'I just met t' wife. Amazing co-incidence, eh?' When I arrived, Sarah already had a Wolfpack t-shirt and the gentle glow of a few wines and maybe a gin and tonic; we were in a new clubhouse of which the Skolars are proud and the fare was onion soup and curry … which I was too late to sample.

Nonetheless, I took my seat next to the RFL's chief operating officer, Ralph Rimmer, whose name my wife found endlessly hilarious, and told him about Thurston's earlier heroics. Also at our table was Paul Faires, the former proprietor of *rugbyleague.com* who owed me money but still bid £400 for a framed and signed FC Barcelona shirt. The journalist Andy Whitaker deadpanned, 'Rugby league — you'd have no idea if the people in this room are going home to a mansion or a blanket under a bridge — or which ones are doing which.'

During the afternoon, I met an Israeli mining investor who Googled 'highest rugby league scores' as Fuifui Moimoi posted a hat-trick (despite being sent off the previous week and not yet having faced a tribunal) in the Wolfpack's 76–0 win. There were Canadians behind me Googling 'average wage of rugby league players' too. The CEO of the Wolfpack, Eric Perez, offered me Iron Maiden tickets in Leeds. 'We'll have backstage passes,' he winked — which left me duty bound to recount the contents of Chapter 6-6-6.

And with five minutes left, your correspondent walked onto the edge of the playing field with a media pass that, by rights, should have barely got me admitted to the stadium. There, behind the in-goal, was the journalist Nigel Wiskar and his son Ted Fuifui Wiskar. Nigel seemed to regard getting the two Fuifuis together as his life's most important work. When the siren sounded, I walked behind the first trans-Atlantic sports club in history as they greeted their exotic group of fans. Moimoi said 'fuck' in his first answer to my iPhone video question … and then talked about sticking to the match plan. Like Penrith's Bryce Cartwright on the other side of the planet, his personal life was recently made public on social media. Afterwards, he asked me where I lived, adding, 'No one really cares about you away from football over here. It's good.'

In this 1500 crowd — it was a club record — are an inordinate number of people who seemed to know who I am. This, the New River Stadium, was the small pond, and I appeared to be a lower medium-sized fish. The self-effacing line, 'I've finally met my reader — I've been waiting for years!' was wheeled out at least three times.

And back at the function, there was Jeff Hagan, the Wolfpack executive from Ann Arbor, Michigan, whom I'd met in Philly, and Skolars owner Hector McNeil, who wants to start a 24-hour rugby league TV station. There was a fellow I once bumped into on a train going to a Challenge Cup final, who said 'My mind is spinning; a team from Toronto playing rugby league in London. What the fuck? Rugby league can't get the basic things right but when it comes to the bizarre and quirky, it's got those things nailed.'

There was former *Rugby League Week* journalist Steve Russo, heckling Fuifui and then posing for a photo with him. Stuart McLennan, another Australian, had flown in from Greece. He reported some stories for me at *rugbyleaguehub.com*; his wife works in the Australian embassy in Athens. And, in the press box I encountered Huw Richards, the journalist and lecturer who paid me to address students back in London at the start of this book. He has had a tough time with his health since, and although things seemed to be improving, he said it took a piece of rugby league history to get him down here. I was overcome by guilt that I did not visit Huw in hospital when I was first told about his illness. If apologising here in print is any consolation, then that's what I will do.

After the game, David Argyle's sister Rebecca told me they were selling Toronto merch — that which I was so dismayed to miss out on in Hull — at the Skolars club shop. Like kids freshly bestowed with pocket money, Andy Whitaker and I hurried around asking for directions to said shop — hastened by the fear of the stuff selling out. To the back of the stand, to the stairwell outside the toilets and finally to a little room below a cramped bar where they were showing Catalans v Widnes live from Perpignan with commentary from a studio a few kilometres from where we were. The gentleman in the shop called me 'Steve' without me introducing myself when I asked about sizes and within five minutes I was the proud owner of an XXL Toronto Wolfpack away jersey (£45).

Then it was back to a gaggle of mining investors, amateur rugby league players, journalists, alleged conmen, small businessmen, North American sports entrepreneurs, gnarled retired pros … and a member of my immediate family. The glasses clinked, I was bought beers by people I didn't know, the clubs exchanged gifts of jerseys. The man of the match said, 'See you in Shoreditch,' and someone from Canada let out a drunken howl.

On the tube back to Shoreditch, I exchanged with Andy story after story of the shysters we have known in rugby league — the man who convinced a millionaire to invest by saying he owned 400 properties in London when in fact he was a handyman at 400 properties in London, and the fellow who donated chicken and champagne for a club raffle in France and then came to collect it at half-time for his family picnic.

But it was hard to portray disgust, even if that was the appropriate response, for too long before laughing. They may have been rip-off artists, but they were *our* rip-off artists. If alienation, media fixation and childhood obsession had brought me to a point where I could have a day like today, if they had led me to these people and these places, then they couldn't be bad things. The following day I flew to Beijing then on to Sydney for yet another season.

This chapter is over: in a literal sense and in terms of relentlessly questioning what is important to me and why. The answer to it all is disarmingly simple: a piece of branded synthetic clothing I had looped studiously around the back of my belt like so many concert t-shirts before.

As subterranean London blurred through the windows of the northern line, in this moment my Wolfpack jersey was my most valued possession; like KISS's *Dynasty* with the original poster intact or a misprinted Des O'Reilly footy card had been in *their* moments.

ON MY THIRD NIGHT back in Australia, I revisited the band responsible for probably the best gig in this book, The Screaming Jets. In the same way the Skolars-Toronto game was like a convention of all the characters in *Touchstones*; this gig at The Entrance Leagues Club, an hour-and-a-half north of Sydney, was a confluence of all the ideas — a storied pub rock band in a leagues club. Before the show, the Broncos-Cowboys NRL game went into extra time on the big screen outside the auditorium and as a piece of peacetime human endeavour, the bravery and athleticism of the footballers rendered completely ludicrous any belief I may have had 12 months ago about the intrinsic worthlessness of professional sport.

What more, physically, could our species do to prove its nobility than provide a spectacle like this?

A couple of fellows who, like those at New River on the other side of the world just five days before, approached me to talk rugby league. One of them had won a trip to the 2016 Four Nations after posing for a photo with his collection of *Big League* magazines next to his swimming pool. His obsession had rewarded him richly over two months; mine has rewarded me over four decades. To underplay that is to insult him.

And as for rock'n'roll? The Jets finished some time after midnight with a magnificent, extended, snarling cover of Neil Young's *Rockin' in the Free World*. No one wrote *Rockin' In Pyongyang*; my 52 gigs have been the greatest expression of freedom of my lifetime and I'll be taking Neil's advice from the chorus to attend many more.

If you imagine this book with closing credits, consider that song the perfect accompaniment.

EPILOGUE

On May 24, 2017, I caught the overground to Wandsworth Town Hall and swore allegiance to the Queen. I qualified for British citizenship thanks to Elizabeth Ann Langley, the Marylebone-born mother I never knew.

Elizabeth's life took a turn for the worse right here in London when a lover committed suicide. The ensuing spiral led her back to Australia and to her being forced to give up two tiny children — one of whom she would never see again and who would grow up in a world largely of his own creation.

It was by learning about Elizabeth from my then-girlfriend that I finally began deconstructing that world and allowing myself to enter a new one. It's where I started the journey to becoming Andrew John Langley, how I learned to turn my obsessions into touchstones, what led me here … to the streets Elizabeth herself walked as a child.

When I was young, she had sent hand-crafted gifts to Andrew on his birthday. They were never passed on to Stephen, who didn't even know she existed. But as I belted out *God Save The Queen*, with my wife Sarah looking on, the biggest gift Elizabeth ever sent me had successfully reached its intended destination.

Thank you, Mum. I dedicate this book to you.

ACKNOWLEDGMENTS

This book has been more than a decade in the making and would never have been completed without my wife, Sarah, whose patience and love realigned my focus, perspective, priorities and knowledge — particularly in relation to where I came from and how I ended up where I am. I would like to thank my publisher in Australia, Geoff Armstrong, editor Larry Writer, typesetter Graeme Jones, cover designer Luke Causby, UK publishers Phil Caplan and Tony Hannan, and a close friend in the publishing industry whose support was invaluable, Charlotte Harper. Three more close friends — Shane Richardson, Jim Savage and Jono Waters — offered boundless encouragement. Also thanks to my mothers, Betty Mascord and Elizabeth Langley, my father Norman Mascord and my sisters, Tammie Mascord and Stephany Jones.

I am grateful to Adam Duritz for permission to reproduce the lyrics to *Mr Jones* in chapter 17, and to Black Stone Cherry for permission to reproduce the lyrics to *The Rambler* in chapter 23.

The photographs in the book are from my collection, from my Aunty Gail (see the top pic on the opening page of the first photo section and all the pics on page 2), or from Getty Images as follows:

Section One

Page 1 (below): Mark Kolbe (Getty Images Sport); Page 3 (above): Alex Livesey (Getty Images Sport); Page 3 (below): Mark Kolbe (Getty Images Sport); Page 6 (above): Kevin Winter (Getty Images Entertainment); Page 6 (below): Shirlaine Forrest (WireImage); Page 7 (above): Mark Kolbe (Getty Images Sport); Page 7 (below): Matt King (Getty Images Sport).

Section Two

Page 2 (above): Paul Bergen (Redferns); Page 2 (below): Katja Ogrin (Redferns); Page 3 (above): Shirlaine Forrest (Redferns); Page 6 (below): Santiago Bluguermann/CON (LatinContent Editorial); Page 8 (above right): Alex Livesey (Getty Images Sport).

My thanks also go to the following people who supported this project by committing to buy a book (and more) before a word was written: Rick Allsopp, Chris Barclay, Scott Barker, Valda Baron, Hudson Burns, Wade Chiesa, Ben Coady, Allan Cooper, Brendan Crabb, Michelle Emmerson, Will Evans, Michael Fallon, Keith Fillingham, Gilles Fleuret, Tim Gore, David Groom, Michael Herlihy, Tim Hishon, Dominic Hughes, Vogue Hughes, Darren Kellett, Matt Lee, Joanna Lester, Terry Liberopoulos, Lewis Lighthowler, James Manning, Aaron Quinn, Howard Scott, Brad Schofield, Damian Sharry, James Sullivan, Brad Tallon, Steve Randall, Brock Schaefer, Brad Smith, Peter Stott, Jim Stringer, Alix Walker, Tim Webb, Clint Wheeldon, Adrian Williams, Stephen Woodcock, Richard York and Robert York.

FOOTNOTE TO PAGE 137

It is true that Russell Crowe, long-time Souths fan and Oscar winning actor, once based aspects of a movie character on me. Brad Walter reported exactly that in the *Sydney Morning Herald* of June 5, 2009:

> Those who know Steve Mascord always thought his life was a movie waiting to be made. But none would have envisaged the lifelong Illawarra Steelers fan, who ran on to Wollongong Showground to claim the corner post at the club's first game, would have such an impact on Hollywood …
>
> Mascord has been revealed as a source of inspiration for Russell Crowe's latest role as a journalist in the crime thriller *State of Play*. Crowe, who grew his hair and put on several kilos to play the investigative journalist Cal McAffrey, knows Mascord from his involvement in the NRL.
>
> In an email to the *Herald*, Crowe confirmed the influence Mascord had on his portrayal and not just the ponytail or physical characteristics developed from years of eating party pies at grounds in Australia and Britain.
>
> 'The question about Steve Mascord has been brought up by a number of people,' Crowe said. 'Certainly, there is an integrity to Mr Mascord that I drew from, I'm surprised so many have noticed. The physicality of the character, the three-quarter coat and the man bag all come from an English journalist, Martyn Palmer. No doubt, Cal McAffrey and Mr Mascord have a similar diet.'

INDEX

Goo Goo Dolls 192
Gotti, John 121
Google 43, 107, 137, 170,
    191, 192, 288
Gould, Phil 16
Graham, Wade 274
Gramm, Lou 108, 147
Grant, John 75–76
Great Britain 6
Gregory, Mike 115
Greenland, Scott 41
Grinspoon 181
Grohl, Dave 57
Grothe, Eric 49
Guardian 60, 257
Gudinski, Michael 107
Guns, Tracii 110
Guns N' Roses (G N'
    R) 29, 56–64, 107,
    127, 136–137, 138,
    139–145, 147, 179,
    210, 262
Gurr, Bernie 96

Hadfield, Dave 116
Hagan, Jeff 289
Hagar, Sammy 67
Halliwell Jones Stadium
    106, 138, 267
Hammersmith Apollo 192
Hannant, Ben 101–102
Hansen, Kelly 108
Hanoi Rocks 112
Harari, Yuval Noah 46
Harding, Jeff 113–114
Hardy, Ed 110–111
Harlem Globetrotters
    205, 212
Harnell, Tony 173
Harrigan, Bill 189, 235
Harrison, Ashley 37
Harrison, Matthew 215
Hasler, Des 101, 164
Hatton, Susie 108
Hawkins, Justin 192
Hayson, Eddie 188
Headingley 5, 6, 279
Head of Steam (bar) 9, 11
Heighington, Chris 58,
    275

Heighington, Eocco 58
Hemel Stags RLFC 15
Henderson, Andrew 258
Hendrix, Jimi 108
Henry, Neil 98
Henwood, Tim 216
Hewar, Gareth 153
Hillyard, Phil 82
Hit Parader 67
Hoad, Cliff 63–64
Hoad, Jeff 63
Hoffman, Philip Seymour
    179
Holdsworth, John 115
Holland, Kerrod 26
Holly, Buddy 116
Holmes, Valentine 209,
    211–212
Honourable Artillery
    Academy 266
Hôtel Terminus 237
Hot Metal 43, 54
Houghton, Danny 153
House of Blues (Boston) 13
House of Blues (West
    Hollywood) 111
House of Blues (Anaheim)
    165
Howland, Daryl 'Spinner'
    184
Huddersfield Giants 120,
    237, 241, 267
Hughes, Glenn 267,
    268–270
Hull FC 106, 153, 241,
    266, 267
Hull Kingston Rovers 266
Hunter, Seb 65
Hunter Stadium 88, 146,
    158
Hurrell, Konrad 74
Hurricane 108, 113
Hustler 200

Iffley Road, 13
Illawarra Cutters 164
Illawarra Steelers 11, 21,
    32, 33, 34, 41, 43, 50,
    52, 154, 155
Illfield, Peter 184

Inside Sport 127
Instagram 29–30, 36, 101,
    146, 201
International Hockey
    Federation 106
International Olympic
    Committee 19, 72
Indio 56
Inglorious 280
Iron Maiden 68, 74,
    76–80, 222, 223,
    266, 280, 288
Islington Academy 267
Italy 90, 206

Jackson, Glenn 204
Jacksonville Axemen 179
Jacob, Ben 164
James Cook High 52
James, Nathan 280–281
James, Sid 217
Jamieson, Don 117
Jett, Joan 163, 171
John, Elton 140
John Coghlan's Quo 250
Johns, Andrew 12, 56, 164
Johns, Chris 44
Johns, Les 92
Johnson, Brian 56, 59,
    139–140
Jones, Brian 108
Jones, Marty 168–169
Jones, Michael 188–189
Joplin, Janis 108
Judas Priest 127, 266
JUKE 43, 60
Junkyard 159

KCOM Stadium 266, 267
Kear, John 279
Kearney, Stephen 205
Keel 68, 69
Kelly, Kevin 11
Kennedy, Myles 143
Kenny, Brett 33
Kent, Paul 50
Kentish Town Forum 126,
    272
Kerrang! 11, 43, 105, 108,
    112, 116, 119, 121

ABOUT THE AUTHOR

Steve Mascord is a writer specialising in rugby league and rock music. His career covering rugby league for newspapers, news agencies, magazines, radio stations, websites and television programs began when he was a 16-year-old student at Port Kembla High School. In the late 1980s he helped launch the iconic Australian magazine *Hot Metal* and began working as a journalist for Australian Associated Press. In 1994, he joined *The Sydney Morning Herald* as a rugby league reporter while continuing to write freelance articles for a variety of music magazines.

From 2006 to 2008, Steve was a league writer at *The Daily Telegraph*, and for the past decade has worked largely on a freelance basis, contributing regularly to the *Herald* (where his weekly 'Discord' column has been a feature of recent seasons) and to a variety of newspapers, magazines and websites based in Australia and the UK, including *Hot Metal*, *Kerrang!*, *Classic Rock presents: AOR*, *The Guardian*, *Rugby League Week*, *League Express*, *Rugby League World*, *Forty20*, *theroar.com.au* and *rugby-league.com*. Steve also has his own website, *stevemascord.com*, has revived *Hot Metal* at *hotmetalonline.com* and runs *rugbyleaguehub.com* and *hardrockhub.com*. His *White Line Fever* podcast is available free via iTunes. He is a regular part of Triple M's NRL coverage.

Steve is married to Sarah and splits his time between Sydney and London.

Touchstones is his first book.

WHERE TO FIND
STEVE MASCORD

Twitter: @touchstonesbook
Facebook: facebook.com/touchstonesbook

stevemascord.com
rugbyleaguehub.com
hotmetalonline.com
hardrockhub.com

White Line Fever podcast via iTunes

Amazon: amazon.com/Steve-Mascord
Facebook: facebook.com/BondiBeat
Flickr: flickr.com/photos/21639081@N00
Foursquare: foursquare.com/therealsteavis
Google: google.com/+SteveMascord
Instagram: Steavis
LinkedIn: linkedin.com/in/steve-mascord-a2264713
SoundCloud: soundcloud.com/therealsteavis
Twitter: @therealsteavis
YouTube: youtube.com/user/WhiteLineFeverTV

To hear Jono Waters interview Steve Mascord, scan here: